Utopias

WILEY-BLACKWELL BRIEF HISTORIES OF RELIGION SERIES

This series offers brief, accessible, and lively accounts of key topics within theology and religion. Each volume presents both academic and general readers with a selected history of topics which have had a profound effect on religious and cultural life. The word "history" is, therefore, understood in its broadest cultural and social sense. The volumes are based on serious scholarship but they are written engagingly and in terms readily understood by general readers.

Other topics in the series:

Published

Heaven	Alister E. McGrath
Heresy	G. R. Evans
Death	Douglas J. Davies
Saints	Lawrence S. Cunningham
Christianity	Carter Lindberg
Dante	Peter S. Hawkins
Spirituality	Philip Sheldrake
Cults and New Religions	Douglas E. Cowan and David G. Bromley
Love	Carter Lindberg
Christian Mission	Dana L. Robert
Christian Ethics	Michael Banner
Jesus	W. Barnes Tatum
Shinto	John Breen and Mark Teeuwen
Paul	Robert Paul Seesengood
Apocalypse	Martha Himmelfarb
Islam 2nd Edition	Tamara Sonn
The Reformation	Kenneth G. Appold

Utopias

A Brief History from Ancient Writings to Virtual Communities

Howard P. Segal

A John Wiley & Sons, Ltd., Publication

This edition first published 2012
© 2012 Howard P. Segal

Blackwell Publishing was acquired by John Wiley & Sons in February 2007. Blackwell's publishing program has been merged with Wiley's global Scientific, Technical, and Medical business to form Wiley-Blackwell.

Registered Office
John Wiley & Sons Ltd, The Atrium, Southern Gate, Chichester, West Sussex, PO19 8SQ, UK

Editorial Offices
350 Main Street, Malden, MA 02148-5020, USA
9600 Garsington Road, Oxford, OX4 2DQ, UK
The Atrium, Southern Gate, Chichester, West Sussex, PO19 8SQ, UK

For details of our global editorial offices, for customer services, and for information about how to apply for permission to reuse the copyright material in this book please see our website at www.wiley.com/wiley-blackwell.

The right of Howard P. Segal to be identified as the author of this work has been asserted in accordance with the UK Copyright, Designs and Patents Act 1988.

Wiley also publishes its books in a variety of electronic formats. Some content that appears in print may not be available in electronic books.

Designations used by companies to distinguish their products are often claimed as trademarks. All brand names and product names used in this book are trade names, service marks, trademarks or registered trademarks of their respective owners. The publisher is not associated with any product or vendor mentioned in this book. This publication is designed to provide accurate and authoritative information in regard to the subject matter covered. It is sold on the understanding that the publisher is not engaged in rendering professional services. If professional advice or other expert assistance is required, the services of a competent professional should be sought.

Library of Congress Cataloging-in-Publication Data

Segal, Howard P.
   Utopias : a brief history from ancient writings to virtual communities /Howard P. Segal.
      pages cm – (Blackwell brief histories of religion ; 44)
   ISBN 978-1-4051-8328-4 (pbk.) – ISBN 978-1-4051-8329-1 (hardcover)
1. Utopias–History. I. Title.
   HX806.S36 2012
   335.8'3–dc23   2011049094

A catalogue record for this book is available from the British Library.

Set in 10/12.5pt Meridien by Thomson Digital, Noida, India
Printed in Malaysia by Ho Printing (M) Sdn Bhd

1   2012

For my wife, Deborah D. Rogers,
for our children, Richard William Rogers Segal
and Raechel Maya Rogers Segal,
and for our beloved shih-tzu, Toms

Table of Contents

Preface   xi
Introduction   1

1   The Nature of Utopias   5
Utopias Defined   5
Utopias Differ from both Millenarian Movements
    and Science Fiction   8
Utopias' Spiritual Qualities are Akin to those
    of Formal Religions   9
Utopias' Real Goal: Not Prediction of the Future
    but Improvement of the Present   12
How and When Utopias are Expected to be Established   13

2   The Variety of Utopias   16
The Global Nature of Utopias: Utopias are Predominantly
    but not Exclusively Western   16
The Several Genres of Utopianism: Prophecies and
    Oratory, Political Movements, Communities,
    Writings, World's Fairs, Cyberspace   24

**3   The European Utopias and Utopians and
    Their Critics**   47
The Pioneering European Visionaries and Their Basic
    Beliefs: Plato's *Republic* and More's *Utopia*   47

Forging the Connections Between Science,
  Technology, and Utopia   50

The Pansophists   53

The Prophets of Progress: Condorcet, Saint-Simon,
  and Comte   55

Dissenters from the Ideology of Unadulterated Scientific
  and Technological Progress: Thomas Carlyle, John
  Ruskin, and William Morris   58

The Expansive Visions of Robert Owen and Charles
  Fourier   60

The "Scientific" Socialism of Karl Marx and Friedrich
  Engels   66

4 **The American Utopias and Utopians and
   Their Critics**   **74**

America as Utopia: Potential and Fulfillment   74

The Pioneering American Visionaries and their Basic
  Beliefs in America as Land of Opportunity: John
  Adolphus Etzler, Thomas Ewbank, and Mary Griffith   78

America as "Second Creation": Enthusiasm
  and Disillusionment   81

5 **Growing Expectations of Realizing Utopia in the
   United States and Europe**   **89**

Later American Technological Utopians: John Macnie
  Through Harold Loeb   89

Utopia Within Sight: The American Technocracy Crusade 96

Utopia Within Reach: "The Best and the
  Brightest "—Post-World War II Science and
  Technology Policy in the United States and Western
  Europe and the Triumph of the Social Sciences   99

On Misreading *Frankenstein*: How Scientific and
  Technological Advances have Changed Traditional
  Criticisms of Utopianism in the Twentieth and
  Twenty-First Centuries   123

6 Utopia Reconsidered   **139**

The Growing Retreat from Space Exploration
   and Other Megaprojects   139

Nuclear Power: Its Rise, Fall, and Possible
   Revival—Maine Yankee as a Case Study   142

The Declining Belief in Inventors, Engineers, and
   Scientists as Heroes; in Experts as Unbiased;
   and in Science and Technology as Social Panaceas   157

Contemporary Prophets for Profit: The Rise and Partial
   Fall of Professional Forecasters   160

Post-colonial Critiques of Western Science and
   Technology as Measures of "Progress"   169

7 The Resurgence of Utopianism   **186**

The Major Contemporary Utopians and Their
   Basic Beliefs   186

Social Media: Utopia at One's Fingertips   193

Recent and Contemporary Utopian Communities   194

The Star Trek Empire: Science Fiction Becomes Less
   Escapist   199

Edutopia: George Lucas and Others   203

The Fate of Books and Newspapers: Utopian and
   Dystopian Aspirations   217

8 The Future of Utopias and Utopianism   **234**

The "Scientific and Technological Plateau" and the
   Redefinition of Progress   234

Conclusion: Why Utopia Still Matters Today and
   Tomorrow   241

Further Reading   **261**
Index   **269**

Preface

I have long found serious, thoughtful utopias and utopians to be fascinating, important, and deserving of respect and inquiry. I remain intrigued by what utopias and utopians tell us about the societies from which they derive and about how those societies might be changed, for better or for worse. In effect, utopianism functions like a microscope: by first isolating and then magnifying aspects of existing, non-utopian societies allegedly needing drastic improvements, it enables us to see more clearly their political, economic, cultural, and psychological mainstreams.

Some students of utopias come to the topic by way of personal experiences, such as time spent either living in a utopian community or trying to perfect the world through political or social movements. In the interest of "full disclosure," let me concede without any apologies that, by contrast, my interest in utopias is largely scholarly. I have never held any passionate beliefs in any remotely utopian projects, have never composed any supposedly utopian manifestoes or other visionary writings, and have never spent time in any self-proclaimed utopian communities or crusades. I am by nature skeptical—if not cynical—about visions and visionaries that claim moral and perhaps intellectual superiority over everything and everyone else. I cannot imagine being seduced by any utopian dream or prophet. Yet I remain fascinated by those who have been so seduced and by the manifestations of their seductions.

As I was completing this book, I happened to receive from my institution's Employee Assistance Program—that is, its counseling service—a four-page pamphlet distributed to all employees entitled "Perfectionism: Too Much of a Good Thing." The timing was ironic. These pamphlets on various topics appear every few months, and the intention—to alert employees to various issues that might confront them, their families, and their friends—is certainly noble. Though hardly surprised by the uniformly negative tone of this critique of "perfectionism," I was reminded of the generally unsympathetic reactions of many others over the years as I studied, wrote about, and presented papers on various aspects of utopianism. Since my Princeton graduate-school days, when I was contemplating writing my doctoral dissertation on some aspect of utopianism, far more often than not I have encountered an implicit if not explicit sense of anxiety that my keen interest in the topic might well reflect some kind of pathology.

As set forth in the pamphlet and in countless earlier warnings from other mental health experts, the quest for "unreasonable standards" of whatever variety for either oneself or others can "waste enormous amounts of time" better spent on more pleasant pursuits. One finds nothing in defense of the idealism likewise associated throughout history with "perfectionism."[1] But, While I cannot refute the pamphlet's list of the harmful effects of "perfectionism"—anxiety, misplaced anger, depression, obsessive compulsive disorders, eating disorders, chronic pain, and procrastination—what of the healthy and positive efforts to improve the world that have characterized the foremost utopian projects and their creators? One need not embrace their sometimes naïve, misguided schemes to be more balanced in assessing utopias and utopians throughout history. Their refusal to accept existing values, customs, institutions, and policies is often admirable if not courageous. True, this book is not a formal moral assessment as such, but it does attempt to treat utopias and utopians—and their critics—with fairness and respect.

In researching and writing this book I was greatly assisted by Samara Gopan, of Bangor, Maine; by University of Maine history major Jason Pote; by Melora Norman, Librarian of Unity College of Maine; and above all by Mel Johnson, University of Maine Fogler Library Reference Librarian.

I am most indebted to my dear and talented wife, Deborah Rogers, Professor of English at the University of Maine. She not only encouraged me to undertake and then complete the book but also vastly improved the manuscript with her editorial skills.

I wish to thank Rutgers University Press for its permission to allow me to use portions of my article "Progress and its Discontents: Postwar Science and Technology Policy," in *The Social Sciences Go to Washington*, ed. Hamilton Cravens (2004); Purdue University Press for its permission to allow me to use portions of my article "Reengineering the Land-Grant University," in *Engineering in a Land-Grant Context*, ed. Alan Marcus (2005) and the Maine Historical Society for its permission to allow me to use portions of my article "Maine Yankee Nuclear Power Plant: A Technological Utopia in Retrospect," in *Maine History*, 44 (April 2009), 120–142.

Notes

1   Mary D'Alessandro, *EAP Messenger, Perfectionism: Too Much of a Good Thing* (Employee Assistance Program, University of Maine, October 2010), 2.

Introduction

The term "utopia" typically conjures up naïve, impractical, unrealistic, superficial notions of an allegedly perfect society. In this book, while not defending all utopian schemes against these connotations, I place more emphasis on utopias' positive qualities, especially their illumination of the non-utopian societies from which all utopias spring. Equally importantly, the book traces the varying forms that utopias have taken over the centuries, from their origins in ancient Greece to their growth in the Renaissance and their persistence in the present, including contemporary "high-tech" utopias and cyberspace utopian communities. No less significantly, I also extend the analysis of utopias from an exclusively Western enterprise to a worldwide one—a facet of utopianism ordinarily neglected.

There have been several classical accounts of utopias to which generations of students and scholars are indebted. But it is surely time to update *The Story of Utopias* (1922), to invoke the title of one of those pioneering studies, which was the first book by the great historian and social critic Lewis Mumford.[1] We are by now past the hostility that greeted most utopian proposals throughout much of the twentieth century, when utopias were commonly equated with the nightmarish and pseudo-utopian totalitarian regimes that shaped most of that century, whether right-wing or left-wing, fascist or communist. The end of the Cold War and the collapse of the Soviet Union in the late twentieth century have provided an

Utopias: A Brief History from Ancient Writings to Virtual Communities,
First Edition. Howard P. Segal.
© 2012 Howard P. Segal. Published 2012 by Blackwell Publishing Ltd.

opportunity for a more balanced assessment of utopias and utopian thought long unavailable when the world was purportedly divided between pure capitalism and pure socialism and when each side routinely demonized the other.[2]

Admittedly, many who are not ideological extremists still remain skeptical of *all* utopian expectations, including the ability of science and technology to improve the planet.[3] Simultaneously, however, other quarters have seen a renewed positive interest in utopias, thanks in part to visions of cyberspace paradises as well as to more material high-tech advances that grant ordinary persons unprecedented access to information, to communication, and to sources of visionary inspiration. These innovations include computers, the Internet, cell phones, satellites, global positioning devices, smart phones, iPods, and biotechnological developments.

On a more mundane plane, one increasingly finds the use of the word "utopian" without apology or defensiveness. Examples include articles in the *New York Times* and elsewhere on a deliberately obscured cluster of homes overlooking the Pacific ("Utopia by the Sea") designed by several prominent architects; Serenbe, an avowedly utopian experiment some thirty miles outside Atlanta that began as a farm, expanded into a bed and breakfast and then into a few cottages, and has since grown into several small communities; and four successful and still desirable housing complexes for common citizens in Lyon, France, termed *Utopies Realisees*, or "Achieved Utopias." Two other, less upbeat articles discuss how in Grenoble, in the French Alps, a failed urban utopian community built in the 1970s has become the site of protests and violence by its now impoverished residents, and how a 2008 exhibit in New York City about a visionary affordable housing project in China contrasts positively, in its small and humane scale, with modern China's common huge and impersonal skyscraper apartment buildings. Further examples are two new books, the first about a small rural Texas town called Utopia that lacks any movie theaters or book or music stores and that only recently became connected to both cable television and the Internet, and the second about someone in search of contemporary utopias, inspired by his having grown up on a street called Utopia Road in a planned community in Southern California. Meanwhile, my own university has a sufficient number of serious scholars of utopia to have warranted favorable articles in the institution's glossy public relations magazine.[4]

Finally, Boston Beer Company, which makes the Sam Adams Beer, highly popular in New England, now also makes a beer named "Utopias." Utopias has the United States' highest alcohol content (twenty-seven percent) and is banned in thirteen states. However, for those who can purchase—and afford—it, Utopias guarantees an exceptional taste.[5] One can only speculate about its potential effects on serious visionaries.

For many advocates of utopia today—be they Utopias drinkers or not—the traditional gap between prophecy and fulfillment has nearly disappeared, enhancing the appeal of these visions. But historical perspectives are generally and painfully absent in such predictions. This simplifies and distorts discussions of the presumed uniqueness of contemporary utopias and so supposedly justifies the frequent absence of any comparisons with their predecessors. As a professional historian, I feel compelled to remedy this neglect.[6]

Notes

1 As I was completing this book I learned of the publication not long before of Lyman Tower Sargent's *Utopianism: A Very Short Introduction* (New York: Oxford University Press, 2010). Sargent is a leading scholar of utopianism, and his book is, not surprisingly, excellent. As I finished my book I read and then cited his at several points. But our books are quite different and are, I believe, complementary studies.

2 Russell Jacoby's *Picture Imperfect: Utopian Thought in an Anti-Utopian Age* (New York: Columbia University Press, 2005) is a powerful indictment of such prominent post-World War II critics of utopia as Hannah Arendt, Isaiah Berlin, Karl Popper, and Leo Strauss.

3 On the history of forecasting and the critical role of technology, see I. F. Clarke, *The Pattern of Expectation, 1644–2001* (New York: Basic Books, 1979). There is no finer general work on this topic, nor any with more examples.

4 See Patricia Leigh Brown, "Utopia by the Sea," *New York Times*, Travel, December 14, 2008, 1, 8; Kevin Sack, "Outside Atlanta, a Utopia Rises," *New York Times*, Travel, March 1, 2009, 5; Sally McGrane,

"Concrete Dreams: France's Housing Utopias," *New York Times*, Travel, August 2, 2009, TR 4; Steven Erlanger, "Grenoble Journal: Utopian Dream Becomes Battleground in France," *New York Times*, April 9, 2010, A7; Nicolai Ouroussoff, "Architecture: In Modern China, 'Little Kingdoms' for the People," *New York Times*, October 13, 2008, C1, C5; Karen Valby, *Welcome to Utopia: Notes From a Small Town* (New York: Spiegel and Grau, 2010); and J. C. Hallman, *In Utopia: Six Kinds of Eden, and the Search for a Better Paradise* (New York: St. Martin's, 2010). Valby's book is infinitely less pretentious and far more interesting than Hallman's superficial and historically ignorant gloss of utopias past and present. On utopian studies at the University of Maine, see Kristen Andresen, "Searching for Utopia," *UMaine Today*, 9 (January/February 2009), 8, 12. The similar unapologetic use of "dystopias" is also increasing. See, for instance, the film *Jonestown* (2006) about Jim Jones' Jonestown, Guyana, mass suicide on November 18, 1978, as reviewed by Stephen Holden in the *New York Times*, October 20, 2006, B11; and a review of the video game Grand Theft Auto IV entitled "Forget It, Niko, it's Liberty City, a Dystopian Dream," in the *New York Times*, April 28, 2008, B1, B6.

5   See Associated Press, "Boston Beer Offers Potential Utopias," *Boston Globe*, December 1, 2009, B6.

6   In its final issue of 2007 (83 (December 24 and 31), 110–111), the *New Yorker*'s cartoons included two full pages by the famous Edward Sorel on "Five Writers in Search of Utopia," with a few lines below each cartoon humorously summarizing each work. The sheer publication of those cartoons bespoke the revival of a broader interest in the history of utopia.

Chapter 1

The Nature of Utopias

Utopias Defined

"Utopia" means the allegedly perfect society. Coined by Thomas More (1478–1535), Lord Chancellor of England, the term is epitomized in his *Utopia* (1516), which was published first in Latin and then translated into French, German, and Italian before it was translated into English in 1551. More had opposed its translation into his native tongue during his lifetime.

"Utopia" refers to the ideal visions themselves. "Utopianism" refers to the movements that bring them about. The particular components of utopia can vary enormously, and one person's or one society's utopia may be another's anti-utopia or "dystopia." In coining the term More was making a pun meaning both "good place" and "nowhere." Nevertheless, we can define "genuine" utopias by comparing them with "false" utopias in three ways.

First, in a genuine utopia, perfection usually entails a radical improvement of physical, social, economic, and psychological conditions. Utopia is—or should be—*qualitatively* different from pre-utopia and non-utopia. Except when pre-utopia is seen as moving toward utopia—as was long assumed by many to be the case with the United States—radical change is critical to the achievement of utopia. Even here, however, considerable improvements are still believed to be necessary. These improvements are to be achieved through the transformation of institu-

Utopias: A Brief History from Ancient Writings to Virtual Communities,
First Edition. Howard P. Segal.
© 2012 Howard P. Segal. Published 2012 by Blackwell Publishing Ltd.

tions, values, norms, and activities. Perfection does not come automatically, and the inhabitants of most utopias remain flawed by nature, except when their flaws might someday be overcome by preliminary versions of genetic engineering. Otherwise, utopian society must maximize virtues and strengths and minimize vices and weaknesses. In evaluating a utopia, the specific objectives and the means devised to reach these objectives define the variety of perfection that is sought. "Perfection," like "beauty," is an empty word unless it is given specific content.[1]

Second, not only their precise contents but also their comprehensiveness further characterize genuine utopias, which seek changes in most, if not all, areas of society. By contrast, false utopias seek changes in only one or two components, such as schools, prisons, diet, or dress. This is because the proponents of utopias are generally more dissatisfied with the basic structure and direction of their own, non-utopian, society than are the proponents of milder changes. Historian of technology Robert Friedel's monumental 2007 study, *A Culture of Improvement: Technology and the Western Millennium*, richly details progress of this more modest degree, a view of the world beginning in the late Middle Ages. He provides myriad examples of persons laboring on farms and in workshops with, in most cases, only limited notions of what they wanted to do, whether they were ultimately successful or not. Yet he does offer repeated examples of what he terms the sustained "capture" of improvement through such means as guilds, professional engineering organizations and engineering schools, and corporate and governmental research and development enterprises. Understandably (if regrettably), Friedel does not discuss technological progress that was largely unintentional and accidental, "un-utopian" instances of "improvement" without an overarching vision. Take, for example, calendar reform, which, according to historian Frank Manuel, would not, in and of itself, qualify as utopian, "but calendar reform that pretended to effect a basic transformation in the human condition might be."[2]

A third and final characteristic of genuine utopias is their seriousness of purpose. Whatever their particular form and content, all genuine utopias share the ethos described by political theorist George Kateb:

When we speak of a utopia, we generally mean an ideal society which is not an efflorescence of a diseased or playful or satirical imagination, nor a private or special dream-world, but rather one in which the welfare of all its inhabitants is the central concern, and in which the level of welfare is strikingly higher, and assumed to be more long-lasting, than that of the real world.[3]

Genuine utopias frequently seek not to escape from the real world but to make the real world better. This objective does not, of course, necessarily translate into practicality or effective action. Compare, for example, fantasies of trips to the moon imagined by Jules Verne and other writers with the Apollo project of NASA that fulfilled its primary objective in 1969 of landing Americans on the moon and returning them safely to earth and that was hailed at the time as an instrument of greater world peace. For years, NASA has identified many pragmatic spin-offs of its Apollo and later space programs that have benefited ordinary Americans and others. NASA missions are indirectly responsible for inventions from MRIs and lasers to more mundane objects such as smoke detectors and dustbusters. In fact, NASA touts the practical implications of its programs on the NASA Spinoff website (http://www.sti.nasa.gov/tto) and on Twitter (@NASA_Spinoff).

One further central characteristic of genuine utopias has been well expressed by Ruth Levitas: "the desire for a different, better way of being" is neither innate nor universal. To suggest otherwise is to indulge in fantasies that may be satisfying to those with utopian desires but that lack any historical basis. Countless examples of non-utopian or outright anti-utopian individuals, groups, cultures, and societies can readily be cited. Utopias are perhaps the foremost "socially constructed response to an *equally* socially constructed gap between the needs and wants generated by a particular society and the satisfactions available to and distributed by it." This social construction in no way diminishes the significance of genuine utopian visions, past or present. The attempted bridging of that gap, in any number of ways, is what utopias are finally all about.[4]

Utopias Differ from both Millenarian Movements and Science Fiction

Depending on human beings rather than on God to transform the world distinguishes utopias from millenarian movements. In millenarian movements, should God enlist humans, much still depends on God. For instance, the ultra-Orthodox Jews who opposed the establishment of the State of Israel in 1948 did so on the grounds that it was up to God to establish Israel, according to their reading of the Old Testament. Only with God's approval would they eventually impose Jewish laws, customs, and institutions upon the blessed new state. By contrast, secular Zionists for decades sought to establish a Jewish state by themselves and, of course, finally succeeded.

Similarly, Christian pre-Millennialists, who believe that Jesus will return without human intervention, do not try to improve the world. If anything, they want conditions to deteriorate precisely to quicken Jesus' return. This was the case with James Watt, the controversial Secretary of the Interior under President Ronald Reagan, regarding the fate of so much of the American environment under his control. By comparison, post-Millennialists believe that Jesus will return only after humans improve their world and themselves, though they do not believe in the perfectibility of either, given original sin.

Utopias differ from science fiction in their basic concern for changing rather than abandoning or ignoring non-utopian communities and societies. Science fiction, on the other hand, consists primarily of escapist fantasies about exploration to distant lands, to depths below the earth, or to outer space. Coinage of the term "science fiction" is credited to Forrest J. Ackerman (1916–2008), but it was applied by him and others to works published before his time.[5] Verne's works such as *Journey to the Center of the Earth* (1864), *From the Earth to the Moon* (1866), and *Twenty Thousand Leagues Under the Sea* (1870) provide classic examples of science fiction. However imaginative they may be, any impact upon the society left behind is quite secondary. As historian Rosalind Williams contends, Verne's various escape routes from his own society's "science-driven globalization" represent far more than a desire to entertain children and adults. Yet, she concedes, his imagined inventions were intended to free his characters from the "entanglements of the modern, industrializing, globalizing world." They were not primarily designed to alter it.[6]

The case of the fairly obscure American writer David Lasser is no less revealing. In the late 1920s and early 1930s, Lasser edited pulp fiction with the legendary Hugo Gernsback. But Gernsback fired Lasser for becoming too concerned with the social and economic crises of the contemporary Great Depression. Lasser then looked to space travel to transcend these and other actual problems, such as nationalism and racism. The first president of the American Interplanetary Society in 1930, Lasser represents the progressive side of science fiction often silenced by technically obsessed persons such as Gernsback but associated in Europe with H. G. Wells above all. During the Cold War, Lasser argued for a world peace that would prevent the extension of tensions between capitalism and communism into space. This distinguished Lasser from better-known post-World War II space scientists and popularizers of space exploration—such as Wernher von Braun, Arthur C. Clarke, Robert Heinlein, and Willy Ley, who favored extending traditional American imperialism into space. Von Braun made a remarkably successful transition from Nazi war criminal to charismatic leader of the American space program. Ben Bova and Gerard O'Neill, later advocates of space exploration, were not, however, the same kind of conservative Cold War warriors.[7]

In recent decades, science fiction has become ever more engaged with the "real world" it would supposedly either transform or escape from. Rejecting the white male technocratic elitism of their predecessors, such contemporary writers as Vonda N. McIntyre, Kim Stanley Robinson, and Allen Steele envision space communities as models of racial and gender diversity. Meanwhile, established writers such as Doris Lessing, Ursula LeGuin, and Margaret Atwood continued with this trend when they moved into science fiction.[8]

Utopias' Spiritual Qualities are Akin to those of Formal Religions

Krishan Kumar argues that there is "a fundamental contradiction between religion and utopia"[9] because of the distinctions drawn above regarding changes to be brought about by human beings versus changes to be brought about by God, or regarding concerns for this world versus those for the next world. But that common stance is simplistic and ignores the fact that most secular utopias that achieve some longevity still have a spiritual dimension. This might be a faith in science and/or technology as panaceas, often as saviors—a focal point of this book—but it does provide a non-material dimension that cannot be ignored. No less importantly, utopias that envision a far longer, happier, more fulfilling life in this world as compared with salvation in another world or reincarnation in this world usually envision a future in which the very poverty, disease, stagnation, and hopelessness that make salvation and/or reincarnation so appealing are eliminated.

Some European and American utopian writings and many communities have had religion in more conventional forms as their principal theme and cause. If, not surprisingly, Christianity has been the commonest faith, Mormonism and Judaism, for example, have also been represented, as have obscure, sometimes mystical creeds. Overall, religion-based communities have lasted longer than those based on secular beliefs such as socialism. Notable exceptions to this generalization have been communities that fell apart after the loss of founding charismatic leaders. For example, the Oneida community established by John Humphrey Noyes in New York State in 1848 could not continue after Noyes fled to Canada in 1879 before he could be arrested for immoral behavior, as elaborated in Chapter 2. There have also been interesting mixtures: for instance, one of the most intriguing sequels to Edward Bellamy's *Looking Backward* (1888) was the work *Young West* (1894), written by a Reform Rabbi, Solomon Schindler, who tried to enlist other American Jews in Bellamy's Nationalist political crusade.[10]

More broadly, the general notion of America as utopia has gradually become part of America's so-called civil religion, whereby a supposedly secular nation repeatedly invokes God at public ceremonies and in the formulation of public policy. The United States became, in these terms, a *de facto* utopia, unique among the world's nations and yet a model for them all.

Americans, including many policy-makers, have argued both that the country's uniqueness makes it morally superior to all other countries and that the United States could somehow still lift up all other, inferior nations to attempt to approach its high standards. To be sure, the apparent paradox of this position—of simultaneous tendencies toward isolationism and toward foreign aggression—is often lost on its policy proponents and on ordinary citizens alike. Moreover, Americans' use of "Manifest Destiny" to rationalize both westward and overseas expansion in the nineteenth and twentieth centuries exemplifies the utopian dimension of mainstream American history. Most recently, the "neo-conservative" planners behind the Iraq War that began in 2003 had illusions similar to those of their predecessors more than a century ago. The George W. Bush Administration naïvely thought not only that American democracy could readily be exported to a land devoid of democratic traditions and values but also that American troops would be enthusiastically welcomed as democratic liberators from the tyranny of longtime dictator Saddam Hussein.[11]

The connections between the rise and fall of religious belief in the twenty-first century and secular substitutes that, at their most optimistic, become utopian are complex and varied. For example, according to both the editor of the highly respected weekly *The Economist* and his Washington bureau chief, religion is supposedly returning to public life and to intellectuals around the world—and is doing so as a matter of individual voluntary choice and commitment. In *God Is Back*, they argue that the resurgence of belief is another facet of the innovation economy and society that most nations profess to seek. Belief in the prospect of a better world obviously need not lead to any utopian embrace, but neither does it preclude that. So-called "megachurches" throughout the world are but one example of this growth.[12]

Still, there is countervailing evidence of declining traditional religious beliefs in the United States and elsewhere. The search for secular alternatives again may include utopianism of different forms. The comprehensive 2008 survey by the Pew Forum on Religion and Public Life showed a complex picture of the more than 35,000 Americans who participated. There was some decline in the percentage of absolute believers and a growing number of believers who nevertheless maintain some doubts. Equally interesting was the lack of firm commitment the survey observed, remarking that the United States "is a nation of religious drifters, with about half of adults switching faith affiliation at least once during their lives."[13] Lisa Miller's *Heaven: Our Enduring Fascination with the Afterlife* (2010) complements these conclusions in its finding that roughly eighty percent of Americans claim belief in an afterlife but remarkably few can provide any specifics about what they mean by an afterlife.

Utopias' Real Goal: Not Prediction of the Future but Improvement of the Present

Utopias are frequently misunderstood as scientific prophecies whose importance should be determined by the accuracy of their specific predictions. In this respect, the notion that utopias can provide "realistic alternatives" to existing society can be misleading. If anything, this view has grown increasingly popular in recent decades, given our unprecedented electronic access to and processing of information and the consequent growth of forecasting as a serious and profitable industry. If, as the late economist John Kenneth Galbraith wittily observed, economists make predictions not because they know but because they're asked, how much more so does that apply to "professional" social forecasters—and how much more superficial and specious are their predictions? This growth of professional forecasting will be discussed in Chapter 6. The intriguing question (also discussed in that chapter) is why thousands of otherwise intelligent people take social forecasting so seriously—and why many of them later hold up those forecasts as scorecards.

Few such true believers in social forecasting, like their counterparts regarding economic forecasting, would ever categorize themselves as utopians. Neither would tens of thousands, maybe millions, of devotees of contemporary social media and of cyberspace communities—discussed in Chapter 7. It is important not to enlarge the pool of utopians in the name of identifying the utopian rhetoric embraced by so many. Yet the critical point is the serious-ness with which such persons treat whatever makes them inter-ested in the future.

Instead, as noted, utopias' principal value is their illumination of alleged problems and solutions back in the "real world" from which they sprang. Utopias should therefore be played back upon the real world rather than be held up as crystal balls.

How and When Utopias are Expected to be Established

It is crucial to keep in mind that not all utopias are intended to be established in the first place. The classic example of such a utopia as an intellectual construct is Plato's *Republic* (360 BCE). Since Plato did not believe in that prospect, *The Republic* is the quintessential "Platonic Form."

The starting point for utopias that *could* be established is More's *Utopia* (1516). For centuries thereafter, and continuing at least as late as James Hilton's *Lost Horizon* (1933), utopia was usually discovered by Western travelers who came upon it by accident, for example through erroneous maps, storms at sea, airplane crashes, or, as in Bellamy's *Looking Backward*, through falling asleep and awakening in utopia. Conditions that eventually brought utopia about included wars, post-war peacetime negotia-tions, natural disasters, and clashes between continents, nations, classes, races, and, yes, sexes. These utopias were usually placed in the contemporary time of their authors. But, as more of the world became explored and known, it became increasingly nec-essary to place utopia in unexplored, exotic places in order to claim some originality—for example, under the sea, inside the earth, or in outer space. However, as these sites themselves became explored and relatively familiar, it became necessary to project utopia into the future. At first, European visionaries (discussed in Chapter 3) harbored vague expectations of utopian fulfillment in the distant future, but usually without particular dates. Even-tually, though, there arose visions that it was forecast would come about in a specified time within reach of the next generation or two—as with *Looking Backward: 2000–1887* (1888)—and later, within one's own lifetime—as with the date of 1960 in the landmark World of Tomorrow exhibit at the 1939–1940 New York World's Fair or, of course, George Orwell's nightmare *1984* (1949). With Buckminster Fuller's *Utopia or Oblivion* (1969) came the elimination of any delay: the future was now.

Notes

1   On the complexity of depictions of human nature by Plato, More, and other utopians, see Gorman Beauchamp, "Imperfect Men in Perfect Societies: Human Nature in Utopia," *Philosophy and Literature*, 31 (October 2007), 280–293.

2   Frank E. Manuel, "Toward a Psychological History of Utopias," in *Utopias and Utopian Thought: A Timely Appraisal*, ed. Manuel (Boston: Houghton Mifflin, 1966), 70.

3   George Kateb, *Utopia and its Enemies* (New York: Free Press, 1963), 6 n. 6.

4   Ruth Levitas, *The Concept of Utopia* (Syracuse, NY: Syracuse University Press, 1991), 181–182. This book is the best general introduction to utopianism as an intellectual and historical phenomenon. But Levitas says little about utopian communities and nothing about non-Western utopias. Also useful is Krishan Kumar, *Utopianism* (Minneapolis, MN: University of Minnesota Press, 1991).

5   See the obituary of Forrest J. Ackerman by Bruce Weber, *New York Times*, December 6, 2008, B10.

6   See Peter Dizikes, "Reporter's Notebook: Jules Verne, Desperado? MIT Historian of Science Rosalind Williams On the Overlooked Legacy of Jules Verne, Anti-Globalization Visionary," *MIT News*, December 10, 2009, web.mit.edu/newsoffice/2009/williams-verne-1210.html.

7   These developments are made clear by De Witt Douglas Kilgore's *Astrofuturism: Science, Race, and Visions of Utopia in Space* (Philadelphia, PA: University of Pennsylvania Press, 2003). By "Astrofuturism" Kilgore means the "tradition of speculative fiction and science writing inaugurated by scientists and science popularizers during the space race of the 1950s" (p. 2).

8   If Kilgore identifies himself as an African American, he goes far beyond lamenting the general absence of African Americans in the literature he analyzes. As he readily concedes, his lifelong fascination with space—despite the absence of "role models"—connects him to

thousands of other Americans, white and non-white alike. See also Marleen S. Barr, *Feminist Fabulation: Space/Postmodern Fiction* (Iowa City, IA: University of Iowa Press, 1993); Robin Roberts, *A New Species: Gender and Science in Science Fiction* (Urbana, IL: University of Illinois Press, 1993); Ellen Susan Peel, *Politics, Persuasion, and Pragmatism: A Rhetoric of Feminist Utopian Fiction* (Columbus, OH: Ohio State University Press, 2002); and Vanessa E. Jones, "Race, the Final Frontier," *Boston Globe*, July 31, 2007, E1, E2.

9   Krishan Kumar, *Utopia and Anti-Utopia in Modern Times* (Oxford: Blackwell, 1987), 10.

10 See Howard P. Segal, "*Young West*: The Psyche of Technological Utopianism," *Extrapolation: A Journal of Science Fiction and Fantasy*, 19 (December 1977), 50–58; and Justin Nordstrom, "Unlikely Utopians: Solomon Schindler, Henry Mendes, and American Judaism in the 1890s," *Utopian Studies*, 20 (2009), 275–297.

11 Susan M. Matarese, *American Foreign Policy and the Utopian Imagination* (Amherst, MA: University of Massachusetts Press, 2001) is a pioneering study of the connections between the two that examines the several dimensions of "national image."

12 John Micklethwait and Adrian Wooldridge, *God Is Back: How the Global Revival of Faith Is Changing the World* (New York: Penguin, 2009) and the critical review by Michiko Kakutani, "Books of the Times," *New York Times*, March 31, 2009, C1, C6.

13 See Eric Gorski, Associated Press, "Survey: Americans Switch Faiths Early, Often," *Bangor Daily News*, April 28, 2009, C8. See also Peter Steinfels, "Beliefs: Uncertainties About the Contemporary Role of Doubt in Religion," *New York Times*, July 19, 2008, B10; and Josie Huang, "Survey Finds Religious Identification Declining," script of Maine Public Radio story, March 20, 2009.

Chapter 2

The Variety of Utopias
Geographical Scope and Genres

The Global Nature of Utopias: Utopias are Predominantly but not Exclusively Western

In their monumental 1979 book on utopian thought, historians Frank and Fritzie Manuel wrote that "the profusion of Western utopias has not been equaled in any other culture." Since the 1970s, the Manuels' point of view has become a matter of considerable debate and historiographical revision, particularly with the flowering of such scholarly fields as post-colonial studies.[1] Lyman Tower Sargent's *Utopianism: A Very Short Introduction* (2010) argues nearly the very opposite of the Manuels: "While the word 'utopia' originated at a particular time and place, utopianism has existed in every cultural tradition."[2] If Sargent is more accurate than the Manuels, he may have gone too far in the opposite direction, at least in terms of visions that look forward rather than backward.

Before proceeding to the chapters that analyze utopia in the Western world, it is imperative to examine the phenomenon of utopianism from a non-Western perspective. Indeed, the claims made by contemporary high-tech proponents of utopia to be

Utopias: A Brief History from Ancient Writings to Virtual Communities,
First Edition. Howard P. Segal.
© 2012 Howard P. Segal. Published 2012 by Blackwell Publishing Ltd.

effected in our own day invariably invoke the familiar argument that we are in a time of unprecedented globalization, so that what happens in the West is either imitated by or initiated in other parts of the world. But here as elsewhere the rhetoric of globalization must be supported by the facts.

It is now evident that there have been significant written utopias and some actual movements to try to achieve utopia in China, Japan, Latin America, and India (those from India will be discussed later, in Chapter 6, as part of the ongoing "post-colonial" critique of Western imperialism, not least Western science and technology). In addition, Israel's many kibbutzim implicitly constitute utopian communities (see Chapter 7).

Utopias in China and Japan   China has a tradition of utopian writings that long predated contact with the West. Such writings were most commonly celebrations of a "primitive" golden age, and their outlook was predominately agrarian and scientifically and technologically stagnant. It is usually assumed that they looked backward, not forward. As Koon-ki Ho put it in a 1983 survey of "The Utopian Tradition in China," on the one hand the utopian concept is not "indigenous" to China. Yet, on the other hand, in "the absence" of the kind of Western utopian writings involving state "socio-political planning," the Chinese "developed their own literary escapist utopias and satirical utopias"[3] that yearned for the past.

Let me be clear: it is by no means necessary that utopian visions either look ahead or be scientifically or technologically advanced. William Morris' *News from Nowhere* (1890) harkens back to his version of medieval England, albeit with some acceptance of modernity. Furthermore, as Ho observes, both escapist and satirical utopias can connect to the future precisely when their treatment of the past is conveyed to readers as being romanticized if not outright invented. For that matter, Ho continues, locating the golden age in the past did not mean that the Chinese were expected simply to await "the spontaneous return of happiness" but were instead expected to work toward it. Hence, these Chinese utopians were more "pragmatic" visionaries than "theoretical" ones.[4]

Going further, in 2002 Zhang Longxi surveyed "The Utopian Vision, East and West" and concluded that many Chinese utopians, especially those adhering to the influential ideas of Confucius, actually looked to the future more than to the past. They used the golden age to spur improvements in the present that ideally would lead to perfection in the future. Both individually and collectively, Chinese visionaries were expected to try to change the world with a "sense of urgency" rather than remain passively nostalgic for the "good old days."[5]

Two Taoist concepts characterize many of these Chinese utopian works: *ta thung* and *thai phing*. *Ta thung* refers to a time of "great togetherness" within one worldwide community, a time of harmony, equality, and justice in a culture without governmental structure, bureaucracies, or social classes. Especially appealing to poor peasant farmers, *ta thung* was invoked over several centuries, and in fact was sustained into the twentieth century through the revolutionary movements led by Sun Yat-Sen and Mao Tse-Tung respectively. *Thai phing*, "the Realm of Great Peace and Equality," was also fundamentally nostalgic even though it looked to a vision of a future state that would restore the golden age and appealed not only to rebellious peasants but also to entrenched ruling classes. Developing the concept of a past that might inspire a different present and in turn a different future, Confucian scholars gradually revised these two concepts to accommodate notions of evolution and progress. But not until European and North American civilizations and cultures began to influence China in the nineteenth century did Western utopian thought, epitomized by Khang Yu-Wei's *Ta Thung Shu (Book of the Great Togetherness)*, start to emerge.[6]

It took Khang (1858–1927) nearly three decades to complete the book, which was not published in full until 1935. During this time he was immersed simultaneously in complementary philosophical and political crusades to transform Confucius into a utopian political reformer and to persuade the emperor to modernize the civil service, to establish both Western-style provincial schools and Beijing University, and to give women basic rights. His was an avowedly modern vision of a democratic world state governed by a world parliament, extending equal rights to women and men, abolishing private property, developing a universal language, and powered both by atomic energy and by a love of science and technology. Institutions would be cooperative and international in scope, the means of production would be publicly owned, goods and services would be provided for all, obsession with money would thereby cease, education would be vocational in orientation, military institutions would be greatly diminished, and the numerous other scientific and technological advances would also be highly practical. Accepting the view that people are innately good, Khang concluded that history could be a story of unceasing progress leading toward utopia rather than the familiar tale of cycles of rising and falling; this constituted an extraordinary leap of faith in his time and culture.[7]

Chairman Mao's utopian visions of the mid-twentieth century did not, of course, ultimately fulfill these dreams. Far from it, as his many multi-year plans, top-down communal establishments, and ruthless tactics have more often been termed dystopian. A review of a 2010 book by Frank Dikotter on *Mao's Great Famine* was entitled "Mao's Utopia a Medley of Death and Destruction." Ironically, as Ho concludes, save for "a report on the condition of hell, we cannot find any genuine dystopia in the history of Chinese literature" until the twentieth century.[8]

Unlike Khang's work, the few pre-nineteenth-century "utopias" in other Asian societies such as Burma (now Myanmar) were primarily satires devoid of substantial alternative visions of existing societies.[9] Little more need be said about them here.

Utopian thought in Japan is another matter. It has been argued that there were no true utopian visions in this country prior to the mid-nineteenth century. But it has been claimed that elements of utopian thought can be found in thinkers of the Tokugawa period (1603–1868) who were influenced by Neo-Confucian thought. That thought was "highly rational, positivistic, and rigidly oriented in its orthodox form toward the exaltation of ethical, harmonious, human relationships."[10]

Examples of such "proto-utopian" Japanese thinkers include Ishida Baigan (1685–1744), who combined an emphasis on the moral cultivation of the self (derived from Neo-Confucian thought) with the value of an intense devotion to work, in contrast to the Neo-Confucian emphasis on study and work. As Eiji

Takemura notes, "It thus became possible, at least in theory, for the masses to cultivate themselves so as to attain unity with nature, and actively participate in social betterment." The goal was not to attain individualistic ends, but instead to cultivate society as a whole.[11] An older visionary, Ogyū Sorai (1666–1727), was apparently "the first to suggest that a true sage is a man who takes thought for the future and seeks to plan social reforms to prevent contingencies from disturbing the institutional order." Sorai's thought was directed against the idea that just action was a direct extension of inner virtue. Rather, he wanted to establish an alternative basis for political action, taking account of human diversity. He used a vision of creation to construct "an open ended vision of historical continuity, an expansive view of the future that theoretically allows no closure."[12] A later thinker, Ninomiya Sontoku (1787–1856), was a commoner who lived most of his life in villages. He founded a movement of agricultural rehabilitation and social engineering important in the Kanto region in the first half of the nineteenth century. As George Bikle notes, "his stress upon the importance of agrarian planning and devotion to the ideal of cooperative self-help served as a model for many utopian visionaries during the Meiji [1868–1912] and Taisho [1912–1926] periods."[13]

After having been "opened" to the West by the 1855 visit of American Commodore Matthew Perry, Japan produced a "flood of utopias," visionary writings that drew upon both traditional Japanese traditions such as those mentioned above and Western utopias. This development of utopian ideas was at least in part a response to modernization.[14] For example, consider the growth of the Japanese socialist and labor movement, founded in Tokyo most importantly by Suzuki Bunji and Abe Iso in the form of socialist study groups. The most significant of these study groups was the *Yūaikai* (Friendly Society), organized in 1912. The *Yuaikai* was heavily influenced by Fabianism, a type of utopian socialism originating in Britain that emphasized social planning. Following World War I, and particularly after the Communist penetration of the labor movement by 1924, utopian socialist ideals gradually declined. After the catastrophic Tokyo earthquake of 1923, Christian messianic utopian movements became especially influential, as did eschatological Buddhist traditions.[15] In the 1930s, the increasingly Fascist political regime persecuted all utopian movements, socialist and religious alike, as they threatened both the imperial colonialist and the anti-socialist monopoly capitalist ideals of the new regime. In the years before and during World War II, Japan's avowedly utopian vision of a "Greater East Asian" colonial empire and culture became all too real for the many Asian neighbors it conquered, using technologies ranging from airplanes to bulldozers. As Bikle has pointed out, the freedoms protected by the post-war Japanese constitution "have encouraged the reemergence of utopian idealism into full flower."[16]

Latin American Utopias   In Latin America, utopian ideas have often been imported from Europe and then applied and transformed in complex ways in response to highly diverse cultures and political situations. While Latin America has rarely spawned utopian communities, utopian ideas have been highly influential, in sometimes indirect ways. In the sixteenth century, the Spanish conquest pitted Iberian conquistadors against highly organized Indian groups—Mayan, Aztec, and Incan—but also against myriad heterogeneous peoples. Though these peoples might be called "Indians" to distinguish them from Europeans, this designation did not "denote some uniform seamless culture."[17] The various cosmological perspectives and world-views of these groups are beyond this book's purview. Nevertheless, they remain critical to Latin America's social and cultural history and to any discussion of utopianism. From the beginning of the period of "discovery" and conquest, Europeans themselves were influenced by what they imagined American Indian societies to be like. Some viewed them as living in a "primitive" Garden of Eden; legends of the golden kingdom, *el dorado*, proliferated, motivating various exploratory expeditions. In fact, the inspiration for More's *Utopia*, the most influential of the European utopias, was his vision of "Amerindian" society.[18]

In subsequent centuries, European ideas were transformed within Latin American societies. In the early nineteenth century, neoclassical Enlightenment culture informed the wars of independence and attempts to build modern, rational, liberal republics. For example, the Venezuelan poet, Andrés Bello (1781–1865), who had tutored the liberating general, Simon Bolívar, advocated cultural reconciliation with Spain, but he also believed that European cultural values would find new life and development in the Americas. He advocated an agriculture that would carefully cultivate the soil and produce abundant fruits as a means to founding a rationally ordered society, based on a partnership of man and nature.[19] Another teacher of Bolívar, Simon Rodriquez (1769–1854), articulated a philosophy that advocated education for all classes and for women as well as men; stressed the importance of practical studies; and believed in human perfectibility through education.[20] Around the same time, another poet, the Argentinian Esteban Echeverría (1805–1851), wrote political essays influenced by the technologically elitist French visionary Henri de Saint-Simon, whose social engineering ideals are discussed in Chapter 3. But this top-down effort eventually failed to impress grass-roots Argentinians and so faded away. Opposing the dictatorship of Juan Manuel de Rosas, Echeverría advocated a new Argentina based on liberty and justice.[21]

In the late nineteenth and twentieth centuries, various forms of Marxism were influential in Latin America. Their impact extended from communist to socialist movements, and from the advocates of violence to those supporting various forms of democracy and non-violence. All were affected by the Cuban revolution of 1959 led by Fidel Castro. As with other forms of utopian thought, the influence of Marxism is highly diverse. Mixed with nationalist-populist as well as reformist ideas, the form taken by utopian Marxist ideals has been contingent on the particular place and political circumstance.[22]

In 2003 an exhibit was held in Brussels on "Cruelty and Utopia: Cities and Landscapes of Latin America." A companion text with the same title appeared in 2005. The many contributors examine the contradictory nature of several leading Latin American cities. These were cities that, unlike older European ones, could be planned from the outset and so avoid the errors found in their European counterparts. But the Latin American cities were often established on the ruins—and the blood and violence—of pre-Hispanic cities destroyed by the European conquerors. In Buenos

Aires, Caracas, Havana, Rio de Janeiro, and (most explicitly utopian) Brasilia, plus some university communities in Mexico and elsewhere, planning often failed amid crime, political instability, corruption, and population growth.[23]

In oil-rich Venezuela, long-time President Hugo Chavez has been building several new utopian cities that would supposedly escape the major problems—the "cruelties"—of those earlier Latin American urban centers. Unlike their predecessors, these urban utopias would be carved from the wilderness, not atop pre-Hispanic communities. In theory, at least, they would be genuinely socialist, environmentally sensitive, and economically self-sustainable.[24]

In many areas of Latin America during recent decades, the movement of indigenous peoples toward autonomy and the assertion of human rights has finally led them to "imagine their own utopia." A prime example is that of the indigenous Chiapas Indians in southeastern Mexico, whose uprising began in 1994. They are steadily freeing themselves from the constricting vision of Indians found in More's *Utopia*. This does not translate into any declaration that "their societies are utopian." Instead, it means that, "like all peoples everywhere," they deserve the basic human rights denied them for far too long.[25]

By contrast, Brazil, Latin America's largest country, has been particularly amenable to antithetical and autocratic religious and millenarian tendencies. A recent study of utopias in twentieth-century Latin American literature finds a similar embrace of the distant past in which anti-democratic, elitist, and pre-industrial values prevail.[26]

Finally, as helpful as it might be to connect these various Asian and Latin American visions of both the future and the past to other, non-utopian political, economic, social, and cultural developments in those respective societies, to do so would go beyond the scope of this book. Suffice it to say that discontent with the status quo in these societies over the centuries, as revealed by the more "aggressive" utopian visions, may well have trickled down to the proverbial masses and may reflect pervasive discontent among them. Direct links between those visions and actual events cannot, however, be established.

The Several Genres of Utopianism: Prophecies and Oratory, Political Movements, Communities, Writings, World's Fairs, Cyberspace

Utopianism has taken various forms over the centuries. In the beginning there were prophecies and oratory from the eighteenth century on declaring the New World as superior to Europe's Old World in its greater natural resources, greater areas of potential settlement, and comparatively greater freedom of speech, religion, and politics. Then came political movements—such as varieties of socialism that went far beyond equal distribution of wages and wealth; forms of engineering-led technocracy; and the American Bellamy-led Nationalist movement. Along with these were actual communities, especially in France, England, and the United States, and, in the twentieth century, in Israel in the form of kibbutzim. A bit later came world's fairs and, most recently, cyberspace "virtual" communities. Because utopianism is usually studied piecemeal, it is important to recognize its multiple dimensions and the relationships between them.

With rare exceptions, neither form of utopian expression—communities or writings—had many followers or much influence. But the exceptions, which include a handful of communities such as the American Shakers and a handful of writings such as Bellamy's *Looking Backward*, do deserve our attention.

Utopian Communities in America: Especially Brook Farm, the Shakers, and Oneida   America's many actual communities varied considerably in viewpoint, organization, size, stability, economic development, and longevity. Because the United States overall had already been proclaimed a potential utopia by many at home and abroad, it was a logical extension of that dream for many prospective communitarians—both European and native-born—to try to establish their particular utopias on a small scale in America. Even when, as with most of the earliest New England colonists such as the Pilgrims and the Puritans, the belief in human beings' permanently flawed character prevailed, there was still the hope of substantial improvement by virtue of the opportunity for the comparative freedom to practice one's religion.[27]

Until Robert Fogarty's *All Things New: American Communes and Utopian Movements, 1860–1914* appeared in 1990, most students of American utopian communities assumed that they had flourished only in the first half of the nineteenth century and had virtually died out until their revival in the 1960s "counterculture." Fogarty examined 141 communities that arose between 1860 and 1914, including mystical Shalam in New Mexico, free-love Spirit Fruit in Ohio and Illinois, all-female Women's Commonwealth in Texas, and socialist, then anarchist, Equality in Washington state. To varying degrees all were inspired by the *Book of Revelations'* injunction to "make all things new" and were self-conscious about their need for journeying elsewhere in America or abroad (usually Palestine) to do so. As such they both reflected and took to extremes the mass migrations and frontier extensions of other, non-utopian Americans of their day.

Contrary to stereotypes, some of these 141 utopias were conservative, not radical—for example, rejecting the growing calls for class action in favor of older ideals of the common good. Certain communities were even "anti-modernist" in various respects. It is therefore wrong to assume that utopian communities in this— or any other—period of American history were invariably on the political or social or cultural fringes, for many were not. Hence no one model fits all American utopian communities.

Equally importantly, as many utopian communities were content with being left alone by the outside world as were eager to convert their contemporaries. The former stance proved sensible insofar as those who held the latter position usually encountered either indifference or hostility from the non-utopians nearest them.

Interestingly, the longest surviving American utopian communities relied on some forms of technology and manufacturing in order to succeed; those that relied primarily on agriculture invariably failed. One of the most famous examples of the latter, built on 170 acres eight miles from Boston, was Brook Farm, which lasted from 1841 until 1847. The experimental community attracted a number of intellectuals inspired in part by the New

England-based philosophy called Transcendentalism, in part by the writings of French utopian Charles Fourier (discussed in Chapter 3), and in part by early versions of socialism. Nathaniel Hawthorne's novel *Blithedale Romance* (1852) was inspired by his experiences while living at Brook Farm from April to November 1841 and by the gap between dreams and reality that he witnessed. The vision of everyone working at whatever he or she desired to do, of men and women being paid equally, and of ample time for leisurely pursuits was naïve. Sales of agricultural products never sufficed. Additional income later derived from selling publications; from selling hand-made shoes and boots, carpentry items, and window sashes and blinds; from charging visitors' fees; and from charging tuition for a school established to cover every level from pre-school through college preparatory. An effort to follow Fourier's blueprints for a special building fell victim to a fire that destroyed the structure. Meanwhile, members' competing ambitions also undermined Brook Farm's prospects.[28]

Ironically, the foremost example of this technological and manufacturing orientation, the Shakers, successfully reproduced new communities while prohibiting their members from "reproducing" themselves. Their official title was the United Society of Believers in Christ's Second Appearing. The Shakers came to America from England in 1774 to practice their religious beliefs freely. Their name derived from the way they shook and whirled to rid themselves of evil. The ecstatic nature of their lengthy services—including hand clapping, stomping, dancing, jumping, having visions, and speaking in tongues—formed an emotional outlet for their otherwise austere lives.

Led by the charismatic Ann Lee (1736–1784)—whom they believed represented Christ's Second Coming (in female form)—the Shakers traveled extensively and attracted converts who accepted celibacy, property held in common, equality of men and women, and pacifism. They believed that Adam and Eve had sinned by having sexual relations in the Garden of Eden and so wanted to avoid that in their own lives and communities. However, given the obvious need to recruit new members from outside their ranks, they had no problem with non-members marrying other non-members and having sex with other non-members.

At their peak in the mid-1800s, the Shakers had six thousand members, far more than any other communitarian enterprise, and nineteen colonies in several New England, mid-Atlantic, and Midwestern states. Their architecture, furniture, household machines, and other products reflected their basic values of simplicity, efficiency, purity, and perfection but were also technologically advanced and commercially successful. Shakers manufactured chairs, brooms, pails, tubs, mops, nails, washing machines, and lathes.[29] In so doing they often improved on existing varieties of these items, and they sometimes invented their own.

The one other prominent technologically oriented utopian community of the period, Oneida, in upstate New York, produced animal traps, chairs, brooms, dishwashers, hats, garden furniture, leather travel bags, and, of course, the silverware that eventually made them famous. It was established in 1848 by John Humphrey Noyes. Far from insisting on celibacy, Oneida insisted on what might today be called "open marriage." Highlights included "complex marriage," whereby every man and every woman were married to one another and so could have sexual relations but not be strictly bound to one another as in conventional marriages; "male continence," a form of birth control precluding ejaculation during and after intercourse; and "ascending fellowship," whereby virgins who were about fourteen years old were put under the guidance of older persons and brought into the practice of complex marriage.

The contrast with the Shakers could hardly be greater. Where the Shakers acknowledged and emphasized human sin, the Oneida Perfectionists claimed that they were without sin once they had accepted Noyes' beliefs. Noyes' revisionist theology contended that Christ's death was not for the sins of human beings but rather was a blow against Satan; those who accepted Christ's death were thereby freed from sin—the very opposite of the Shakers. Noyes also claimed that Christ had already returned to earth in the year 70 and that human nature was thereby perfectible. (The post-Millennialists, by contrast, could also improve the world but, unlike Noyes' followers, still awaited Christ's return to complete the salvation process and still believed in original sin.)

Oneida's road to perfection included "mutual criticism," whereby each community member was brought before a committee of older members to be evaluated for strengths and weaknesses. The committees rotated every three months and eventually included all adult members so that every adult could take turns being critic and being criticized. The goal was not punishment but correction, not singling out individuals but increasing cooperation, creating a consensus, and making the community ever more harmonious.

Initially, Noyes envisioned Oneida with an economic focus on growing and selling fruit. As with so much else, he believed that Oneida's horticulture could be perfected. A decade later, the community was instead turning to business and manufacturing for economic survival. Not until 1877, however, did it begin manufacturing its signature silverware.

In its social dimensions, Oneida remained remarkably successful under Noyes' leadership for over thirty years; however, unlike the Shakers, the Oneida Perfectionists' efforts to create other communities largely failed. These "offspring" were located in Wallingford, Connecticut; Newark, New Jersey; Putney, Vermont; and Cambridge, Vermont. All but Wallingford, which survived until it was destroyed by a tornado in 1878, were closed in 1854.

Noyes successfully involved himself in every major aspect of both the original and the branch communities. But in 1879, threatened with legal action for immoral behavior, Noyes fled to Canada to escape arrest and trial. Before leaving, he got the community to accept the abolition of complex marriage, reducing outside scrutiny and condemnation. Within two years, though, the community had broken up. Oneida then became the joint-stock corporation Oneida Limited, which concentrated on silverware.[30]

Meanwhile, the Shaker communities began to close in the late nineteenth century and today continue only in Maine.[31] The insistence on celibacy, on spirituality, and, no less important, on detachment from the outside world (save for commerce) increasingly condemned the Shakers to the margins of an ever more urbanized and secularized America. (Still, Shaker-style furniture continues to be admired and sold, as does Oneida silverware.)

Edward Bellamy on Writings versus Communities The failure of the Shaker, Oneida, and other experiments to transform the United States is the reason why Edward Bellamy (1850–1898) concluded that complex times demanded utopian writings rather than the continued creation of communities. Long before he began composing *Looking Backward*, the visionary credited with the establishment of American utopian writings as a serious, modern intellectual genre determined that only thoughtful, reflective tracts could respond convincingly to industrialization, urbanization, immigration, poverty, disease, and class conflict. The continued creation and, if possible, duplication of small-scale communities no longer constituted an effective means of social or economic change. As Bellamy observed retrospectively in 1892, "In a broad sense of the word the Nationalist movement [the political movement growing out of the popularity of his book] did arise fifty years ago" in the form of "the Brook Farm Colony and a score of phalansteries for communistic [i.e., communal] experiments." Note Bellamy's reference to Brook Farm and to the Fourierist material and organizational structure attempted by that community, which, alas, went up in flames as its construction was nearing completion. But then the overriding concern for ending slavery redirected the energies of "these humane enthusiasts." By the 1890s, the time for such small-scale enterprises had passed.[32]

For Bellamy, utopian speculation was obviously less risky and less costly when attempts were made to put words down on paper than when attempts were made to place it on the actual landscape. Bellamy's Nationalist movement eventually subordinated its independence in joining with the Populist party under the leadership of William Jennings Bryan in two unsuccessful presidential campaigns. As Bellamy put it, "We nationalists are not trying to work out our individual salvation, but the weal of all, and no man is a true nationalist who . . . wishes to be saved unless all the rest are." Consequently, he concluded, "A slight amendment in the condition of the mass of men is *preferable to elysium attained by the few*."[33]

Without for a moment marginalizing utopian communities as merely exotic phenomena, as has too often been done even by sympathetic scholars, their very diversity—whether of architecture or religious beliefs or economic schemes or sexual practices—

Figure 2.1 Photograph of Edward Bellamy about a year after his *Looking Backward: 2000–1887* (1888) was published. The book became the most popular and influential utopian work ever to appear in the United States, but Bellamy's efforts to effect short-term political and economic changes largely failed. *Source*: Courtesy of Prints and Photographs Division, Library of Congress, Washington, DC.

inevitably limited the possible connections between them and so undermined their respective causes. There was no unified movement of the nation's utopian communities in pursuit of common goals. Nor, for that matter, can one take too seriously the argument of economist Brian Berry that the pattern of America's utopian communal formation correlates with long-wave economic rhythms. Specifically, the Kondratiev theory held that periodic deflationary troughs produced economic crises and that those crises led to utopian experiments as havens for those hurt financially. (Named after the Russian economist Nikolai Kondratiev (1892–1938), this theory contends that, in the modern capitalist world economy, high sectors of growth in certain economic sectors alternate with low sectors of growth every fifty or sixty years.) Unlike the communitarians, utopian writers usually agreed on the nature of the fundamental problems of the day even if they often disagreed about solutions. These problems were called "industrialization," "urbanization," "immigration," or "labor unrest." For the utopian writers, economic crises were certainly significant but not always critical.[34] *Looking Backward* reflects this consensus, notwithstanding its unique popularity and influence.

Why Bellamy's Looking Backward *was so Popular*   Curiously, *Looking Backward*'s spiritual qualities may have been as important to the book's persistent popularity as its technological utopian vision. A professional journalist and accomplished fiction writer before *Looking Backward* appeared, Bellamy knew how to captivate an audience. His readers are transported along with Julian West, a wealthy young Bostonian who somehow sleeps for 113 years, from the poverty, disease, crowding, violence, and corruption of late-nineteenth-century industrial America to a nation of well-planned cities and towns whose citizens enjoy full employment, material abundance, good health, and social harmony. In the process, they join Julian in his quest to understand how utopia emerged without bloodshed, much less revolution.[35]

At its heart, Bellamy's novel is about cooperation, a modest form of socialism, the "Religion of Solidarity," and material and administrative advances. It is also about romance. Yet technology is at once a principal cause of and solution to the major problems Bellamy addresses, including inefficiency (overproduction and underproduction, excessive competition, mismanagement); inequality of opportunity and of income; immorality (greed, monopoly, exploitation); and urban blight. Technology's purposeful, positive use—from improved factories and offices to new highways and electric lighting systems to innovative pneumatic tubes for delivering goods, electronic broadcasts, and credit cards—is critical to America's predicted transformation from living hell to heaven on earth.

Without question, Bellamy's envisioned twenty-first-century United States is an avowed technological utopia, an allegedly ideal society not simply dependent upon machines but outright modeled after them, its citizens quite willing cogs in a "great industrial machine." Bellamy grasped technology's potential to create a reformed social and civic order out of what, to many of his fellow Americans, was material and moral chaos. Not surprisingly, the Nationalist movement his book inspired sought to reform America's political system, not to overthrow it.[36]

Still, unlike numerous other technological utopians of his day whose writings were commercial failures, Bellamy was not a rigid technocrat demanding complete conformity. Instead, he was exceptionally sensitive to technology's potential for satisfying citizens' varying needs and desires. In this he recalls the insights of Marx and Engels. Occupation, residence, and leisure would be matters of choice; only those seeking top positions in the industrial army would work after age forty-five. Marriage would be for love, never wealth, because everyone would live comfortably. Crime would barely exist because poverty would no longer exist. In these ways, *Looking Backward* is a more complex and more humane work than William Morris in his *News From Nowhere* (1890)—discussed in the next chapter—would ever acknowledge.

Interestingly, Bellamy predicted only a few specific technological advances: those pneumatic tubes to deliver goods, electronic broadcasts, and credit cards instead of money. Other predictions such as department stores were primarily logical extensions of existing American society. Nevertheless, *Looking Backward* remains timely in its concern for using cutting-edge technologies efficiently, for distributing the opportunities and wealth derived from technological advances fairly, for offering varieties of work and living arrangements, and, not least, for constructing a vision of the future out of moral conviction.

Looking Backward's enormous popularity inspired a political movement, the Nationalist crusade, but its influence, as indicated, was modest. Moreover, in general, utopian writings were no more successful than utopian communities in general in providing either practical or popular solutions to the problems of American society at any juncture in the nineteenth and twentieth centuries.

World's Fairs World's fairs constituted yet another expression of American utopianism beyond communities and writings. Contrary to popular stereotypes, world's fairs have been more than harmless diversions from everyday life. They are significant social and cultural artifacts that must be approached seriously since they reveal more about the times and places that produced them than about future times and places. Moreover, fairs offer a microcosm of the dreams and fears not only of their planners and sponsors but also of many ordinary visitors. Furthermore, the very impermanence of world's fairs allows them to function as innovative, *de facto* model cities, combining architecture and city planning.

Figure 2.2 Crystal Palace, London, 1851. From hand-colored lithograph, circa 1851. The site of the first world's fair. *Source*: Courtesy of Prints and Photographs Division, Library of Congress, Washington, DC.

The first world's fair was London's Crystal Palace Exhibition of 1851. It was followed a mere two years later by a smaller version of the same event held in New York City.[37] Then came dozens of international extravaganzas throughout the West, including several in various other American cities.[38] The fairs brought together in one site countless world leaders, inventors, and scholars and their various platforms and projects. World's fairs were, in effect, temporary utopias.[39]

But it was in the 1930s that there were four times the number of fairs of any previous decade. Fairs were hosted by Antwerp, Glasgow, Leipzig, Oslo, Paris, and Stockholm. The popularity of earlier fairs spurred much of this increase. So, too, however, did a growing faith, especially in the United States, in the ability to shape the future through science and technology. Previous world's fairs in both the United States and Europe had certainly had a scientific and technological bent, as they still do. This bent was present and persists in the strictly commercial and ideologically unpretentious trade fairs whose history antedates the 1851 Exhibition. Yet the 1933–1934 Century of Progress International Exposition in Chicago, the 1935 California-Pacific Exposition in San Diego, the 1939 Golden Gate International Exposition in San Francisco, and, above all, the 1939–1940 World of Tomorrow in New York City, still more than their predecessors, manifested the idealism that a veritable utopia would come about in America in the very near future—by 1960, to be exact, according to the World of Tomorrow, the only fair to set a specific date.[40] Thus the fair moved the deadline for (a version of) scientific and technological utopia from a century or more ahead—as with the date of 2000 given by 1887's *Looking Backward*—to just two decades.

No less importantly, the four major architects of the World of Tomorrow—Walter Dorwin Teague, Henry Dreyfuss, Raymond Loewy, and, most notably, Norman Bel Geddes—were pioneering industrial designers who readily assumed that the achievement of a scientific and technological utopia only awaited their design.[41] Having begun their careers by designing the individual components of a new world, discrete artifacts ranging from home appliances to vehicles to buildings, they enlarged and redirected their efforts to designing the new world itself. This proudly synthetic environment would replace much of the natural environment. The chronological and psychological gap between the real and ideal realms had thus been all but bridged.[42]

The gaps between these fantasy worlds and the real one proved far wider than was anticipated by the fair's designers, by their government and corporate sponsors, and by most of their visitors. By 1960, the America that Geddes and others envisioned had come about only in bare outline—in its sleek skyscrapers and smooth superhighways and in its newer cities and renovated older ones. But there was nothing of the social and economic equality or the cultural riches that, like many other technological visionaries, Geddes and his associates assumed would follow automatically in the wake of the scientific and technological advances. For that matter, the very dream of world peace through international gatherings such as fairs, a traditional belief that permeated the 1939 fair season, was shattered by World War II, a scientific and technological nightmare, well before the 1940 season.

The Spanish Civil War coincided with the 1937 Paris exposition's celebration of science and technology, which was at variance with the mass bombing of the city of Guernica weeks earlier. That deliberate attack on civilians inspired Pablo Picasso's famous painting, first shown in the Spanish pavilion. Meanwhile, the Tower of Peace dwarfed the highly nationalistic German, Italian, Soviet, and Japanese pavilions, along with the Palestinian one that boasted growing Jewish settlements.[43]

As hopes for universal peace through world's fairs have diminished, fairs in recent decades have provided fewer social, economic, and cultural predictions and have been less avowedly idealistic regarding "the shape of things to come" (to invoke the tile of H. G. Wells' 1933 book). Moreover, the computerization of the world and the unprecedented ability to communicate instantaneously with people almost everywhere have rendered world's fairs obsolete. Why travel to distant points to see the future if satellites, computers, cell phones, iPhones, faxes, and the Internet can now immediately deliver needed information to one's office, factory, home, or palm? For that matter, the cutting-edge mass entertainment that once also drew visitors to fairs can now be found on a more permanent basis at theme parks such as Disney and Universal. And then, of course, there's always Las Vegas.

Missing from recent world's fairs and theme parks alike is any genuine moral critique of the present, any serious effort to alter society in the manner of earlier world's fairs. This is not to deny the widely accepted historical interpretation of these prior fairs as socially and culturally conservative, given their origins and funding as promotions of business, industry, and corporate-oriented government. As far back as the 1851 London and 1853 New York fairs, world's fairs have attempted to promote a consensus on national and international issues and to downplay conflicts within and between nations.

Robert Rydell, John Findling, and Kimberly Pelle, the authors of *Fair America: World's Fairs in the United States* (2000), have neatly summarized American world's fairs into four categories: (1) "Fairs in the Age of Industrialism's Advance" sought to replace lingering Civil War tensions with examples of post-Reconstruction America's industrial and cultural advances; (2) "Fairs of the Imperial Era" tried to legitimize American expansion and imperialism by exhibiting "primitive" peoples—whether Native Americans or Africans or Filipinos or Eskimos—who allegedly needed our educational and economic assistance and moral uplift; (3) "Fairs between the World Wars" tried to promote faith in science and technology as means of securing permanent world peace and prosperity; and (4) "Fairs in the Atomic Age" attempted to allay Cold War anxieties and, later, environmental concerns with visions of peaceful uses of nuclear power and other energy sources.

This is not to reject the argument of Rydell himself in other books that the American fairs from Philadelphia in 1876 through San Francisco in 1915 and San Diego in 1915 and 1916 were at least implicitly sexist, racist, and imperialist. *Fair America* makes clear that some world's fairs endured periodic protests from those who did not embrace their exaggerated notions of national consensus. Protesters included anti-imperialists, suffragists, citizens displaced by demolition and construction, and, not least, African Americans. Thus, at the 1893 World's Columbian Exposition in Chicago—which had excluded African Americans from all of its planning committees—abolitionist Frederick Douglass delivered a speech on August 25, designated Colored People's Day. Unimpressed by this blatant tokenism, he condemned white Americans for violating the constitution by refusing to grant equal rights to their fellow blacks.

Although Rydell reduces those late-nineteenth- and early-twentieth-century American fairs to a single theme that surely did not encompass all the varied experiences of every attendee at any fair, ranging from scholarly presentations to entertainment to shopping, he does illuminate part (but only part) of the varying messages conveyed by many organizers.[44] American history textbooks routinely observe that historian Frederick Jackson Turner's famous address about the alleged closing of the American frontier was delivered at the 1893 Chicago fair. Early fairs in both America and Europe were highly respected as settings for powerful intellectual discourse, where scholarly papers on cutting-edge topics were given before eminent authorities in various fields.

It is, of course, impossible to determine precisely what influence, if any, fairs had on visitors, but it is reasonable to contend that, because those fairs often attracted huge numbers of visitors, they had at least some longer-term effects. Moreover, twentieth-century fairs everywhere increasingly replaced nationalist sentiments with more universal consumer consciousness. As "Selling the World of Tomorrow," a temporary (1989–1990) exhibit at the Museum of the City of New York on the 1939–1940 fair (which was widely known as "The World of Tomorrow") demonstrated, the fair was selling not just a genuine vision of a utopia that could come about in the next two decades but also commercial products and mass entertainment. This is reflected both in overall messages and in specific structures. Where private corporations had a modest presence in pre-1900 fairs in terms of building their own exhibits, post-world-war fairs have steadily become the province of multi-national corporations whose exhibits primarily advertise and sell their products.

Despite world's fairs having become cultural dinosaurs amid declining public interest and governmental support, they remain of considerable interest. Not even the cancellation of the proposed Chicago fair of 1992 and the disappointing attendance and financial disasters at others that did open—especially Knoxville in 1982, New Orleans in 1984, and Hanover, Germany, in 2000—has stopped this trend. In fact, the latest world's fair, the six-month-long Expo 2010 in Shanghai, China, attracted some seventy-two million, surpassing the previous record of sixty-four million set by the 1970 fair in Osaka, Japan. Expo 2010 included many national and corporate pavilions and the by now requisite attention to environmental as well as commercial and cultural themes. A principal purpose was to stimulate discussion of "urban maladies" under the slogan of "Better city, better life." Expo 2010 included new electric buses and carts, energy-saving air-conditioning, water filters to reduce bottled water, recycled rain water, solar power, and an Urban Best Practices Area. It claimed to have recycled all waste when the fair ended. The forceful relocation of some 55,000 people to clear the fair's site was, of course, conveniently overlooked.[45]

On the fair's final day, China's Premier, Wen Jiabao, proclaimed it to have been a great success, above all as the first world's fair held in a developing country. That was a dubious claim, since the second world's fair—in New York City in 1853–1854—was in an avowedly developing country. Meanwhile the Chinese economy, while still "developing," is now the second largest in the world.

Interestingly, unlike previous fairs, Expo 2010's public relations arm addressed the crucial topic of the continuing relevance of world's fairs. As Chen Shuai, a twenty-four-year-old Chinese tourist, wrote in *China Daily* (using "World Expo" to mean world's fairs in general),

> The World Expo has seen its influence wane over the past two decades, especially with the advent of the information era ... countries need to exhibit ... things that cannot so easily be shown in the virtual world—in order to keep the Expo a valid and credible event ... most countries [at the Shanghai fair] are marketing what they are [most] proud of, whether it is their natural environment, their sights and attractions, or their public policies.[46]

Shuai's rationale is intriguing if not entirely convincing, for older world's fairs, of course, likewise marketed what their exhibitors were most proud of and likewise enjoyed large numbers of visitors from the home nations. But it is also true that, for most Chinese, obtaining passports for foreign travel is challenging, thanks to restrictions on human rights and bureaucratic obstacles. Thus, if the majority of the visitors were Chinese, they may in fact have been limited in their foreign travel. Moreover, Shuai at least recognized the dilemma of world's fairs' continuing relevance today.[47]

The next world's fairs will also have basic themes intended to underline the fairs' persistent importance: the 2012 fair in the South Korean port city of Yeosu will focus on marine-based sustainability, while the 2015 fair in the Italian city of Milan will emphasize food safety.

Notes

1 Frank Manuel and Fritzie P. Manuel, *Utopian Thought in the Western World* (Cambridge, MA: Belknap Press of Harvard University Press, 1979), 1. See also Frank Manuel and Fritzie P. Manuel, "Introduction," in *French Utopias: An Anthology of Ideal Societies*, trans. Manuel and Manuel (New York: Schocken, 1971), 1, where they state that within Europe utopianism "for four centuries . . . has remained predominantly English and French." See also Krishan Kumar, *Utopia and Anti-Utopia in Modern Times* (Oxford: Blackwell, 1987), 33.

2 Lyman Tower Sargent, *Utopianism: A Very Short Introduction* (New York: Oxford University Press, 2010), 126.

3 Koon-ki T. Ho, "Several Thousand Years in Search of Happiness: The Utopian Tradition in China," *Oriens Extremus*, 30 (1983), 19–20. See also Koon-ki T. Ho, "Utopianism: A Unique Theme in Western Literature? A Short Survey on Chinese Utopianism," *Tamkang Review*, 13 (1982), 87–108; and Wolfgang Bauer, *China and the Search for Happiness: Recurring Themes in Four Thousand Years of Chinese Cultural History*, trans. Michael Shaw (New York: Seabury, 1976).

4 Ho, "Several Thousand Years," 21.

5 Zhang Longxi, "The Utopian Vision, East and West," *Utopian Studies*, 13 (2002), 8.

6 The generalizations in this paragraph come from Kumar, *Utopia and Anti-Utopia* (33–35) but the actual scholarship derives from Laurence

G. Thompson's introduction to his abridged English translation of *Ta Thung Shu: The One-World Philosophy of Khang Yu-Wei* (London: Faber and Faber, 1958); and from Joseph Needham, "Social Devolution and Revolution: Ta Thung and Thai Phing," in *Revolution in History*, eds. Roy Porter and Mikulas Teich (New York: Cambridge University Press, 1986), 61–73. Khang Yu-Wei's book was also entitled *The United States of the World* according to Roger L. Emerson, "Utopia," in *Dictionary of the History of Ideas*, ed. Philip P. Wiener (New York: Scribner, 1973–1974), vol. 4, 459.

7   Kumar, *Utopia and Anti-Utopia*, 33–35; Thompson, "Introduction," in *Ta Thung Shu*; and Needham, "Social Devolution and Revolution." See also Kung-Chuan Hsiao, *A Modern China and a New World: K'ang Yu-Wei, Reformer and Utopian, 1858–1927* (Seattle, WA: University of Washington Press, 1975).

8   Ho, "Several Thousand Years," 33.

9   Jean Chesneaux, "Egalitarian and Utopian Traditions in the East," *Diogenes*, 62 (Summer 1968), 100. See Longxi, "The Utopian Vision" (6) for criticisms of Chesneaux's influential article.

10 George B. Bikle, Jr., "Utopianism and the Planning Element in Modern Japan," 41. See Seija Nuita, "Traditional Utopias in Japan and the West: A Study in Contrasts," in *Aware of Utopia*, ed. David W. Plath (Urbana, IL: University of Illinois Press, 1971). Nuita provides a list of Japanese utopias from 1775 to 1902, most published after 1880 (24, 31), and agrees with Kumar, Needham, and others about there being no tradition of utopianism in any Asian country save China (17). However, see also the whole of Bikle, "Utopianism."

11 Eiji Takemura, *The Perception of Work in Tokugawa Japan: A Study of Ishida Baigan and Nonomiya Sontoku* (Lanham, MD: University Press of America, 1997), 61.

12 Bikle, "Utopianism," 43; and Tetsuo Najita, *Tokugawa Political Writings* (Cambridge: Cambridge University Press, 1998), xv–xvi, which contains translations of some of Sorai's writings.

13 Bikle, "Utopianism," 44; and Takemura, *Perception of Work*, esp. 109–135.

14 Nuita, "Traditional Utopias," 29. See also Bikle, "Utopianism," 44–51. For a broad background and an introduction to more recent scholarship, see the following chapters in *The Cambridge History of Japan, vol. 5: The Nineteenth Century*, ed. Jansen (Cambridge: Cambridge University Press, 1989): Marius B. Jansen, "The Meiji Restoration" (308–366), Stephen Vlastos, "Opposition Movements in early Meiji, 1868–1885" (367–431), Hirakawa Sukehiro, "Japan's Turn to the

West" (432–498), and Kenneth B. Pyle, "Meiji Conservativism," (674–720, esp. 676–679).

15 Bikle, "Utopianism," 46–50; and Stephen S. Large, *The Rise of Labor in Japan: The Yuaikai, 1912–1919* (Tokyo: Sophia University Press, 1972).

16 Bikle, "Utopianism," 50–52. For a broader context, see Marius B. Jansen, *The Making of Modern Japan* (Cambridge, MA: Belknap Press of Harvard University Press, 2000), 555–564; and James L. McClain, *Japan: A Modern History* (New York: Norton, 2002), esp. 357–397. Regarding the 1930s, World War II, and the present, see, for example, the abstracts of papers delivered at Session 129, "Utopias of Japanese Colonialism," Association of Asian Studies, San Diego, March 9–12, 2000. As a prime and graphic example, see Iris Chang's remarkable and chilling *The Rape of Nanking: The Forgotten Holocaust of World War II* (New York: Basic Books, 1997). For an introduction to the context of these developments, see Jansen, *Making of Modern Japan*, 577–624; McClain, *Japan*, 405–481; and the following chapters in *The Cambridge History of Japan*, vol. 6: *The Twentieth Century*, ed. Peter Duus (Cambridge: Cambridge University Press, 1988): Gordon M. Berger, "Politics and Mobilization in Japan, 1931–1945" (97–153), Mark R. Peattie, "The Japanese Colonial Empire, 1895–1945" (217–270), Ikuhiko Hata, "Continental Expansion, 1905–1941" (271–314), and Alvin D. Coox, "The Pacific War" (315–382). For post-war utopianism, see Bikle, "Utopianism," 52–54.

17 Edwin Williamson, *The Penguin History of Latin America* (London: Penguin, 1992), 84. For a succinct description of these groups, see 37–76. For a detailed introduction, see Leslie Bethell, *The Cambridge History of Latin America, vol. 1: Colonial Latin America* (Cambridge: Cambridge University Press, 1984).

18 See Arthur J. Slavin, "The American Principle from More to Locke," in *First Images of America: The Impact of the New World on the Old*, eds. Fredi Chiappelli with Michael J. B. Allen and Robert Benson (Berkeley and Los Angeles, CA: University of California Press, 1976), 139–164, esp. 142–147, 149–151, and 159–160; and, more recently, Candace Slater, *Entangled Edens: Visions of the Amazon* (Berkeley and Los Angeles, CA: University of California Press, 2002), esp. 29–53, which cites further literature.

19 Williamson, *History of Latin America*, 287–288. For Andrés Bello's views on agriculture, see, for example, "Ode to Tropical Agriculture," in *Selected Writings of Andres Bello*, ed. Ivan Jaksic, trans. Frances M. Lopez-Morillas (New York: Oxford University Press, 1997), 28–37.

There is a large literature on Bello that includes Rafael Caldera, *Andres Bello: Philosopher, Poet, Philologist, Educator, Legislator, Statesman*, tr. John Street (London: G. Allen and Unwin, 1977) and Ivan Jaksic, *Andres Bello: Scholarship and Nation-Building in Nineteenth-Century Latin America* (New York: Cambridge University Press, 2001).

20 See especially Jorge Lopez Palma, *Simon Rodriquez: Utopia y Socialismo* (Caracas: Catedra Pio Tamayo Expediente, 1989) and Maria del Rayo Ramirez Fierro, *Simon Rodriquez y su utopia para America* (Mexico: Universidad Nacional Autonoma de Mexico, 1994).

21 Frank Safford, "Politics, Ideology, and Society in Post-Independence South America," in *The Cambridge History of Latin America, vol. 3: From Independence to c.1870*, ed. Leslie Bethell (Cambridge: Cambridge University Press, 1985), 347–421, esp. 368; Edgar C. Knowleton, *Estaban Echeverría* (Bryn Mawr, PA: Dorrance, 1986); William H. Catra, *The Argentine Generation of 1837: Echeverria, Alberdi, Sarmiento, Mitre* (Madison, NJ: Fairleigh Dickinson University Press, 1996); Juan Carlos Mercado, *Building a Nation: The Case of Echeverria* (Lanham, MD: University Press of America, 1996); and Williamson, *History of Latin America*, 288–289.

22 For an introduction to this complex subject, see especially Alan Angell, "The Left in Latin America since c.1920," in *Cambridge History*, ed. Bethell, 163–232; and Jorge G. Castañeda, *Utopia Unarmed: The Latin American Left after the Cold War* (New York: Knopf, 1993).

23 See Jean-Francois Lejeune, ed., *Cruelty and Utopia: Cities and Landscapes of Latin America* (New York: Princeton Architectural Press, 2005).

24 See Juan Forero, *Washington Post*, "As Chavez's First 'Socialist City' Rises, A Utopian Vision Takes Shape," *Boston Sunday Globe*, December 2, 2007, A4.

25 Shannon L. Mattiace, "Mayan Utopias: Rethinking the State," in *Mayan Lives, Mayan Utopias: The Indigenous Peoples of Chiapas and the Zapatista Rebellion*, eds. Jan Rus, Rosalva Aída Hernánez Castillo, and Mattiace (Lanham, MD: Rowman and Littlefield, 2003), 185–186. See also 185–190.

26 See Juan Carlos Grijalva, "Looking for the Remains of America: Exoticism, Utopia, and Latin American Identity in the 20th Century," unpublished Ph.D. dissertation, University of Pittsburgh, 2004.

27 On the variety of utopian communities throughout history, see the illuminating summary and analysis in Lyman Tower Sargent, "The Three Faces of Utopianism Revisited," *Utopian Studies*, 5 (1994), 2, 13–19.

28 There are many studies of Brook Farm, but among the most recent, and most interesting, is Sterling F. Delano, *Brook Farm: The Dark Side of Utopia* (Cambridge, MA: Harvard University Press, 2004).

29 Carl J. Guarneri, *The Utopian Alternative: Fourierism in Nineteenth-Century America* (Ithaca, NY: Cornell University Press, 1991) is the foremost study of the complex relationships between utopian communities and mainstream American politics and culture.

30 On the Shakers and technology, see John A. Kouwenhoven, *The Arts in Modern American Civilization* (New York: Norton, 1967), 92. On the Oneida Perfectionists and technology, see John H. Noyes, *History of American Socialisms* (New York: Dover, 1966 [1870]), 19; and Charles Nordhoff, *The Communistic Societies of the United States* (New York: Schocken, 1965 [1875]), 389–390. Relatively recent scholarship on the Shakers and their crafts includes June Sprigg, *By Shaker Hands: The Art and the World of the Shakers* (Hanover, NH: University Press of New England, 1990); Stephen J. Stein, *The Shaker Experience in America* (New Haven, CT: Yale University Press, 1992); John T. Kirk, *The Shaker World: Art, Life, Belief* (New York: Harry N. Abrams, 1997); and Clarke Garrett, *Origins of the Shakers: From the Old World to the New World* (Baltimore, MD: Johns Hopkins University Press, 1998). Works that treat Shaker and Oneida beliefs about sexuality and community living include Louis J. Kern, *An Ordered Love: Sex Roles and Sexuality in Victorian Utopias: The Shakers, the Mormons, and the Oneida Community* (Chapel Hill, NC: University of North Carolina Press, 1981); and Lawrence Foster, *Women, Family, and Utopia: Communal Experiments of the Shakers, the Oneida Community, and the Mormons* (Syracuse, NY: Syracuse University Press, 1991). For a more negative treatment of the Shakers, see Elizabeth De Wolfe, *Shaking the Faith: Women, Family, and Mary Marshall Dyer's Anti-Shaker Campaign, 1815–1867* (New York: Palgrave, 2002); *Domestic Broils: Shakers, Antebellum Marriage, and the Narratives of Mary and Joseph Dyer*, ed. De Wolfe (Amherst, MA: University of Massachusetts Press, 2010); and Ilyon Woo, *The Great Divorce: A Nineteenth-Century Mother's Extraordinary Fight Against Her Husband, the Shakers, and Her Times* (New York: Grove/Atlantic, 2010).

31 On the "agreement between Maine's Shaker community and a coalition of preservation and conservative organizations [that] will help protect the unique village [in New Gloucester] and the 1700 acres surrounding it from becoming carved into subdivisions," see Associated Press, "Deal to Protect Shakers' Land Coming Together," *Bangor Daily News*, August 15, 2005, B2.

32   Edward Bellamy, "Progress of Nationalism in the United States," *North American Review*, 154 (June 1892), 743.

33   Edward Bellamy, "Concerning the Founding of Nationalist Colonies," *The New Nation*, 3 (September 23, 1893), 434; italics added.

34   See Brian J. L. Berry, *America's Utopian Experiments: Communal Havens From Long-Wave Crises* (Hanover, NH: University Press of New England, 1992). See also the insightful reviews by Robert S. Fogarty, *American Historical Review*, 99 (April 1994), 635; Carl J. Guarneri, *Journal of Economic History*, 53 (December 1993), 976–977; Susan Matarese, *Utopian Studies*, 6 (1995), 144–145, and Timothy Miller, *Journal of American History*, 81 (September 1994), 691.

35   There are several paperback editions of *Looking Backward* available, but the most accessible—and with the best introduction and other materials for general readers—is the one edited by Daniel H. Borus (Boston and New York: Bedford Books of St. Martin's, 1995). But see also the superb edition prepared by John L. Thomas (Cambridge, MA: Harvard University Press, 1967). Scholarship on Bellamy includes Sylvia E. Bowman, *Edward Bellamy* (Boston, MA: Twayne Publishers, 1986); *Looking Backward, 1988–1888*, ed. Daphne Patai (Amherst, MA: University of Massachusetts Press, 1988); Toby Widdicombe and Herman S. Preiser, *Revisiting the Legacy of Edward Bellamy (1850–1898): American Author and Social Reformer* (Lewiston, NY: Edwin Mellen Press, 2002), which includes scholarly essays and a collection of Bellamy's writings; and two bibliographical works—Nancy Snell Griffith, *Edward Bellamy: A Bibliography* (Metuchen, NJ: Scarecrow Press, 1986) and Toby Widdicombe, *Edward Bellamy: An Annotated Bibliography of Secondary Criticism* (New York: Garland, 1988).

36   Withdrawn, frail, and often sickly, Bellamy was hardly the strong charismatic leader his millions of readers dearly sought. Yet he worked diligently, at the sacrifice of his remaining health, to try to effect the reforms he envisioned in his book and in other works. The Nationalist crusade eventually failed, and he devoted his last years to writing *Equality* (1897), his sequel to *Looking Backward*.

37   For a facsimile of the illustrated 1851 catalog of the Exposition see *The Great Exhibition: London's Crystal Palace Exposition of 1851* (New York: Gramercy Books, 1995). See also Patrick Beaver, *The Crystal Palace, 1851–1936: A Portrait of Victorian Enterprise* (London: Hugh Evelyn, 1970) and Giovanni Brino, *Crystal Palace: Cronaca di un'avventura progettuale* (Genoa: Sagep, 1995).

38   For an early account, see Benjamin C. Truman, *History of the World's Fair: Being a Complete and Authentic Description of the Columbian Exposi-*

tion from its Inception (New York: Arno Press, 1976 [1893]). See also Reid Badger, *The Great American Fair: The World's Columbian Exposition and American Culture* (Chicago: N. Hall, 1979); Robert Muccigrosso, *Celebrating the New World: Chicago's Columbian Exposition of 1893* (Chicago: I. R. Dee, 1993); and John E. Findling, *Chicago's Great World's Fairs* (New York: St. Martin's, 1994).

39   John E. Findling, ed., *Historical Dictionary of World's Fairs and Expositions, 1851–1988* (Westport, CT: Greenwood, 1990) is the foremost reference work on this topic even if now more than two decades old.

40   See Findling, *Chicago's Great World's Fairs*; Armour H. Nelson, *The Conquest of Chicago: Visiting the 1933 World's Fair*, ed. Alice C. Nelson (Manhattan, KS: Sunflower University Press, 2004) and Matthew F. Bokovoy, *The San Diego World's Fairs and Southwestern Memory, 1889–1940* (Albuquerque, NM: University of New Mexico Press, 2005). For the 1939 New York World's Fair, see David Hillel Gelernter, *1939, The Lost World of the Fair* (New York: Free Press, 1995); Larry Zim, Mel Lerner, and Herbert Rolfes, *The World of Tomorrow: The 1939 New York World's Fair* (New York: Harper and Row, 1988); and Andrew F. Wood, *New York's 1939–1940 World's Fair* (Charleston, SC: Arcadia, 2004).

41   On Teague, see W. Dorwin Teague, *Industrial Designer: The Artist as Engineer* (Lancaster, PA: Armstrong World Industries, 1998). On Dreyfuss, see Russell Flinchum, *Henry Dreyfuss, Industrial Designer: The Man in the Brown Suit* (New York: Cooper-Hewitt National Design Museum, Smithsonian Institution, and Rizzoli, 1997). On Loewy, see Raymond Loewy, *Industrial Design* (Woodstock, NY: Overlook Press, 1979) and Raymond Loewy, *Never Leave Well Enough Alone* (Baltimore, MD: Johns Hopkins University Press, 2002). On Geddes, see especially C. D. Innes, *Designing Modern America: Broadway to Main Street* (New Haven, CT: Yale University Press, 2005); but also Jennifer Davis Roberts, *Norman Bel Geddes: An Exhibition of Theatrical and Industrial Designs* (Austin, TX: University of Texas Press, 1979).

42   See Jeffrey L. Meikle, *Twentieth-Century Limited: Industrial Design in America, 1925–1939*, 2nd edn. (Philadelphia: Temple University Press, 2001 [1979]).

43   See Jay Winter, *Dreams of Peace and Freedom: Utopian Moments in the Twentieth Century* (New Haven: Yale University Press, 2006), ch. 3.

44   See Robert W. Rydell, *All the World's A Fair: Visions of Empire at American International Expositions, 1876–1916* (Chicago, IL: University of Chicago Press, 1984) and Robert W. Rydell, *World of Fairs: The*

Century-of-Progress Expositions (Chicago, IL: University of Chicago Press, 1993). Several generally positive reviews of either or both books—not just my own readings—have lamented Rydell's refusal to acknowledge both that many fairgoers came simply to have a good time and that most fair organizers were not intentionally sexist, racist, or imperialist.

45 See "Living the Dream," *The Economist*, 395 (May 1, 2010), 41–42.

46 Chen Shuai, "Internet Redefining Expo's Role, Content," *Expo 2010 Visitors*, October 15–21, 2010, 7.

47 This additional information on the Expo 2010 derives from Elaine Kurtenbach, Associated Press, "Shanghai World Expo Ends: Drew 72 Million Visitors," *boston.com*, October 30, 2010; and Aileen McCabe, *Postmedia News*, "73 Million People Saw the World at Shanghai Expo," *canada.com*, October 31, 2010. See also Melinda Liu and Duncan Hewitt, "Shanghai Surprise," *Newsweek*, 155 (April 26, 2010), 40–42; and Austin Ramzy and Jessie Jiang, "Shanghai is Ready for its Close-Up," *Time*, 175 (May 17, 2010), 38–41.

Chapter 3

The European Utopias and Utopians and Their Critics

From Thomas More to Karl Marx

The Pioneering European Visionaries and Their Basic Beliefs: Plato's Republic and More's Utopia

Besides Plato's *Republic*, other utopian writings appeared before More's *Utopia* but were not categorized as such. They probably derived from even earlier visions that were conveyed orally before they were written down. The principal themes of these earlier visions were either a golden age of some kind set in the distant past or a more contemporary earthly paradise akin to the Garden of Eden. Endless speculation about worlds beyond Europe and, in time, actual voyages of discovery to those lands, generated many of these oral and written visions alike.

The foremost pioneering examples of writings about a golden age were "Works and Days" by Hesiod, a Greek poet of the eighth century BCE; *Fourth Eclogue* by Vergil (70–19 BCE), a Roman poet; and *Metamorphosis* by Ovid (43 BCE–17 CE?), a Roman poet. Comparable influential pioneering examples of writings about the Garden of Eden are *Genesis* 2:8–2:25 and 3:1–3:24; *Fragments* 129 and 130 by Pindar (522?–443 BCE), a Greek poet; and *Epode* 16: "Islands of the

Utopias: A Brief History from Ancient Writings to Virtual Communities,
First Edition. Howard P. Segal.
© 2012 Howard P. Segal. Published 2012 by Blackwell Publishing Ltd.

Blest" by Horace (65–8 BCE), a Roman poet and satirist. With the rise of Christianity, both versions of utopia took on a more systematic cast with a more coherent narrative and theme and, of course, with divine intervention of one kind or another.[1]

More—beheaded by Henry VIII for refusing to subscribe to the Act of Supremacy, which impugned the Pope's authority and made Henry the head of the Church of England—is best known to history as a martyr of the Roman Catholic Church. But More is also a pivotal figure in the history of utopianism, for his *Utopia* marks a crucial shift in the image of utopia. Previously, as in Plato's *Republic*, there was no expectation of genuine improvement. Instead, the insurmountable gap between the real and ideal worlds was lamented. "Platonic forms" such as the *Republic* reflected that avowedly human condition. More, however, was the first to offer the prospect, albeit dim, of actually establishing a perfect society and thereby altering human nature. Recall that the term utopia, which More coined from Greek roots, means "nowhere" as well as "good place," and bear in mind that More considered human nature depraved. For that matter, the first book of *Utopia* concedes some persistent human weaknesses in discussing the ills facing Europe at that time. (The second and final book describes Utopia.) Nevertheless, More considered utopia a possibility. From More came the idea that "utopian" need not signify forlorn. And from More came a utopian tradition eventually traced back to Plato.[2]

The evidence for More's qualified optimism is threefold. First, he locates utopia in contemporary semi-feudal society rather than in either an agrarian paradise of long ago or a far-off tomorrow. That More strives implicitly to perfect his own society rather than forsaking it altogether surely bespeaks a grain of optimism. Second, like the pre-Millennialists, More expects *people*, not God, to establish utopia. Dependence on God would mean a vote of no confidence in people and, in the wake of Christ's delayed return, would consign utopia to a very distant future. Third, More provides a detailed description of utopia, not merely a set of abstract principles, and his description reflects a close evaluation of his own society, not unanchored speculation. Here More foreshadows the systematic social planning of later full-fledged technological utopians such as the Pansophists (discussed below).

Figure 3.1 Woodcut showing the Island of Utopia, from the frontispiece of the 1516 Louvain edition of Thomas More's *Utopia* (published first in Latin in that year and not in English until 1551), the book that, more than any other, created the tradition of utopian writings (at least in the West). *Source*: Thomas More, *De Optimo Reipublicae Statu deque Nova Insula Utopia* (Leuven [Louvain]: Dirk Martens, 1516).

Yet More provides his utopians with only three scientific and technological improvements, none of them decisive: the hatching of eggs by artificial heat in incubators, the charting of planetary movements by means of various instruments, and the invention of

unspecified "clever ... war machines." To achieve economic subsistence, his utopians rely on the efficient use of established
agrarian techniques and craft devices. To achieve improvements
in human nature, they rely on the introduction of novel social and
cultural arrangements—above all, the abolition of money and
private property, rather than a new prosperity wrought by technological means. Like the later full-fledged scientific and technological utopians, More's utopians are hungry for new scientific and
technical knowledge of the world, but their purpose is as much to
serve God as to improve society: "They think that the investigation
of nature, with the praise arising from it, is an act of worship
acceptable to God."[3]

True, Plato's *Republic* is often cited as the first serious utopian
work. Yet the fact that Plato never envisioned the actualization of
utopia because of flawed human nature has usually relegated the
Republic to the periphery of utopian studies. Still, *Utopia*'s own
dependence on the *Republic* has been well established. The society
depicted by Plato was not wholly imaginary. But the most critical
distinction between the works is that Plato's vision inspired virtually no other utopias for nearly nineteen hundred years—until
More's. More, in contrast, inspired that whole utopian tradition
eventually made retroactive to Plato. More rendered utopianism a
full-fledged mode of thought and discourse.[4]

Forging the Connections Between Science, Technology, and Utopia

As visions that might actually come about rather than as mere
thought experiments, utopianism is rooted in two European
developments. First, starting in the sixteenth century, faith in the
power of reason to achieve steady human improvement grew.
(In the eighteenth century this would become the Enlightenment.) A logical outcome of this perspective was unprecedented
belief in the prospects for utopia. Second, beginning in England's
textile industry in the mid-eighteenth century, rapid technological
advances led to the English Industrial Revolution, which, in time,
spread to most of the rest of the world.[5] We know this as the

revolution of "rising expectations." These developments are intertwined. Only when technology advanced sufficiently to offer the prospect of general affluence did utopian schemes begin to appear at all realistic. Such schemes presupposed the availability of adequate food, clothing, and shelter, and only in modern times could their availability be taken for granted.[6]

Technology was crucially linked to the rise of utopian thought. In 1932, when historian Charles Beard provided a new introduction to the American reprint of J. B. Bury's 1920 classic, *The Idea of Progress: An Inquiry into its Growth and Origin*, he stressed the eminent British scholar's failure to appreciate the importance of technology:

> Although Bury made efficient use of the bearing of one aspect of natural science, that represented by Darwinism, upon the idea of progress as the clue to history, he did not dwell upon the significance of another branch, applied science [as technology was still commonly conceived], for his philosophy of interpretation. Yet technology is the fundamental basis of modern civilization ... [but] has received little attention from historical thinkers and from those social observers who scan the horizon of the future .... Of all the ideas pertinent to the concept of progress, to the interpretation of what has gone on during the past two hundred years and is going on in the world, none is more relevant than technology.[7]

Yet, if progress depended on technology, the path from technological—and scientific—progress to the achievement of utopia was (and remains) neither simple nor inevitable.

It is imperative to clarify here the semantic and historical differences between science and technology. Before the word "scientist" was coined in 1833 by English scientist, philosopher, and Anglican priest William Whewell, the term "natural philosopher" was commonly used to designate those who pursued discovery in any area. As science became more specialized, and as aspiring scientists became able to take specialized undergraduate-level and then graduate-level courses in astronomy, biology, chemistry, geology, and physics, "scientist" became commonly used.[8]

Coinage of the term "technology" cannot be ascribed to any one person but the term began to be used at roughly the same time. In

America, Harvard professor Jacob Bigelow popularized the term through his lectures in the 1810s and then in his *Elements of Technology*, which first appeared in 1829. Like Whewell, Bigelow had transatlantic influence. Bigelow divided technology into elements—separate fundamental units designating categories of human productions—and maintained that these elements were bound together by a particular mode of thought.[9]

Thirty-six years after *Elements of Technology* first appeared, in 1865, Bigelow delivered a major address at the recently founded Massachusetts Institute of Technology. Here he illuminated the growing public understanding of and approval of technology—as represented by the institution's very name, which, he acknowledged, would not have been imaginable in 1829.[10]

Princeton University civil engineer David Billington has distinguished between science and engineering: "Science is discovery, engineering is design. Scientists study the natural, engineers create the artificial. Scientists create general theories out of observed data; engineers make things, often using only very approximate theories." Engineers' goal is to create things that work. As Stanford aeronautical engineer Walter Vincenti has demonstrated in case studies from aeronautical history, whereas the knowledge generated by scientists is ordinarily used by them to generate more knowledge, the knowledge generated by engineers is ordinarily used by them to design artifacts. If engineering knowledge is used to generate more knowledge, that is a quite secondary objective.[11]

Various European utopians forged the first real connections between utopianism and fulfillment through science and technology. They included the Pansophists, a small number of late sixteenth- and early-seventeenth-century visionaries. The most prominent Pansophists were Tommaso Campanella (1568–1639), an Italian Dominican friar; Johann Valentin Andreae (1586–1650), a German Lutheran minister and teacher; and Francis Bacon (1561–1626), a scientist, philosopher, man of letters, and, like More, Lord Chancellor of England. Other European utopians who connected science and technology were the Enlightenment philosopher Marquis de Condorcet (1743–1794); the Frenchmen Henri de Saint-Simon (1760–1825) and Auguste Comte (1798–1857), the former's one-time protégé; the British industrialist and communitarian Robert Owen (1771–1858); the French communitarian Charles Fourier (1772–1837); and the communists Karl Marx (1818–1883) and Friedrich Engels (1820–1895). Yet, for all of their commitment to the power of science and technology, none of these men endorsed unadulterated scientific and technological advance. That is, they did not see science and technology as the royal road to utopia. All insisted no less on a mixture of what each deemed appropriate values for varied kinds of ideal societies. For example, Fourier insisted that there could be no utopia unless individuals could fulfill their varying sexual and other pleasure-providing desires. Meanwhile, Marx and Engels insisted upon a variety of work and leisure activities to avoid exhaustion and boredom in the highly mechanized future they envisioned.

All offered different versions of what I call a plateau of scientific and technological progress (see Chapter 8). Scientific and technological advances, it was believed, could not exceed advances of other kinds. The aim was to achieve progress in non-scientific and non-technological areas at roughly the same rate as in science and technology. Until social, political, economic, and cultural progress caught up with scientific and technological progress, scientific and technological progress would have to level off in selected areas.

The Pansophists

In their greater optimism, the Pansophists stood closer than does More to scientific and technological utopianism. Their religious orientation, however, sharply differentiated them from secular-minded scientific and technological utopianism, for they sought a civilization, called Pansophia, that would harmoniously join Christianity, science, and technology. Their ideas were articulated in three works that appeared over a period of eight years: Andreae's *Christianopolis* (1619),[12] Campanella's *The City of the Sun* (1623),[13] and Bacon's *The New Atlantis* (1627).[14] Like More's *Utopia*, these works recount the adventures of travelers who have discovered societies unknown to Europeans and have returned home to announce their findings. The civilizations they describe prove not merely to have equaled the cultural and material achievements of the West but to have surpassed them.[15]

From the outside, each of these three utopias, like More's, resembles a medieval European town—modest in size, with high towers and thick walls. Within those walls, however, life is considerably more pleasant than life in any medieval European town ever was in actuality. The inhabitants of all three utopias enjoy comfortable living and working quarters; handsome public buildings and gardens; academic and vocational schooling; limited working hours; diverse cultural activities; a rough equality of opportunity; government untainted by politics; and, above all, Christian practice and preaching.

The historical significance of these utopias is the attention they give to science and technology. For example, Campanella's utopia boasts efficient water supply and sewerage systems, labor-saving agricultural machines, and mechanically propelled ships. Similarly, Andreae's utopia prides itself on its water, sewerage, and lighting systems and its fireproof stone buildings. Bacon's ideal society vaunts the most impressive technological achievements of all: the harnessing of water power, the prediction of weather, the invention of clocks, the production of new metals, the creation of vehicles for underwater and air travel, the preservation of bodies after death, the curing of diseases, and indeed the prolongation of life. Finally, the utopias of Andreae and Bacon harbor comprehensive research institutions, which aim at achieving further scientific and technological advances. Campanella's utopia lacks such institutions but does include circular walls that function like computers, displaying an encyclopedic breath of knowledge.

To say that their scientific and technological advances are what make these utopias utopian would be too bold. Clearly, these advances improve life. They make it pleasanter, easier, healthier, and safer—in short, happier. Nevertheless, scientific and technological progress in these utopias is only a means to an end and not, as in full-fledged scientific and technological utopianism, an end in itself. As with More's utopia, the ultimate goal of Pansophism is the service of God.

Although their utopias are based on confidence in the possibility of improving human nature, Campanella, Andreae, and Bacon all

Figure 3.2 Engraving of a view of Johann Valentin Andreae's Christianapolis (Strasburg: Zetzner, 1619); he was one of the three major Pansophists who forged the first real connections between utopianism and science and technology. *Source*: Johann Valentin Andreae, *Christianapolis* (Strasburg: Zetzner, 1619).

remain sufficiently wary of mankind that they propose establishing limits within utopia in order to keep human nature in check. Each of them envisions a fixed, unchanging society; each seeks surcease from toil not simply to enjoy leisure but, more importantly, to contemplate and worship God. Release from ceaseless labor, provided by science and technology, is for them a means and not an end.

The Prophets of Progress: Condorcet, Saint-Simon, and Comte

The empiricism of Bacon (that is, his belief in the significance of experience in the acquisition of knowledge)—along with the scientific discoveries of Isaac Newton, the rationalism of Rene Descartes, and the circulation of many other intellectual currents—fostered a belief in "natural law," a confidence in human reason, and a faith in progress. Together these fed into the Enlightenment.

Two works by Condorcet, a leading Enlightenment philosopher, broke radically with the notion of utopia as a means of contemplating and worshipping God and with many other characteristics of previous utopias. Condorcet's two utopian writings were both published posthumously in 1795. *Sketch of a Historical Picture of the Progress of the Human Mind* traces the remarkable economic, political, and social progress made by mankind from ancient times to the 1790s and predicts even greater progress in the future, whereas Condorcet's commentary on *The New Atlantis* forecasts scientific and technological advances surpassing those envisioned by Bacon. In both works, Condorcet departs fundamentally from previous utopias by envisioning endless progress rather than endless tranquility and by denigrating rather than embracing organized religion.[16]

Condorcet's break with other aspects of earlier utopias is no less marked. He evinces an unprecedented optimism about the prospects for realizing utopia, and he grants science and technology unprecedented roles in establishing it. Yet he is no scientific or technological utopian himself, for he credits mankind's advances not to science and technology but rather to the increase of secularization (the view that public policy should be conducted without reference to religion), the spread of education, and the growth of the ideal of equality. Further, he envisions ongoing eternal progress rather than the eventual culmination of all past progress in a specific kind of society. Thus, the scientific and technological advances he so carefully and lovingly delineates are only indications of the way society is moving generally, not blueprints for the future.

Of all the European visionaries, Saint-Simon and Comte (the former's one-time protégé) most nearly approximate outright technological utopianism. Interestingly, at age nineteen Saint-Simon volunteered for the rebellious colonists during the American Revolution and fought at the Battle of Yorktown. At the same time, he distanced himself from the French Revolution.

He became wealthy through his land speculation and used his funds to establish a lavish salon where scientists and men called "industrialists" could meet. In later years, however, Saint-Simon suffered a reversal of fortune and lived in poverty, sustained by a few disciples and by his conviction that his message for humanity should be propagated continuously. His most famous work, left unfinished at his death, was *The New Christianity* (*Le Nouveau Christianisme*), published in 1825.[17]

Despite his personal setbacks, Saint-Simon not only became one of the most popular nineteenth-century utopians but also has continued to attract followers throughout the West. Saint-Simon's vision rested on his analysis of the Europe of his own day. He argued that the intellectual, social, political, and cultural unity that Europe once enjoyed had collapsed under assault by various forces and that a new unity must be forged, based on science. Science was to be applied in the practical form of "industry," including both the manufacture of goods and their distribution, which together amounted to "technology" (not yet a widely used term in Europe or North America).[18] Priests and politicians were to supplant the old rulers of Europe.

Far more the philosopher of utopia than its designer, Saint-Simon offered no blueprints and therefore falls short of being a full-fledged scientific and technological utopian. Moreover, near the end of his life he backed away from his exclusively scientific and technological vision, urging a religious as well as a scientific and technological panacea. He came to feel that people had spiritual as well as material needs. In addition to scientists and technicians, now industrialists and managers, artists, teachers, and philosophers (but no dogmatic clerics) would be involved.

Comte became Saint-Simon's disciple in 1817 and remained with him until the year before the latter's death, when he broke with his master over both personal and intellectual matters. Of importance here, however, is their persistent agreement, despite their parting, on six fundamental aspects: (1) the need for a new social order in Europe, and perhaps elsewhere, in the wake of the disorder brought about by the English Industrial Revolution and the political revolution in France; (2) the need for science and technology to solve major social as well as technical problems; (3) the need for technical experts to run society; (4) the need to control the unenlightened masses in order to effect these changes; (5) the need to establish a new European hierarchy based not on social origins but on natural talent and society's requirements; and (6) the need to abandon mass democracy and politics.

Comte was a more systematic thinker than Saint-Simon. Not content with Saint-Simon's comparatively modest philosophical formulations, he created a full-fledged philosophical system that aimed to encompass every aspect of human existence. Sometimes called the "New Social System," but now more often called "Positivism," it provided an intellectual foundation for the modern discipline of sociology that grew out of it. Its principal expressions were Comte's multi-volume *Cours de philosophie positive* (1830–1842) and his *Systeme de politique positive* (1851–1854). Yet Comte eventually followed Saint-Simon in expanding his vision to accommodate spirituality. Both men were reluctant to embrace a purely scientific and technological utopian vision.[19]

In short, all of the European prophets of scientific and technological progress—from More to the Pansophists to Condorcet to Saint-Simon and Comte—either refrained or retreated from endorsing unadulterated scientific and technological advance. Their reasons differed, but none was a scientific and technological utopian in the final analysis. To each, other aspects of life were (or became) no less important than scientific and technological advancement.

Dissenters from the Ideology of Unadulterated Scientific and Technological Progress: Thomas Carlyle, John Ruskin, and William Morris

Reservations about scientific and technological advance, articulated especially by Saint-Simon and Comte, were echoed in very different quarters in late-eighteenth- and nineteenth-century Western Europe, in conservative and socialist circles alike, particularly in England and France. Thomas Carlyle (1795–1881; born in Scotland), John Ruskin (1819–1900), and William

Morris (1834–1896), prominent English social critics, all sought a renewed organic England with a re-emphasis on traditional arts and crafts as opposed to large-scale mechanization and factories.[20]

Morris was a designer and craftsman whose furniture, wallpaper, stained glass, designs of books printed at his famous Kelmscott press, and designs in other media led to the Arts and Crafts movement in England. A major influence on Victorian taste, his design and craft work has shaped design culture up to the present day. Morris was a socialist who went further than Carlyle and Ruskin in developing his utopian ideas. His prolific writings include *News From Nowhere* (1890), about a utopian communist society that was heavily influenced by both Ruskin and Marx. The narrator falls asleep after returning from a meeting of the Socialist League and awakens to find himself in a future society wholly different from his own Victorian London. Based on common ownership and democratic control of the means of production, this utopia lacks money, classes, governmental structures, congestion, poverty, crime, and industrial pollution. Like Ruskin, Morris envisions a prevalence of medieval buildings, clothing, and musical instruments. In *News From Nowhere*, all large towns have been downsized to increase the extent of the countryside; huge industrial cities such as Manchester have disappeared; and large-scale factories have given way to small workshops scattered throughout the land and catering to the exercise of craftsmanship and art. Agriculture is again popular. Even smoke has been eliminated, thanks to a new power called "force."

Yet Morris was hardly opposed to technology: work that would be painful to do by hand is done by machines vastly superior to those in medieval times or the nineteenth century. Moreover, products are made both because society needs them and because citizens enjoy making them—not for the purpose of making a few people rich and powerful. Creativity, freedom, and happiness prevail. *News From Nowhere* is, in effect, a medieval bridge to the future as well as a look back to a supposedly more organic culture. It is an early example of an implicit scientific and technological plateau (elaborated upon in Chapter 8).

Morris also wrote in reaction to the kind of soulless and mechanical vision of socialism he found in Bellamy's *Looking*

Backward, the popular and influential American utopian work that had been published two years before *News From Nowhere*—although Morris' reading of that book was simplistic and one-sided.[21] Similar pleas among French social critics whose names are less well-known today—for example, the Vicomte de Bonald (1754–1840) and Pierre Edouard Lemontey (1762–1826)—originated as reactions to the French Revolution but were later applied to the English Industrial Revolution as well.[22] Worries concerning the mechanization and specialization of work and leisure, the decline of communal institutions such as the family and church, the unprecedented growth of materialism and utilitarianism, and the breakdown of social and political order thus gave radical and conservative social critics alike some grounds for agreement about restricting scientific and technological development.

The Expansive Visions of Robert Owen and Charles Fourier

Owen, Fourier, and Marx and Engels were among the handful of critics who offered serious schemes for making beneficial use of various scientific and technological achievements without letting scientific and technological advance—or, for that matter, the threat of scientific and technological advance—become virtually ends in themselves. More than other "radical" European visionaries, and more than the "conservative" critics of industrialization such as Morris and Ruskin, they proposed specific means of regulating and accommodating—as opposed to merely stopping or severely limiting—scientific and technological advance.

Robert Owen The son of an English ironmonger and saddler, Owen had only an elementary education before being apprenticed to a draper. After several years' work in that and other occupations, he became, at age twenty, the manager of a cotton mill. Under his direction, the mill was reputed to produce Britain's finest yarn. At twenty-four, Owen became managing partner of another prominent concern that four years later purchased Scotland's New Lanark Mills. For the next three decades Owen headed this, the largest of Britain's cotton-spinning enterprises, establishing a model factory community that greatly improved working and living conditions, reducing working hours and educating workers' children in innovative ways. Gradually, Owen acquired considerable fame and fortune.

However, dissatisfied with what seemed a slow rate of social improvement not only at New Lanark but throughout Britain, Owen journeyed to America in 1824, using his personal savings to found a model utopian community at New Harmony, Indiana. Unlike New Lanark, New Harmony failed completely, and five years later Owen returned to Britain, though not to his business, from which he retired. For the rest of his life he worked tirelessly on behalf of the British laboring classes. Meanwhile, his disciples founded other Owenite communities in Britain and the United States.[23]

Owen was not a profound thinker, nor, despite his entrepreneurial skills, was he a very practical communitarian. Yet, unlike Condorcet and the Continental prophets of technological progress,

Figure 3.3 View of New Harmony, Indiana, established by English manufacturer and visionary Robert Owen in 1825. *Source*: *United States Illustrated* (1855), based on a drawing by Karl Bodmer during a visit from 1832 to 1833.

Owen actually lived and worked amid profound technological change, clearly benefiting personally from the English Industrial Revolution. Gradually he became aware of the drawbacks of industrialization, which he hoped might be alleviated. He did not advocate wholesale retreat from technological change but rather restrictions on its development; moreover, and no less importantly, he showed as much concern for improving the social, cultural, and moral lot of industrial workers and their families as for improving machinery.

Owen's solutions to the problems of industrialization were at once colored and undermined by his unapologetic paternalism, a trait he acquired as a successful manager, and by his naïve twin beliefs in the power of human reason to discern, treat, and eliminate all social ills and in the power of an appropriately structured environment to shape human character in desired directions. Owen's intended beneficiaries readily recognized his paternalism and often resented it. But he held fast to the reins of control and to his faith in both reason and the environment. Owen envisioned a rational, enlightened, and compassionate business and governmental elite determining the environment, and so the character, of the industrial masses. He adopted outright his friend Jeremy Bentham's utilitarian idea of "the greatest good for the greatest number"—the "good" to be defined by that same elite. These convictions were most clearly spelled out in two of his earliest and most famous works, *A New View of Society* (1813) and *Report to the County of Lanark* (1821).

A New View of Society concerns Owen's achievements at New Lanark. Owen understood, as few other industrialists did, that the discipline required for the efficient operation of any large-scale factory-based system must be undergirded by as pleasant a factory life as possible under the circumstances and also by a comfortable domestic environment. Thus, Owen provided decent, reasonably priced food, clothing, and shelter for all his workers. He also reduced their working hours. He furnished them and their families with opportunities for educational, religious, and recreational activities. Mandatory schooling for all children between five and ten was free. Repeatedly, and in the workers' presence, Owen linked high moral standards to high profits.

Owen's 1813 book contains only cryptic remarks concerning his hopes for educating the whole of the British working population. But not so his *Report to the County of Lanark*, published eight years later: here is a detailed plan to transform that segment of British society, not by renovating existing communities but by creating new ones. Owen advocated a return to the soil on a mass scale—not to abandon technology but to redeem and purify it. By means of well-designed and tightly organized cooperative communities to be set up throughout the British countryside, he hoped to restore that oft-lauded sense of community that supposedly had been lost in the transition from agrarian to industrial society. Such communities would engage primarily in farming and only secondarily in manufacturing, but they would utilize the latest machinery and draw on the best agricultural science. Moreover, they would be able to grow enough food to supply an expanding population that, according to some economists such as Thomas Malthus (1766–1834), was doomed to increase faster than the means of subsistence. The affluence necessary for nearly all serious utopian schemes would thus be available.

As envisioned by Owen, these communities would consist of multi-storied "parallelograms," each housing between three hundred and two thousand men, women, and children. More than either New Lanark or New Harmony, these communities would be scientifically planned. So, too, would the work and leisure spaces and activities of their inhabitants. Diversity of daily routines would be institutionalized and, ideally, exhaustion and boredom would be avoided. These communities would be virtually self-sufficient, would attract citizens from all classes, and would eventually be part of one large communal family, replacing smaller separate families.

Alas, Owen's parallelograms were never established to his specifications, and those that were set up ultimately failed. For all their scientific planning and incorporation of technological advances (such as special valves in each room to regulate heating, cooling, and ventilation), the parallelograms were so predominantly agrarian that they were more retreats from industrializing society than accommodations to it. Still, they were intended as means of balancing and integrating technological progress with social progress, and, whether or not they succeeded, Owen's beneficial intent deserves to be recognized.

In 2010 the Scottish Parliament debated whether or not to feature Owen's portrait on Scottish banknotes in time for the United Nations International Year of Cooperatives in 2012. Although Owen was not Scottish, his New Lanark site has achieved permanent recognition as an experiment in social progress.[24]

Charles Fourier   Like Owen, Charles Fourier had a modest formal education and early exposure to the marketplace as the son of a moderately successful cloth merchant. His early years in Lyons allowed him to observe the efforts of silk workers to organize. In contrast to Owen, who enjoyed his apprenticeship to a draper, Fourier despised his less elevated position as a merchant's assistant. The experience, moreover, was responsible for Fourier's obsession with ridding the world of greed and hypocrisy. His contempt for existing society was deepened by his traumatic experiences as an unwilling participant in the French Revolution. After losing his paternal inheritance—and nearly his life—because of false accusations against him, he served unhappily for several years in the army. In 1795 he managed to secure work as a clerk in a cloth-making concern and, a few years later, as a traveling salesman. In 1826 he finally settled in Paris.

Fourier's first book appeared in 1808; his second not until 1822. These as well as his subsequent works received little attention, thanks to his terrible writing style. Only late in life did he gain a following, but he remained a reclusive bachelor whose complex theories of passionate attraction were cosmically distant from his personal practices.[25]

Fourier persistently preached that his version of utopia could come about only in small communities whose inhabitants actually knew one another, not in big cities filled with anonymous masses. He asserted the economic and moral superiority of agriculture over manufacturing. Yet Fourier recognized that communal living in itself was no panacea. For true happiness, the passions must be released completely. He insisted, as had Owen, that new societies must replace old ones. Like Owen's communities, Fourier's "phalansteries," as he called them, would be models for the reconstruction of his own society and, eventually, of all Western civilization.

Phalansteries would reorder society by replacing separate families with a large single family for each phalanstery (a goal akin to Owen's); institutionalizing varieties of work, leisure, and pleasure; encouraging and enticing rather than coercing children to become socialized and educated, for example by giving them tasks pleasant for them but not for adults; and promoting and rewarding creativity within every citizen, including scientists and technicians as much as artists and other humanists. The rigidly symmetrical multi-story rectangles he envisioned for each phalanstery would simultaneously foster group fulfillment and self-fulfillment. Fourier's scheme was at once more meticulous than that of Owen and more tolerant of both passion and diversity.

Admittedly, Fourier lived in a largely pre-industrial society and so, unlike Owen, did not write in direct reaction to the English Industrial Revolution. His proposed communities were predominantly agrarian and rural. He missed the significance of the profound economic and social changes that Saint-Simon, twelve years his elder, as well as Owen, his contemporary, readily grasped. Nevertheless, Fourier's concern, bordering on obsession, with fulfilling mankind's psychological as well as material needs was

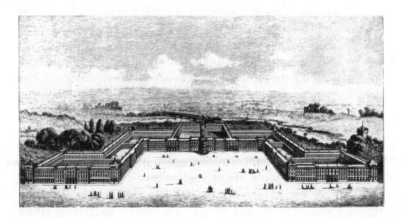

Figure 3.4 Sketch of Charles Fourier's envisioned "phalanstery" building, in which the fortunate would live in small communities and have ample living areas, a theater, great hallways, gardens, and stables. *Source*: A. Bebel, *Charles Fourier* (Stuttgart: J. H. W. Dietz, 1907).

not just provocative but also prophetic. Long before twentieth-century critics of depersonalized working and living conditions, Fourier recognized the problems that ensued from treating people as mere cogs in machines. Equally importantly, he rejected the idea that the proliferation of technology was necessary for the achievement of utopia.

The "Scientific" Socialism of Karl Marx and Friedrich Engels

Marx and Engels remain the most famous of all modern European visionaries because of the enormous impact their ideas have had throughout so much of the world. They famously criticized several leading contemporaries—including Saint-Simon, Owen, and Fourier—for being "utopian" socialists in their adherence to excessively rigid blueprints of a future they could hardly anticipate so precisely. By contrast, Marx and Engels were, in their own words, "scientific" socialists exactly in their refusal to specify the kind of society that would follow the collapse of capitalism and the triumph of the proletariat.

Marx and Engels were more sensitive than those "utopian" socialists to the liberating as well as enslaving potential of modern science and technology. They repeatedly hinted at a society radically superior to the existing capitalist order, a society that would utilize modern, especially automated, technology as a principal means of freeing the proletariat—that is, the class dependent for its very existence on daily employment. The proletariat would be liberated from their longstanding alienation from their work and freed for more varied and fulfilling activities. More than Owen and even Fourier, they readily perceived the psychological as well as the physical consequences of work in industrializing Western society. As they wrote about "communist" (that is, for them, utopian) society in *The German Ideology* (1845–1846), nobody would have an "exclusive sphere of activity." Everybody could become accomplished in any desired activity under a system in which "society regulates the general production and thus makes it possible for me to do one thing today and another tomorrow, to hunt in the morning, fish in the afternoon, rear cattle in the evening, criticize after dinner, just as I have a mind, without ever becoming hunter, fisherman, shepherd or critic."[26] Moreover, Marx and Engels saw technical activities such as devising and improving machinery as no less creative than the artistic activities usually so labeled. In contrast to Fourier, who left little room for technical work of any kind apart from agriculture, Marx and Engels saw creative technicians as engaging more in mental work than in physical labor.

For Marx and Engels, then, the same science and technology that would help destroy capitalism would thereafter help to build a genuinely good, if not utopian, society. And, if the automated equipment at the heart of the new technology could be enslaving, it could also be liberating. Contrary to what is often said about them, Marx and Engels were not crude technological determinists; they did not believe that the form taken by technology determines the social conditions under which humans live.[27] They primarily emphasized the mode of production, insisting that the prevailing kind of labor or productive activity was *conditioned by the existing state of technology*. The mode of production was predominantly social, and the mode of production under capitalism was wage labor.[28]

On the one hand, Marx and Engels, along with Owen and Fourier, turned utopianism into a legitimate mode of thought by making utopia seem possible rather than impossible. On the other hand, all of these men (whose visions, alas, generally marginalized women) offered different versions of what I have called a plateau of scientific and technological progress beyond which scientifically and technologically advanced societies would proceed cautiously, in order to effect a roughly equivalent measure of non-technological and non-scientific—that is, of social, political, economic, and cultural—progress. None approached the concept explicitly, but all provided a glimpse of such a stage of technological, scientific, and social development. That kind of plateau, as discussed in Chapter 8, may offer a real-life alternative to technological utopianism.

Notes

1   On these and other important utopias before *Utopia* appeared, see Gregory Claeys and Lyman Tower Sargent, eds., *The Utopia Reader*

(New York: New York University Press, 1999), ch. 2. The book provides the actual texts of the works mentioned here.

2 The most accessible translation of, introduction to, and discussion of Thomas More's *Utopia* remains the Norton Critical Edition: Thomas More, *Utopia: A Revised Translation, Backgrounds, Criticism*, 2nd edn., ed. and tr. Robert M. Adams (New York: Norton, 1992). The standard critical edition with Latin text and English translation is part of the Yale edition of the complete works of Thomas More: Thomas More, *Utopia*, ed. Edward Surtz (New Haven, CT: Yale University Press, 1964). A useful new Latin edition and translation is Thomas More, *Utopia: Latin Text and English Translation*, eds. George M. Logan, Robert M. Adams, and Clarence Miller (Cambridge: Cambridge University Press, 1995). There are numerous studies of Thomas More and of his writings, including *Utopia*. See especially John Guy, *Thomas More* (New York: Oxford University Press, 2000); Richard Marius, *Thomas More: A Biography* (New York: Knopf, 1984); John Olin, *Interpreting Thomas More's Utopia* (New York: Fordham University Press, 1990); Quentin Skinner, "Thomas More's Utopia and the Virtue of True Nobility," in *Visions of Politics*, 3 vols. (Cambridge: Cambridge University Press, 2002), vol. 2: 213–244; and Gerard B. Wegemer and Stephen W. Smith, eds., *A Thomas More Source Book* (Washington, DC: Catholic University of America Press, 2004). For extensive further bibliography on More's *Utopia*, see R. I. Lakowski, "A Bibliography of Thomas More's *Utopia*," *Early Modern Literary Studies*, 1 (1995), 6.1–10, http://purl.oclc.org/emls/01-2/lakomore.html.

3 More, *Utopia*, ed. Surtz, 128 and 137.

4 On that tradition, see Surtz's introduction in More, *Utopia*, xii–xviii; Frank E. Manuel's introduction to *Utopias and Utopian Thought: A Timely Appraisal*, ed. Manuel (Boston: Houghton Mifflin, 1966), vii–viii; J. H. Hexter, *The Vision of Politics on the Eve of the Reformation: More, Machiavelli, and Seyssel* (New York: Basic Books, 1973), 117–118; Adams' preface to *Utopia: A Revised Translation*, viii–ix; Frank Manuel and Fritzie P. Manuel, *Utopian Thought in the Western World* (Cambridge, MA: Belknap Press of Harvard University Press, 1979), 12–15; J. C. Davis, *Utopia and the Ideal Society: A Study of English Utopian Writing, 1516–1700* (New York: Cambridge University Press, 1981), introduction and ch. 2; and Lyman Tower Sargent, "The Three Faces of Utopianism Revisited," *Utopian Studies*, 5 (1994), 1–37. On Plato's relatively limited influence before *Utopia* appeared, see John Ferguson, *Utopias of the Classical World* (Ithaca, NY: Cornell University Press, 1975), chs. 9–10, 12–13, 18–20.

5   On the English Industrial Revolution and its aftermath, see Phyllis
     Deane, *The First Industrial Revolution*, 2nd edn. (Cambridge: Cambridge
     University Press, 1979), a fine survey; Melvin Kranzberg,
     "Prerequisites for Industrialization," in *Technology in Western Civiliza-
     tion*, eds. Kranzberg and Carroll W. Pursell, Jr., 2 vols. (New York:
     Oxford University Press, 1967), vol. 1: 217–230, an illuminating
     comparison of England and France in the eighteenth century and the
     reasons why the former led the latter into industrialization despite
     France's superiority in many ways over England; David S. Landes, *The
     Unbound Prometheus: Technological Change and Industrial Development in
     Western Europe from 1750 to the Present* (Cambridge: Cambridge Univer-
     sity Press, 1969), the best work of its kind; E. P. Thompson, *The Making
     of the English Working Class* (New York: Pantheon, 1963), still the
     foremost study of the English Industrial Revolution from "the bottom
     up," as compared with Landes' "top-down" work; and *The Impact of the
     Industrial Revolution: Protest and Alienation*, ed. Peter N. Stearns (Engle-
     wood Cliffs, NJ: Prentice-Hall, 1972), still the best brief collection of
     primary documents that complements Thompson's work. For an
     introduction to recent work on the industrial revolution, a highly
     active area of scholarship, see T. S. Ashton, *The Industrial Revolution,
     1760–1830* (Oxford: Oxford University Press, 1997), which has a new
     preface and bibliography by Pat Hudson; Maxine Berg, *The Age of
     Manufactures, 1700–1820: Industry, Innovation, and Work in Britain*, 2nd
     edn. (London: Routledge, 1994); Julian Hoppit and E. A. Wrigley, eds.
     The Industrial Revolution in Britain, 2 vols. (Oxford: Blackwell, 1994);
     Joel Mokyr, *The British Industrial Revolution: An Economic Perspective*, 2nd
     edn. (Boulder, CO: Westview Press, 1999); Kenneth Morgan, *The Birth
     of Industrial Britain: Social Change, 1750–1850* (Harlow: Pearson Long-
     man, 2004); Patrick K. O'Brien and Roland Quinault, *The Industrial
     Revolution and British Society* (Cambridge: Cambridge University Press,
     1993); and Peter N. Stearns, *The Industrial Revolution in World History*,
     2nd edn. (Boulder, CO: Westview Press, 1998).
6   On this fundamental change, the best overall work—and the one
     with the most examples—remains I. F. Clarke, *The Pattern of Expecta-
     tion, 1644–2001* (New York: Basic Books, 1979).
7   Charles A. Beard's introduction to J. B. Bury, *The Idea of Progress: An
     Inquiry Into its Origin and Growth* (New York: Macmillan, 1932 [1920]),
     xx–xxi.
8   A very helpful summary of the development of the sciences in the
     United States and, by extension, Western Europe, is found in the
     following entries in Paul S. Boyer, ed., *The Oxford Companion to United*

States History (New York: Oxford University Press, 2001): Ronald L. Numbers, "Science: Overview," Simon Baatz, "Science: Colonial Era," James Rodger Fleming, "Science: Revolutionary War to World War I," Judith R. Goodstein, "Science: From 1914 to 1945," Michael A. Dennis, "Science: Since 1945," Numbers, "'Science and Religion," and Marcel C. LaFollette, "Science and Popular Culture" (collectively found on pages 685–692).

9   See Jacob Bigelow, *Elements of Technology, Taken Chiefly from a Course of Lectures Delivered at Cambridge, on the Application of the Sciences to the Useful Arts* (Boston, MA: Hillard, Gray, Little, and Wilkins, 1829). The book appeared in several later editions, including a two-volume expanded edition in 1840 under the title *The Useful Arts*. On Bigelow's life, see the sketch in the *Dictionary of American Biography* (New York: Scribner, 1929), vol. 2: 257–258; and the memorial in the *Proceedings, Massachusetts Historical Society*, 17 (March 1880), 383–467.

10   See Jacob Bigelow, *An Address on the Limits of Education* (Boston, MA: Dutton, 1865). For an illuminating refinement of Bigelow's role in the popularization of "technology" and its relationship to the opening of MIT, see Eric Schatzberg, "*Technik* comes to America: Changing Meanings of Technology before 1930," *Technology and Culture*, 47 (July 2006), 486–512.

11   David P. Billington, "In Defense of Engineers," *The Wilson Quarterly*, 10 (New Year's 1986), 87 and 89; and Walter Vincenti, *What Engineers Know and How They Know It: Analytical Studies From Aeronautical History* (Baltimore, MD: Johns Hopkins University Press, 1990).

12   See Johann Valentin Andrea, *Christianopolis: An Ideal State of the Seventeenth Century*, ed. and tr. Felix Held (New York: Oxford University Press, 1916); and Johann Valentin Andrea, *Christianopolis*, tr. Edward H. Thompson (Dordrecht: Kluwer Academic, 1999).

13   English editions include Tommaso Campanella, *The City of the Sun*, in *Peaceable Kingdoms: An Anthology of Utopian Writings*, ed. Robert L. Chianese (New York: Harcourt Brace Jovanovich, 1971), 8–41; an Italian/English edition: Campanella, *La Citfa del Sole: Dialogo Poetico / The City of the Sun: A Poetical Dialogue*, tr. Daniel J. Donno (Berkeley and Los Angeles, CA: University of California Press, 1981); and a combined reprint of *The New Atlantis and City of the Sun* (Mineola, NY: Dover, 2003). See also Phyllis A. Hall, "The Appreciation of Technology in Campanella's 'The City of the Sun,'" *Technology and Culture*, 34 (July 1993), 613–628; and John M. Headley, *Tommaso Campanella and the Transformation of the World* (Princeton, NJ: Princeton University Press, 1997).

14 Francis Bacon, *The Great Instauration and New Atlantis*, ed. J. Weinberger (Arlington Heights, IL: AHM, 1980). On Bacon, the most important of the Pansophists in the context of *The New Atlantis*, see especially Benjamin Farrington, *Francis Bacon: Pioneer of Planned Science* (New York: Praeger, 1969) and Antonio Perez-Ramos, *Francis Bacon's Idea of Science and the Maker's Knowledge Tradition* (Oxford: Clarendon, 1988).

15 On the Pansophists, see also Manuel and Manuel, *Utopian Thought*, chs. 9–11.

16 For the full text, see Marquis de Condorcet, *Sketch for a Historical Picture of the Progress of the Human Mind*, tr. June Barraclough (New York: Noonday, 1955 [1795]). With the same translation, it is reprinted in part in Keith Michael Baker, ed., *Condorcet: Selected Writings* (Indianapolis, IN: Bobbs-Merrill, 1976), 209–282, with the full text of Condorcet's *Fragment on the New Atlantis*, 283–300. Baker's *Condorcet: From Natural Philosophy to Social Mathematics* (Chicago, IL: University of Chicago Press, 1975) is the foremost study, while his introduction to *Condorcet: Selected Writings* is an excellent summary of that book. See also Frank Manuel, *The Prophets of Paris: Turgot, Condorcet, Saint-Simon, Fourier, Comte* (New York: Harper Torchbooks, 1965), ch. 2, reprinted largely intact as ch. 20 of Manuel and Manuel, *Utopian Thought*. The flood of more recent scholarship on Condorcet includes the following comprehensive biography: Elisabeth Badinter and Robert Badinter, *Condorcet, 1743–1794: Un intellectual en politique* (Paris: Fayard, 1988). See also Edward Goodell, *The Noble Philosopher: Condorcet and the Enlightenment* (Buffalo, NY: Prometheus, 1994); Emma Rothschild, *Economic Sentiments: Adam Smith, Condorcet, and the Enlightenment* (Cambridge, MA: Harvard University Press, 2001); and David Williams, *Condorcet and Modernity* (Cambridge: Cambridge University Press, 2004).

17 The best selections of and introductions to Henri de Saint-Simon's writings are Felix Markham, ed., *Social Organization, The Science of Man and Other Writings* (New York: Harper Torchbooks, 1964); Keith Taylor, ed., *Henri de Saint-Simon (1760–1825): Selected Writings on Science, Industry, and Social Organisation* (London: Croom Helm, 1975); and Ghita Ionescu, ed., *The Political Thought of Saint-Simon*, tr. Valence Ionescu (London: Oxford University Press, 1976). For further analyses, see Robert B. Carlisle, "The Birth of Technocracy: Science, Society, and Saint-Simonians," *Journal of the History of Ideas*, 35 (July–September 1974), 445–464; Carlisle, *The Proffered Crown: Saint-Simonianism and the Doctrine of Hope* (Baltimore, MD: Johns

Hopkins University Press, 1987); and Manuel, *Prophets of Paris*, chs. 3–4, reprinted largely intact as chs. 25–26 of Manuel and Manuel, *Utopian Thought*. Recent scholarship includes François Dagognet, *Troi philosophies revisitees: Saint-Simon, Proudhon, Fourier* (Hildeshim: Georg Olms Verlag, 1997) and Oliver Pétré-Grenouilleau, *Saint-Simon: L'Utopie ou la raison en actes* (Paris: Editions Payot & Rivages, 2001).

18 See especially Schatzberg, "*Technik* comes to America."

19 The best selections of and introductions to Auguste Comte's writings are Gertrud Lenzer, ed., *Auguste Comte and Positivism: The Essential Writings* (New York: Harper Torchbooks, 1975) and Kenneth Thompson, ed., *Auguste Comte: The Foundation of Sociology* (New York: Wiley, 1975). See also Manuel, *Prophets of Paris*, ch. 6, reprinted largely intact as ch. 30 of Manuel and Manuel, *Utopian Thought*. Recent scholarship includes Mary Pickering, *August Comte: An Intellectual Biography* (Cambridge: Cambridge University Press, 1993); Robert C. Scharff, *Comte after Positivism* (Cambridge: Cambridge University Press, 1995); Juliette Grange, *Auguste Comte: La politique et la science* (Paris: O. Jacob, 2000); Michel Bourdeau and F. Chazel, *Auguste Comte et l'idee de science de l'homme* (Paris: L'Harmattan, 2002); and Mike Gane, *Auguste Comte* (New York: Routledge, 2006).

20 The foremost studies of Thomas Carlyle, John Ruskin, and William Morris in this context are Raymond Williams, *Culture and Society, 1780–1950* (New York: Harper Torchbooks, 1966), chs. 4, 7; and Herbert L. Sussman, *Victorians and the Machine: The Literary Response to Technology* (Cambridge, MA: Harvard University Press, 1968), chs. 1, 3, 4. See also Edward P. Thompson, *William Morris: Romantic to Revolutionary* (New York: Pantheon, 1976 [1955]); Peter Stansky, *Redesigning the World: William Morris, the 1880's, and the Arts and Crafts* (Princeton, NJ: Princeton University Press, 1985); and *William Morris: Catalog for Centenary Exhibit of William Morris, 1834–1896, Victoria and Albert Museum, 1996*, ed. Linda Parry (London: Philip Wilson/Victoria and Albert Museum, 1996).

21 The most accessible selection of and introduction to Morris' utopian and related writings is Asa Briggs, ed., *News from Nowhere and Selected Writings and Designs* (New York: Penguin, 1984 [1962]).

22 See David K. Cohen, "Lemontey: An Early Critic of Industrialism," *French Historical Studies* 4 (Spring 1966), 290–303; and Cohen, "The Vicomte de Bonald's Critique of Industrialism," *Journal of Modern History*, 41 (December 1969), 475–484.

23 The foremost selection of and introduction to Robert Owen's writings, as discussed below, is *A New View of Society and Report to the County*

of Lanark, ed. V. A. C. Gatrell (Baltimore, MD: Penguin Books, 1970). J. F. C. Harrison, *Quest for the New Moral World: Robert Owen and the Owenites in Britain and America* (New York: Scribner, 1969) remains a fundamental study. Recent scholarship includes Anne Taylor, *Visions of Harmony: A Study in Nineteenth-Century Millenarianism* (Oxford: Clarendon Press, 1987); Ian L. Donnachie, *Robert Owen: Owen of New Lanark and New Harmony* (East Linton: Tuckwell Press, 2000); Brian Thompson, *Devastating Eden: The Search for Utopia in America* (London: HarperCollins, 2004); and Donnachie, *Robert Owen: Social Visionary* (Edinburgh: John Donald, 2005).

24 BBC News, "MSPs Debate Robert Owen Banknotes Call," June 3, 2010, http://news.bbc.co.uk/2/hi/uk_news/scotland/10219504.stm.

25 The most accessible selection of and introduction to Charles Fourier's writings remains Jonathan Beecher and Richard Bienvenu, eds., *The Utopian Vision of Charles Fourier: Selected Texts on Work, Love, and Passionate Attraction* (Boston: Beacon, 1971). The most significant study (in English, at least) is Beecher, *Charles Fourier: The Visionary and His World* (Berkeley and Los Angeles, CA: University of California Press, 1986). But Nicholas V. Riasanovsky, *The Teaching of Charles Fourier* (Berkeley and Los Angeles, CA: University of California Press, 1969) remains an important study. Fourier studies are flourishing. A small selection of recent work includes Claude Morilhat, *Charles Fourier: Imaginaire et critique sociale* (Paris: Méridiens Klincksieck, 1991); Urias Corrêa Arantes, *Charles Fourier, ou, l'art des passages* (Paris: L'Harmattan, 1992); and Patrick Tacussel, *Charles Fourier, le jeu des passions: Actualité d'une pensée utopique* (Paris: Desclée de Brouwer, 2000).

26 Karl Marx and Friedrich Engels, *The German Ideology*, in *The Marx-Engels Reader*, ed. Robert C. Tucker, 2nd. edn. (New York: Norton, 1978), 146–220, 160. An excellent brief introduction to this topic is Shlomo Avineri, "Marx's Vision of Future Society and the Problem of Utopianism," *Dissent*, 20 (Summer 1973), 323–331.

27 See especially Donald Mackenzie, "Marx and the Machine," *Technology and Culture*, 25 (July 1984), 473–502.

28 The most accessible collections of writings by Marx and Engels and their followers and critics are Tucker, *Marx-Engels Reader* and David McLellan, ed., *Marxism: Essential Writings* (New York: Oxford University Press, 1988). Excellent short secondary studies are Tom Bottomore, ed., *Karl Marx* (Englewood Cliffs, NJ: Prentice-Hall, 1973); McLellan, *Karl Marx* (New York: Viking, 1975); and McLellan, *Friedrich Engels* (New York: Penguin, 1978).

Chapter 4

The American Utopias and Utopians and Their Critics

America as Utopia: Potential and Fulfillment

For all the rhetoric about the New World being superior to the Old World, it is critical to distinguish utopian yearnings and expectations from more conventional ones, not least sheer survival in a very different climate in all senses of the term. Despite the overwhelmingly agricultural nature of colonial America, technologies of various kinds were instrumental in sustaining its first permanent English settlements. Established as mercantile ventures to provide raw materials to Mother England and to purchase its finished products, the colonies mined and modified the New World's abundant resources, first to maintain themselves and eventually for export. By the 1760s, the success with which the colonists plied their skills, many brought with them from the Old World, placed them in direct competition with England. Although the American Revolution broke formal connections with England, it neither lessened the New World's reliance on mercantilism nor completely separated America from Europe.

The United States Constitution was a product of mercantilistic notions, but Americans soon recognized that their country was a land of seemingly limitless possibilities. They endeavored to fulfill the promise of a democratic republic by

Utopias: A Brief History from Ancient Writings to Virtual Communities,
First Edition. Howard P. Segal.
© 2012 Howard P. Segal. Published 2012 by Blackwell Publishing Ltd.

rejecting aristocracies of wealth and heredity and by expanding the right to vote to ever more white males. By the first decade of the nineteenth century, Americans had abandoned mercantilism, concentrating instead on exploring the New World's possibilities and providing opportunities for them to be tapped by its citizens.

In this milieu, technologies became equated with the provision of individual opportunity. State and federal governments sponsored or built turnpikes, canals, bridges, and railroads to facilitate commerce, and created an unprecedented number of corporations to take advantage of these internal improvements. A shortage of skilled and inexpensive labor plagued many of these enterprises. Entrepreneurs responded by encouraging immigration from Europe of individuals possessing special skills, by copying European production machines, and by replacing workers with machinery. They also established institutions to provide learning opportunities and to join capital with new inventions. That factories quickly dotted the nation's landscape was an indication that opportunity had been provided. All of these developments were widely seen as measures of "progress."

Although various parts of the world outside Europe were considered suitable locations for utopias, North America finally became the Europeans' most popular locale. (From here on "America" refers to what became the United States, not what became Canada.) The most basic notions underlying the vision of America as a utopia derive from prior European notions about America not as a permanent primitive paradise but as a potentially advanced society—scientifically and technologically as well as politically, economically, socially, and culturally. Yet the American scientific and technological utopians reassessed and revised these basic ideas in light of experiences unforeseen by those original European exponents. Specifically, America was to be a *probable*, not merely a possible, utopia that would come about primarily by scientific and technological changes. Indeed, scientific and technological progress equaled *progress itself*, not merely the means to progress; scientific and technological utopia was to be modeled on the scientific instruments and machines that made it probable.[1]

What made America a potential utopia was its status as a blank slate on which a new society could be written and its possession of enough natural resources to provide material plenty for all.[2] Nevertheless, the *potentiality* rather than reality of America as a utopia must be emphasized. Too often it has been assumed that abundant natural resources alone guaranteed that America would become an advanced society, possibly a utopia, and that virtually all Americans from the seventeenth century onward agreed with that proposition. But there is a considerable gap between the possession of abundant resources on the one hand and the proclamation of them as utopia on the other. The simple conversion in America from resources into utopia was inhibited by the inheritance of a European tradition of utopianism, the need to convert natural resources into finished products, the existence of a Native American civilization that viewed European civilization as an invader and as a rival for territory, and the consequent existence of a partly settled territory rather than a virgin land.[3]

To most new arrivals and their offspring, the threat of permanent scarcity loomed far larger than the promise of eventual abundance. Until at least the mid-nineteenth century, most people conceived of America's natural resources as finite, not infinite. The finished products developed from the nation's resources and the wealth realizable from their manufacture, purchase, and distribution were also seen as finite, not only because the raw materials were limited but also because other sources of wealth could not apparently be created. Hence, most Americans before the Civil War saw their economic realm as ultimately a closed system and so saw America as merely a *potential* utopia.

What, beginning in the mid-nineteenth century, changed these assumptions about scarcity was the invention of various devices that not only converted raw materials into finished products at an infinitely greater pace but also provided opportunities at last to create new wealth. This was made possible not only by the invention and manufacture of synthetic raw materials and later finished products but also by the use of tools and machines to locate, extract, and transport previously unknown or unmovable natural resources and to build canals, steamboats, and railroads, and in due course farms, towns, and cities. These developments transformed much of America's vast lands into fluid—and infinitely expandable—capital. The extent to which the relative dearth of common laborers, as compared with the situation in Europe, spurred Americans to begin to invent more than their European counterparts remains a controversial topic.[4]

By the late 1830s, Americans were increasingly eschewing identification with the Old World and beginning to define themselves in a new way, as a people exhibiting a distinctive and unique character. Rather than remaining primarily as providers of individual opportunity, technologies now were championed as means of unifying and homogenizing the nation. Uniformity and coherence became the new basic objectives. Mid-nineteenth-century Americans adopted those technologies that measured the distinctly American character, furnished the nation's citizens with a common material experience, or enhanced the country's standing within the world of nations. This quest for a new American identity took place despite the nation's increasing divisions over whether to end slavery altogether, to allow it to continue only in existing Southern states, or to extend it to new territories and states.

A 1795 book by two noted American millwrights, Oliver Evans and Thomas Ellicott, *The Young Mill-Wright and Miller's Guide*, was a *de facto* utopian tract beneath its ostensible character as a conventional water-milling text. Yet its utopian dimensions have never been appreciated. Writing in the closing days of pervasive belief in mercantilism, Evans and Ellicott concentrate on flour milling and other large, complex milling operations not normally associated with the modest enterprises of their day. They indicate that cutting-edge technology would allow the new nation to create and sustain virtually limitless growth. The book envisioned the establishment of countless factories and the steady increase of national wealth.

The identification between America as a distinctive social collection and its idyllic crusade for nationwide coherence and homogeneity collapsed in the decade following the Civil War. Obviously the war undermined national unity for decades to come. But the growing nation was becoming fractionalized in other ways and for other reasons. Mass immigration from Central and Eastern Europe, more than any other factor, resulted in an increasingly diverse

America that, unlike in contemporary times, was lamented more than celebrated. Unlike their mid-nineteenth-century counterparts, late-nineteenth- and early-twentieth-century Americans routinely made firm, fixed, and critical distinctions between peoples, places, and things. Who, for example, was a "real" American? Only native-born citizens whose ancestors came here from Western Europe generations earlier? Was it imperative to discard one's native language, dress, and culture? Who would or should decide? Regardless, Americans steadily realized that their respective distinctions did not stand alone but instead were parts of *systems*.

"System" was the touchstone of late-nineteenth and early-twentieth-century America and influenced virtually every aspect of American life. It manifested itself primarily in ever larger and more complex transportation and communications systems. Those systems were frequently the backbone of utopian visions, however else those visions might differ. All Americans agreed that establishing a "true" hierarchy based on objective methods and criteria was critical for operating a system at optimum efficiency. In the roughly fifty years after 1870, Americans, in effect, remade their nation.

The Pioneering American Visionaries and their Basic Beliefs in America as Land of Opportunity: John Adolphus Etzler, Thomas Ewbank, and Mary Griffith

Reasonably accurate opinion polls did not exist before the 1940s. Yet newspapers, magazines, editorials, speeches, and sermons; historical, literary, and travel writings; and worker and labor union publications provide abundant evidence that, until at least the late 1960s, most Americans were quite positive about scientific and technological advances, which they equated with social and moral progress. Technological and scientific advances resulted in the reconceptualization of America as an *open system*. It is hardly accidental that the first American technological utopian writings—those of John Adolphus Etzler (b. 1791), Thomas Ewbank (1792–1870), and Mary Griffith (1800?–1877)—appeared just as those advances were starting to become evident, in the second quarter of the nineteenth century. As the idea developed of

America as *people-made* rather than as natural, utopia became a distinct possibility. The original Puritan idea of America as the site of God's millennial kingdom on earth faded in popularity. And, of course, dependence on people rather than on God is what distinguishes utopianism from millenarianism.

Etzler was a German engineer best known for *The Paradise Within the Reach of All Men, Without Labor, By Powers of Nature and Machinery* (1833) and *The New World; Or, Mechanical System to Perform the Labours of Man and Beast by Inanimate Powers, that Cost Nothing* (1841). He became a close friend of the famous bridge builder and Hegelian visionary John Roebling, whom he accompanied to America in 1822. Etzler remained there until 1829, when he returned to Germany to recruit others for the New World. Throughout his life, Etzler seduced followers and patrons with vague promises of great wealth to be based on limitless natural resources, especially in less populated lands such as the western United States and parts of South America. In the 1840s Etzler led a group of some two hundred English emigrants to Venezuela under the banner of the Utopian Socialist Society. He offered them a dream of a tropical paradise of endless sunlight, fertile land, and good health; the reality was misery, poverty, and disease for all and death for many. Etzler apparently survived this dystopian ordeal, but the date and circumstances of his death are unknown.

To the extent that Etzler became familiar to American and Western European audiences, it was as the object of a sarcastic 1843 essay by Henry David Thoreau in the *United States Magazine and Democratic Review*. Thoreau faulted Etzler's *Paradise* for excessive optimism, materialism, and authoritarianism.

In *The Great Delusion* (2008), historian Steven Stoll vividly describes the September 22, 1845 launching near Oxford, England, of Etzler's greatest invention, the Satellite, proclaimed to be capable of doing "anything on the ground: plow, pulverize and sift soil, level a field, sow grain, pull weeds, cultivate between plants, mow, harvest, hammer, saw, cut down trees, pull out stumps, notch rocks, excavate and elevate, dig ditches and canals, form terraces, operate in water or mud, dig mines, and generate its own power." Stoll calls it "a Swiss Army knife on wheels, a cross between a plow and the Batmobile"—or a "philosophical machine" that supposedly

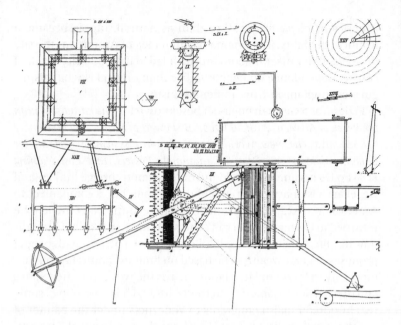

Figure 4.1 Detail of a technical drawing by John Adolphus Etzler of his invention that would supposedly allow one person to control all the sails of any ship "using the power of the wind itself." This was typical of the fanciful if seemingly scientific proposals by one of the earliest American scientific and technological utopians, an immigrant from Germany who successfully attracted financial backers to his schemes. *Source*: J. A. Etzler, *Description of the Naval Automation Invented by J. A. Etzler* (Philadelphia, PA: Gihon, Fairchild, 1841 or 1842).

would "generate infinite wealth by concentrating infinite power on infinite resources." As large as two modern-day shipping containers, the experimental machine promptly failed. Etzler had not taken account of entropy. Energy departed as useless heat, which was caused by friction over the long ropes the Satellite used, along with wind, water, and a pivot for movement. The roughly eight hundred spectators were dismayed.[5]

Like Etzler, Ewbank hoped to make his fortune in America. Leaving his native England in 1819, he had a much more successful career than Etzler, working successively as an inventor, as a manufacturer, and from 1849 to 1852 as United States Commissioner of Patents. He published several essays and tracts, including *The World a Workshop: Or the Physical Relationship of Man to the Earth* (1855) and *Thoughts on Matter and Force: Or, Marvels that Encompass Us* (1858). Some of his essays and tracts were published (not without attracting criticism) in official annual reports of his high office as patent commissioner.[6]

Less is known about Mary Griffith than about either Etzler or Ewbank. She was apparently born about 1800 and was living in New Jersey when she wrote her one utopian work, "Three Hundred Years Hence" (1836). A novella, it was published as the longest part of a collection entitled *Camperdown; or, News from Our Neighbourhood*. Her other writings primarily concerned horticulture. She died in 1877.[7]

Notwithstanding Etzler's Satellite, these early American utopian writings were considerably less detailed than those that appeared later—not only in the technical specifics but also in the non-technological dimensions of their utopias. Because of the countless differences in the development of American society between the early and late nineteenth century, Etzler, Ewbank, and Griffith could barely imagine what their successors could readily conceive.

America as "Second Creation": Enthusiasm and Disillusionment

If Bigelow could celebrate the popularization of the term "technology" at the opening of MIT in 1865, the introduction of new technologies did not always win unanimous acclaim. In his *America as Second Creation* (2003), David Nye argues that colonial and early Republican transportation and communications technologies traditionally equated with progress also had their less familiar dark sides. On the one hand, these advances were considered by many optimistic Americans to be extending and complementing God's first creation. They constituted a second creation story that manifested itself in four "foundation narratives": the axe, the mill, the canal and the railroad, and the dam. On the other hand, these advances generated five "counter-narratives" embraced by increasingly marginalized inhabitants: Native Americans deprived of their forests, fishermen adversely affected by dams, yeoman farmers victimized by the railroads, workers exploited by mill-owners and railroad magnates, and pioneering environmentalists dismayed by exploitation and waste of natural resources. Nye terms his version of a technological plateau a "recovery narrative."[8]

Despite these counter-narratives and the protests accompanying them, the eventual triumph of the nation's major transportation and communications systems brought into being two related concepts that became part of most Americans' basic beliefs long before they were formally categorized by scholars: "technological determinism," or the conviction that technology shapes society and culture; and the "technological imperative," or the conviction that technological advances must be pursued and implemented simply because they *can* be pursued and implemented, regardless of the consequences for society.

Not surprisingly, the unprecedented abundance brought about by technological advances hardly benefited everyone. Not only was the distribution of raw materials, finished products, and the wealth accruing from them grossly unequal, but concerns arose about the impact of wealth on its very recipients, the newly rich or at least newly comfortable middle class. Puritan concerns that abundance might produce moral corruption resurfaced, rendered more acute by unparalleled abundance and by the absence of the kind of rigorous ethical restraints that the Puritans had imposed on themselves.

The first of the late-nineteenth-century technological utopias was John Macnie's *The Diothas; Or, A Far Look Ahead*, published in 1883.[9] By the time it appeared, prosperity was widely viewed as a problem in itself as well as a solution to other problems. In *Progress and Poverty* (1879), social critic Henry George had argued that poverty invariably accompanied material progress. Like George, however, the technological utopians were confident that the problems could be solved. To use technological advances to solve problems created in some measure by technological advances (or their misuse) struck them as neither paradoxical nor problematic.

Yet in his classic 1907 autobiography, *The Education of Henry Adams*, Henry Adams asked what constituted genuine progress. Comparing the technological power of the dynamo at the 1900 Paris world's fair with the spiritual power that had inspired the builders of the great medieval cathedral at Chartres, Adams wondered whether the former power was genuinely superior to the latter and whether sheer technological progress necessarily meant comparable social or moral progress. His answers were negative: "All the steam in the world could not, like the Virgin, build Chartres."[10]

No less importantly, many Americans throughout the nineteenth and early twentieth centuries debated whether industrialization in the United States would entail the kind of urban blight then plaguing England and whether "dark satanic mills" (a phrase commonly attributed to the British poet William Blake) would consume the American countryside and decimate farms and villages, as had already happened in much of England. This concern was also voiced by many European visitors to the United States. For some foreign and native critics alike, the prospect of America as a potential utopia had become the prospect of a potential dystopia—with results just the opposite from what were sought.

Still, an overwhelming majority of Americans from colonial times to the present have accommodated themselves and their communities to technological change, if not always enthusiastically. Criticism by Americans of technological change has rarely taken the form of the outright destruction of machinery. There is no American version of the legendary English Luddites, or "machine breakers," of the early days of the English Industrial Revolution, who tried in vain to prevent the introduction of textile machinery that eliminated their skilled jobs.[11] Instead, oratory, protest literature, and work stoppages or strikes have been the normal American expressions of dissatisfaction over working and living conditions, pay, health, and safety.

During the Great Depression of the 1930s, for the first time in American history the public held inventors, engineers, and scientists responsible for economic bad times as greedy industrialists—most notably, President Herbert Hoover, a distinguished mining engineer before he entered politics. Nevertheless, the very machinery that had helped to create "technological unemployment" was almost never smashed by laid-off workers. Not wishing to oppose technological progress—and in so doing risk being scorned as "un-American"—workers and their union leaders have traditionally sought only their fair share of economic benefits from mechanization and reduced costs of production, or, as necessary, unemployment insurance or retraining assistance. This stance is reflected in many worker and labor union publications over several decades.[12]

The accommodation that Americans have made to technological advance cannot be overemphasized. Far too often, historians have insisted that accommodation between the technology of the Industrial Revolution and the nation's predominantly agrarian and pre-industrial society was neither widely sought nor widely achieved. The two have been depicted as utterly antagonistic (the machine *versus* nature, the city *versus* the country, or civilization *versus* wilderness). Such a misreading of American history is epitomized by Leo Marx's influential *The Machine in the Garden: Technology and the Pastoral Ideal in America* (1964). Too many of Marx's conclusions derive from his otherwise insightful readings of a handful of great writers such as Henry David Thoreau and Ralph Waldo Emerson. Such men were hardly representative of ordinary Americans. By definition, as great writers they transcended their own times and places, and they *themselves* were hardly averse to all forms of technology. Their principal target was the intrusion of the railroad into pastoral settings.

This distortion of American history leads to the kind of pseudo-romantic quest for a pre-technological past that was popular with the "counterculture" of the 1960s. It was reflected in the movement of urban and suburban youth (and sometimes older folks) to farms and still more remote and more "primitive" locales such as caves. Their reliance on selective forms of modern technology to survive, much less to live comfortably, did not strike them as inconsistent, or dare I say hypocritical. Like the infamous Unabomber—Theodore Kaczynski, a 1962 Harvard graduate who lived alone on a 1.4 acre plot lacking electricity and running water in a remote part of Montana—a countercultural generation depended upon up-to-date communications and transportation technologies to spread their anti-technology messages (or worse, in Kaczynski's case, to kill three persons and to injure twenty-three other alleged enemies by mailing separate letter bombs that resulted in sixteen explosions). In truth, these would-be rebels, like most ordinary Americans throughout the nation's history, successfully reconciled machine and nature, city and country, and civilization and wilderness. What they frequently have sought is a *turn*, but not a wholesale *return*, to nature, to the countryside, to wilderness. Besides automobiles and recreational vehicles, their technological arsenal now often includes computers, cell phones, and global positioning devices.[13] Ironically, Leo Marx himself popularized the term that best describes this reconciliation: the "middle landscape."[14]

Notes

1 Besides J. B. Bury, *The Idea of Progress: An Inquiry Into its Origin and Growth* (New York: Macmillan, 1932 [1920])—including Charles A. Beard's introduction—see Arthur A. Ekirch, Jr., *The Idea of Progress in America, 1815–1860* (New York: Columbia University Press, 1944); W. Warren Wagar, *Good Tidings: The Belief in Progress from Darwin to Marcuse* (Bloomington, IN: Indiana University Press, 1972); Rush Welter, *The Mind of America, 1820–1860* (New York: Columbia University Press, 1975); Robert Nisbet, *History of the Idea of Progress* (New York: Basic Books, 1980); Theodore Olson, *Millennialism, Utopianism, and Progress* (Toronto, ON: University of Toronto Press, 1982); and Lyman Tower Sargent, "Utopianism in Colonial America," *History of Political Thought*, 4 (Winter 1983), 483–522.

2 On America as an existing paradise with abundant natural resources, see Hugh Honour, *The New Golden Age: European Images of America from the Discoveries to the Present Time* (New York: Pantheon, 1975).

3 For elaboration on this and the following three paragraphs, see Howard P. Segal, "Eighteenth-Century American Utopianism: From the Potential to the Probable," *Utopian Studies*, 11 (2000), 5–13. See also Daniel J. Boorstin, *The Genius of American Politics* (Chicago, IL: University of Chicago Press, 1953); David M. Potter, *People of Plenty:*

Economic Abundance and the American Character (Chicago, IL: University of Chicago Press, 1954); Francis Jennings, *The Invasion of America: Indians, Colonialism, and the Cant of Conquest* (New York: Norton, 1976); and Zane L. Miller, "Scarcity, Abundance, and American Urban History," *Journal of Urban History*, 4 (February 1978), 131–155.

4   The starting point for this issue remains H. J. Habakkuk, *American and British Technology in the Nineteenth Century: The Search for Labour-Saving Inventions* (Cambridge: Cambridge University Press, 1962).

5   Steven Stoll, *The Great Delusion: A Mad Inventor, Death in the Tropics, and the Utopian Origins of Economic Growth* (New York: Hill and Wang, 2008), 9, 11. On the review by Henry David Thoreau, see "Paradise (to be) Regained," *United States Magazine and Democratic Review*, 13 (November 1843), 451–463. Etzler's works have been reprinted in Joel Nydahl, ed., *The Collected Works of John Adolphus Etzler* (Delmar, NY: Scholars' Facsimiles and Reprints, 1977). Nydahl's introduction is a good starting point for further analysis, as is Robin Lindstromberg and James Ballowe, "Thoreau and Etzler: Alternative Views of Economic Reform," *Midcontinent American Studies Journal*, 11 (Spring 1970), 20–29.

6   See Thomas Ewbank, *The World a Workshop: Or the Physical Relationship of Man to the Earth* (New York: Appleton, 1855) and Ewbank, *Thoughts on Matter and Force: Or, Marvels that Encompass Us* (New York: Appleton, 1858). There is no biography or other substantial study of Ewbank, but see his entry in the *Dictionary of American Biography* (New York: Scribner, 1943), vol. 6: 227–228.

7   See Mary Griffith, "Three Hundred Years Hence," in *Camperdown; Or, News from Our Neighbourhood* (1836; reprinted in Arthur O. Lewis, Jr., ed., *American Utopias: Selected Short Fiction* (New York: Arno Press, 1971)). On Griffith and this work, see Nelson F. Adkins, "An Early American Story of Utopia," *Colophon*, 1 (Summer 1935), 123–132; and Beverely Seaton, "Mary Griffith," in *American Women Writers: A Critical Reference Guide from Colonial Times to the Present*, ed. Linda Mainiero (New York: Ungar, 1980), vol. 2: 183–185. All of these texts list her date of death as 1877—but without firm sources. However, Rutgers University Library's manuscript collections—which has some of her letters—says in its description of those letters that she "died at Red Hook, Dutchess County, New York, in 1846. Note: Griffith's death date is listed incorrectly as 1877 in some sources" (Women's History Sources: A Guide, Letter G; see http://www.libraries.rutgers.edu/rul/libs/scua/womens_fa/wfa_e_g.shtml).

8   See David E. Nye, *America as Second Creation: Technology and Narratives of New Beginnings* (Cambridge, MA: MIT Press, 2003). Nye's work

continues his primary project, extending and enriching the principal themes of his mentor, Leo Marx, as presented in Marx's classic work, *The Machine in the Garden: Technology and the Pastoral Ideal in America* (New York: Oxford University Press, 1964).

9   John Macnie (Ismar Thiusen, pseud.), *The Diothas; Or, A Far Look Ahead* (New York: Arno Press, 1971 [1883]). On Macnie, see Webster Merrifield et al., "In Memorium: Professor John Macnie," *University of North Dakota Bulletin*, 1 (November 1909), 3–33; and Louis G. Geiger, *University of the Northern Plains: A History of the University of North Dakota, 1883–1958* (Grand Forks, ND: University of North Dakota Press, 1958), 52–55, 99, 109.

10   Henry Adams, *The Education of Henry Adams: An Autobiography* (1907; reprinted in part in Thomas Parke Hughes, ed., *Changing Attitudes Toward American Technology* (New York: Harper and Row, 1975), 174). This is the best introduction to Adams' work in terms of his evolving attitude toward technology and society and the implicit dystopia that Adams fashioned, as discussed later in the chapter. On Adams' historical outlook, the foremost study remains William H. Jordy, *Henry Adams: Scientific Historian* (New Haven, CT: Yale University Press, 1952). The most recent major analysis of Adams is Garry Wills, *Henry Adams and the Making of America* (Boston, MA: Houghton Mifflin, 2005).

11   See E. J. Hobsbawm, "The Machine Breakers," in *Labouring Men: Studies in the History of Labour* (London: Weidenfeld and Nicolson, 1964), 5–22; Malcolm I. Thomis, *The Luddites: Machine Breaking in Regency England* (New York: Schocken, 1972); and Brian J. Bailey, *The Luddite Rebellion* (New York: New York University Press, 1998).

12   See Amy Sue Bix, *Inventing Ourselves Out of Jobs? America's Debate Over Technological Unemployment, 1929–1981* (Baltimore, MD: Johns Hopkins University Press, 2000).

13   On the opportunity to purchase the Unabomber's plot of land—minus the cabin—see Michael E. Altman, "Unabomber's Secluded Plot of Land for Sale," *Harvard Crimson*, December 6, 2010, http://www.thecrimson.com/article/2010/12/6/harvard-kaczynski-currently-plot. On the online auction of the Unabomber's personal items, with the proceeds going to his victims and their families, see Paul Elias, Associated Press, "Auction of Unabomber Items Raises $175,000 for His Victims," *Bangor Daily News*, June 3, 2011, A10. On efforts to live more simply in contemporary times based on a year's experiences in a Mennonite community, see Eric Brende, *Better Off: Flipping the Switch on Technology* (New York: HarperCollins, 2004) and

the witty exchange between Brende—a dropout from MIT's Science, Technology, and Society Program—and Jonathan Coopersmith (who reviewed the book in *Technology and Culture*, 46 (July 2005), 623–624) in *Technology and Culture*, 47 (July 2006), 704–706.

14 For elaboration, see Howard P. Segal, *Future Imperfect: The Mixed Blessings of Technology in America* (Amherst, MA: University of Massachusetts Press, 1994), ch. 2. See also Jeffrey L. Meikle, "Classics Revisited: Leo Marx's *The Machine in the Garden,*" *Technology and Culture*, 44 (January 2003), 147–159. Within metropolitan areas, one can point to countless "middle landscapes" as represented by suburban communities with their backyards and nearby commuter trains, and by city parks (above all, those such as New York City's Central Park, designed by pioneering landscape architect Frederick Law Olmstead (1822–1903)). Going outside cities and suburbs, one can identify regional "middle landscapes," particularly the Tennessee Valley Authority (TVA), which began in 1933 under President Franklin Roosevelt's New Deal. The nation's foremost example of regional planning, TVA achieved a great deal in the way of dam construction, flood control, land reclamation, and cheap electrical power. The many examples of reconciliation between nature and technology throughout American history cannot be overemphasized.

Chapter 5

Growing Expectations of Realizing Utopia in the United States and Europe

Later American Technological Utopians: John Macnie Through Harold Loeb

If no prominent Europeans were genuine technological utopians, this was not true of Americans—though there were hardly as many as one might think. For all the rhetoric in American history about the uniqueness of the nation's natural and man-made wealth, about an American "exceptionalism" that favored scientific and technological progress, and that equated human progress with scientific and technological progress, surprisingly few Americans have provided actual blueprints for a better society. Thousands of orations, sermons, poems, essays, articles, and books provide generalizations about utopia, but the vast majority never go beyond such generalizations.

However, between the appearance of Macnie's *The Diothas* in 1883 and Harold Loeb's *Life in a Technocracy: What It Might Be Like* in 1933, twenty-five individuals published fundamentally similar visions of the United States as a technological (and, to a lesser extent, scientific) utopia. Most of these twenty-five were obscure as visionaries, though some were prominent in their respective professions, businesses, or other pursuits. George Shattuck Morison (1842–1903), for example, a civil engineer, became the leading American bridge

Utopias: A Brief History from Ancient Writings to Virtual Communities,
First Edition. Howard P. Segal.
© 2012 Howard P. Segal. Published 2012 by Blackwell Publishing Ltd.

engineer of his day, while Robert Henry Thurston (1839–1903) became an equally distinguished mechanical engineering administrator, first at Stevens Institute of Technology and later at Cornell University. Meanwhile, King Camp Gillette (1855–1932) invented the safety razor and, thanks to his portrait on the wrapper of every Gillette blade, became famous. The youngest of the twenty-five, Harold Albert Loeb (1891–1974), lived among a group of prominent American expatriates in Paris in the 1920s and, as a wealthy aspiring writer, bankrolled an avant-garde magazine that published early works by Ernest Hemingway and other emerging literary giants. Loeb later became a leading member of the Technocracy movement of the 1930s. Still, the only technological utopian made famous by his writings was Bellamy, whose remarkable success with *Looking Backward* was wholly unexpected.

All of these American utopians were composing utopias not out of literary indulgence but, on the contrary, out of concern for the concrete, real problems of their day. They saw utopianism not as fanciful escapism but precisely as a practical solution to these woes.

Obtaining information on some of these twenty-five techno-logical utopians is extremely difficult. Nevertheless, what the data on occupation, education, race, religion, and gender suggest are that economically and socially, at least, these visionaries were not marginal, alienated, disaffected figures but, on the contrary, successful, well-integrated Americans. This indicates that technological utopianism was not a movement of revolt but rather a movement seeking to alter the speed instead of the direction in which American society was moving. Others who have studied larger groups of American utopians for roughly the same period have reached conclusions similar to mine.[1]

All of the twenty-five technological utopians were male. The absence of women is disappointing but hardly surprising. Their absence here is certainly not for my lack of trying to find them.[2] Save for Griffith, American women with visionary outlooks tended to be reformers rather than utopians. Interestingly, Mary Shelley's *Frankenstein* (1818), considered the greatest Gothic novel of the early nineteenth century (and one that, as discussed in Chapter 5, has continuing relevance for utopian thought), did not carry her name until the novel became popular years after its

MODERN PARADISE

AN

Outline or Story of How Some of the
Cultured People will Probably Live,
Work and Organize in the
Near Future.

BY

PROFESSOR HENRY OLERICH

FULLY ILLUSTRATED

EQUALITY PUBLISHING COMPANY
2219 Larimore Avenue
Omaha, Neb.
1915.

Figure 5.1 Frontispiece of Henry Olerich, *Modern Paradise: An Outline or Story of How Some of the Cultured People Will Probably Live, Work, and Organize in the Near Future* (Omaha, NE: Equality, 1915). A typical respectable book cover that is intended to appeal to middle-class and perhaps wealthy readers—and, ideally, organizers—with expectations of fulfillment in the not-too-distant future, unlike utopian visions before the late nineteenth and early twentieth centuries.

initial publication. Few male readers of the early nineteenth century would have thought a woman capable of such provocative and insightful writing. Similarly, Griffith's "Three Hundred Years Hence" (1836) did not lead to further utopian writings by American women in the nineteenth century. Two decades later, with comparable restrictions still placed on American female writers, few could risk writing for an overwhelmingly male audience.

Significantly, exceptions to this generalization commonly took the form of fiction about Amazons, physically strong and usually beautiful women who dominated men but who, notably, lacked "social graces," much less formal education. This was the case in works by both men and women. As Krishan Kumar noted in 1981, a focus on pre-industrial "primitivism" in feminist visions of a perfect or at least radically better future could be found in Ursula LeGuin's *The Left Hand of Darkness* (1969) and *The Dispossessed* (1974), Marge Piercy's *Woman on the Edge of Time* (1976), Joanna Russ' *The Female Man* (1975), and Mary Staton's *From the Legend of Biel* (1975).

Unbeknown to most scholars when Kumar wrote was *Mizora: A Prophecy*, written by one Mary E. Bradley Lane and published in serialized form in the *Cincinnati Commercial* from 1880 to 1881 and reprinted in book form in 1890. Published under a pseudonym, the novel is significant because its characters are all pretty and refined females who are advanced technologically and scientifically. They would have fitted comfortably into middle-class Victorian homes of late-nineteenth-century America and Britain. Moreover, the Mizorans maintain single-family rather than communal homes, where each mother is directly responsible for her young daughters' well-being. The Mizorans' scientific and technological elevation finds expression in the development not only of a highly industrialized and automated state but also of a means of procreation without reliance on men.[3] Only Charlotte Perkins Gilman's far better known utopian novel *Herland* (1915) has a similar scheme.

Interestingly, the twenty-five (male) technological utopians did not predict a world without women, nor one in which women were completely equal to men. These men reflected their own largely middle-class values despite their wish to change many aspects of contemporary American society. Women were to obey their husbands and, in other situations, their fathers, brothers, or other males. Yet women in technological utopia could vote, hold office, hold jobs, and attend college. These women thus possessed a greater degree of equality than did women at the time that most of the utopians wrote.[4]

At least in part, these technological utopians were responding to widely perceived late-nineteenth- and early-twentieth-century problems. Like countless other Americans, they were obsessed about seemingly unprecedented social disorder, including crowding, competition, aggression, selfishness, and rudeness. They feared the ever-present threat of disease (whose source in

Figure 5.2 "The Town Mansion," from the frontispiece of a typically envisioned utopian (small) city with orderliness in every physical respect. *Source:* Thomas Kirwan (William Wonder, pseudo.), *Reciprocity (Social and Economic) in the Thirtieth Century: The Coming Co-operative Age* (New York: Cochrane, 1909).

microorganisms was just beginning to be understood); the unsanitary habits and habitats that spread the agents of epidemic and death; the growing secularism and declining belief in God and an afterlife; and the pervasive sense that individuals had lost control over self, family, and community. And, again like countless other Americans, these technological utopians feared that, a century or more after the Declaration of Independence and ratification of the Constitution, the United States had lost the quality of extraordinary leadership, integrity, and vision that had made it a unique beacon of democracy and opportunity. The run of mediocre presidents from Andrew Johnson through William McKinley epitomized this sense of moral decline. The utopians' anxieties were thus rooted in particular historical circumstances.

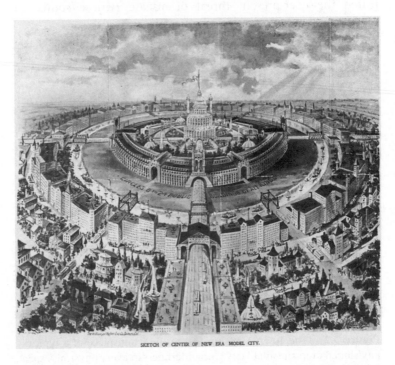

SKETCH OF CENTER OF NEW ERA MODEL CITY.

Figure 5.3 The metropolitan center of a scientific and technological utopia with suburbs connected directly to the city. *Source:* Charles Caryl, *New Era* (Denver, 1879).

Figure 5.4 Cover of Edgar Chambless, *Roadtown* (New York: Roadtown Press, 1910). Chambless imagined skyscrapers laid on their sides rather than extending vertically—the common vision of his fellow American utopians—and spanning the entire American countryside.

What these prophets of technological utopia envisioned was not a mass of soot-belching smokestacks, clanging machines, and teeming streets. Instead, the dirt, noise, and chaos that invariably accompanied industrialization in the real world would have given way to perfect cleanliness, efficiency, quiet, and harmony. With the taming of technology would come the taming of nature. Wind, water, and other natural resources would be subdued and harnessed in the form of clean, quiet, powerful electricity. Electrification was a widely held dream that had become a reality for most Americans by the late 1930s, by which time President Franklin Roosevelt's Rural Electrification Administration and the Tennessee Valley Authority (TVA) had accomplished their initial missions. By the time Loeb's book appeared in 1933, most of the envisioned transportation and communications systems had become facts of life throughout America.

Although many elements of utopia have not been realized, those who dreamed up these ideas ought not to be dismissed as mere crackpots. Neither, however, were these utopian visions simply pale reflections of what was sought by contemporary reformers. Instead, they were significant precisely *as* utopian visions. They took to extremes the vision and values of mainstream Americans who were seeking changes strictly within their society. Recall the metaphor of the microscope to understand how these utopians functioned vis-à-vis mere reformers: by first isolating and then magnifying aspects of existing, non-utopian societies allegedly needing drastic improvements, the utopians enable us to see more clearly the political, economic, cultural, and psychological mainstreams in which utopians and reformers alike lived. Reformers pushed movements ranging from conservation to corporate control and government reorganization, from city planning to national planning, and from scientific management to technocracy. But, unlike the utopians, they saw no need for wholesale alterations in the fabric of American society.

Utopia Within Sight: The American Technocracy Crusade

Of all the reform crusades of the late nineteenth and early twentieth centuries throughout the world, the American Technocracy movement of the 1930s and 1940s most closely approximated scientific and technological utopianism. It was the crusade that relied most fully on science and technology as the panacea for the problems of American society. Yet, paradoxically, it is precisely because of its preoccupation with science and technology that Technocracy cannot be considered the equivalent of technological utopianism. In seeking to increase efficiency and production, the overwhelming majority of Technocrats ignored the social ramifications of scientific and technological advance. Only a few were concerned with government, education, religion, culture, recreation, and social relations. The most prominent of these was none other than Harold Loeb, who was an authentic utopian. But Howard Scott, the leader of the Technocrats, had no such concerns and eventually competed with Loeb for leadership.[5]

Of the countless panaceas for the Great Depression, few enjoyed so spectacular, if so spectacularly brief, a reign. As the popular journal *Literary Digest* proclaimed in December 1932, "Technocracy is all the rage. All over the country it is being talked about, explained, wondered at, praised, damned."[6] Although the movement still persists, Technocracy's heyday lasted only from June 16, 1932, when the *New York Times* became the first influential press organ to report its activities, until January 13, 1933, when its leader, Scott, in attempting to silence his critics delivered a rambling, confusing, and uninspiring address on a well-publicized national radio hookup. Before, during, and after those seven crucial months, Scott and other Technocrats preached ceaselessly about their "scientific" (and therefore presumably foolproof) scheme for not merely ending the depression but also effecting unprecedented and permanent abundance for all Americans. Their technical jargon and complex charts invariably simultaneously impressed and perplexed their growing audiences. The great expectations thus raised were never met, and the present-day equation of a "technocracy" with a distinctly *un*utopian society reflects the movement's dismal legacy.

The origins of Technocracy are shrouded in controversy, but most of its future leaders were apparently inspired by their association between 1919 and 1921 with the social critic Thorstein Veblen, then teaching at New York City's New School for Social Research. Veblen offered a strategy, spelled out in *The Engineers and the Price System* (1921), for ridding American society of the waste and extravagance that he and other reformers had long con-demned. Under Scott's leadership, the Technocracy movement used some of Veblen's analysis, but they ignored his social criti-cism, his passionate desire to do more than operate a more efficient America. Veblen finally gave up on the prospect of engineers, scientists, and other technical experts changing the basic structure of American society. As he conceded, "by settled habit the tech-nicians, the engineers and industrial experts, are a harmless and docile sort, well fed on the whole, and somewhat placidly content with the 'full dinner-pail' which the lieutenants of the Vested Interests habitually allow them."[7]

It was later revealed that Scott had pathetically lied about his alleged extensive European engineering education and interna-tional project experience. In fact, he had absolutely no certified technical training or formal engineering experience and was actually a one-time foreman of a cement-pouring gang who had been fired for, of all things, incompetence and inefficiency! What Scott, alas, *did* have was a desire to become a national leader of either the genuine scientific and technological elite or, failing that, of the masses of lay citizens. He failed on both crusades. Yet Technocracy's eventual acquisition of a militaristic demeanor, rigid hierarchical structure, special insignia and salute, grey uni-forms, and fleet of grey automobiles raised the specter of fascism (already manifested in more overt American imitations of Mussolini's Italy).

By contrast, as Anna-K. Mayer has pointed out, technocracy was nowhere as popular in the "Anglophone world" of the same period and was instead equated with "unwelcome modern realities" in "exotic locations" outside of Britain. This disen-chantment with technocratic values and visions did not, how-ever, begin in the 1920s or 1930s. It can be traced back at least as far as the debates between Matthew Arnold and T. H. Huxley in the 1880s. Yet even their disagreements, along with those later debates between the world wars over possibly expanding science and technical education, were all premised upon a "collective opposition to technocracy" in the American style. The British still embraced a liberal humanistic education of some kind and did not place undue faith in numbers and in numbers-crunching as the royal road to progress. Hence, Mayer characterizes the British participants in these debates as "reluctant technocrats."[8]

In addition, during the same years (1883–1933), social critics who were pessimistic about America's future engaged in what historian Frederick Cople Jaher has called "cataclysmic thought."[9] Their ranks included such notables as Ignatius Donnelly, Homer Lea, Mary Lease, Jack London, and brothers Brooks and Henry Adams. Like the scientific and technological utopians, they stressed the overwhelming force of various upheavals taking place., but they despaired of solving the problems these upheavals entailed. All would culminate in a cataclysm, they predicted. They looked forlornly to the past, to a more settled, more agrarian, and more ethnically, religiously, and racially homogeneous golden age that could never be restored—if, in fact, it had ever existed. By contrast, technological utopians looked confidently to the future, to salvation through technological development.

Utopia Within Reach: "The Best and the Brightest"—Post-World War II Science and Technology Policy in the United States and Western Europe and the Triumph of the Social Sciences

In the introduction to his seminal 1945 report, *Science—The Endless Frontier*, Vannevar Bush wrote that

> We have no national policy for science. The Government has only begun to utilize science in the Nation's welfare. There is no body within the Government charged with formulating or executing a national science policy . . .. Science has been in the wings. It should be brought to the center of the stage—for in it lies much of our hope for the future.[10]

Five years after the report appeared, and following extensive debate inside and outside Congress and the White House, the National Science Foundation (NSF) finally came into being.

In its early formulations and applications, post-war science and technology policy largely excluded the social sciences. Bush himself had no use for the social sciences, which he deemed mushy, propagandistic, and—most damningly—unscientific. Bush's influence on immediate post-war science and technology policy overall was so great that his characterization of the social sciences pervaded many quarters. True, Bush was hardly alone in his assessment, and similar comments can still be heard from some "pure" scientists.[11]

But Bush likewise excluded "applied science" from the intended focus of post-war federal support, which would instead go to "basic science," or biology, chemistry, and physics. By "applied science" Bush meant engineering. This was not because Bush was either uninterested in the application of scientific discoveries or insensitive to America's historic "practical culture."[12] As a distinguished MIT electrical engineering Ph.D. recipient, professor, department chair, and eventually vice president and Dean of Engineering, Bush had more than a passing interest in both. He, himself, had many inventions and patents to his credit and became the leading designer of electromechanical analog computers.

Yet Bush's own career and his pre-war and wartime experiences had impressed on him the value—but also the unpredictable path—of basic science for ultimately practical purposes. Prominent wartime examples included basic research in nuclear physics leading to the atomic bomb and in microbiology leading to penicillin. Better to let private industry operating in the free marketplace fund avowedly applied science and to save precious federal funds for the kind of basic science that private industry ordinarily wouldn't fund.[13] As Bush put it repeatedly, "Applied research invariably drives out pure."[14] From such sentiments came the name National *Science* Foundation, not National Science *and Engineering* Foundation (though Bush actually wanted the name National *Research* Foundation).

Bush thereby perpetuated in a monumental way the modern hierarchy that places science above technology; that treats engineers and other technical experts as handmaidens to scientists; that deems technology merely applied science; and that thereby misses the unique intellectual qualities of technology itself. The modern hierarchy that Bush embraced was based on a false foundation. If, however, "applied science" did not in Bush's and other powerbrokers' views warrant anywhere as much federal support as "pure science," what claims on federal largesse could the social sciences possibly make? And how could the social sciences ever justify their own intellectual stature?

By contrast, Bush's principal antagonist, Senator Harley Kilgore of West Virginia, pushed for large federal spending in the social sciences as well as in basic (and applied) science. A New Deal liberal, Kilgore linked the social sciences with supplying ordinary citizens with direct assistance to ordinary citizens, such as better housing and better public schools. To him, the benefits of expanded science and technology research would likewise filter down to the grass roots by the same route. Neither Kilgore nor Bush invoked "utopianism," but what might have been a positive application for the former was, in its alleged naïveté, a negative connotation for the latter. In any case, the final legislation favored Bush, not Kilgore, save, ironically, in the naming of the new organization, Kilgore having proposed "National Science Foundation."[15]

By the late 1950s and early 1960s, however, things had turned around for the social sciences and, consequently, for their use in science and technology policy. To begin with, the self-confidence by then enjoyed by American science and, to a growing degree, American technology in a time of unprecedented federal support and citizen enthusiasm allowed increasing room on the policy pedestal for the social sciences. Indeed, some prominent social scientists virtually shaped debates over public policy, justifying social scientists' increasing respect and power. For example, economist John Kenneth Galbraith's bestseller *The Affluent Society* (1958) convinced many not only that affluence had by now pervaded most of American society but also that major economic and social problems either had been or soon would be solved. Moreover, professional economists in policy-making roles were, according to Galbraith and others, heavily responsible for this persistent prosperity. Even the belated discovery of poverty in Appalachia and other predominantly white areas, as detailed in Michael Harrington's *The Other America* (1963), could not diminish this utopian optimism that economists could attain affluence for all. If anything, the Council of Economic Advisors under both

President Kennedy and President Johnson believed in their ability to develop policies to help to eradicate poverty, a belief expanded by Johnson with his "War on Poverty."

Similarly, sociologist Daniel Bell's influential *The End of Ideology* (1960), even though it was misread as endorsing this consensus over the end of strongly ideological politics in affluent America, nevertheless gave enormous intellectual legitimacy to it. Furthermore, the purported consensus on America's present and future was now traced to the nation's past by influential historians such as Daniel Boorstin in *The Genius of American Politics* (1953) and David Potter in *People of Plenty: Economic Abundance and the American Character* (1954). Both discovered an American history supposedly marked by far more agreement than disagreement on fundamental values and policies, and both deemed dissenters from that consensus marginal figures if not outright subversives. Neither Boorstin nor Potter claimed to be a social scientist, but Potter in particular based much of his analysis of the "American character" on the findings of social scientists.

During this same period, in foreign policy, the social sciences also played a crucial role directly related to science and technology. Political scientists, sociologists, and economists provided models for the maturation of countries in Latin America, Africa, and Asia. Their expertise would help to turn "underdeveloped" areas into more industrialized and more democratized nations emulating the United States. At the peak of the Cold War, their models were invaluable political as much as academic tools. Area studies, international studies, and development studies became prominent interdisciplinary subfields.

Overarching these fields was "Modernization" theory. "Modernization" became the buzzword of politicians and social scientists alike. Both groups believed that the exportation of American science and technology, such as agricultural chemicals and equipment, to the aforementioned "backward" lands would turn the tide within them from communism to capitalism or undermine any efforts to remain ideologically neutral. These politicians and social scientists used a very traditional notion of "technological determinism" and ignored historical contexts that might have tempered their utopian expectations. They assumed that the sheer transfer abroad of American and Western European science and technology would steadily alter centuries-old native cultures in the direction of American and Western European culture, not least American and Western European democracy. The United States' own revolutionary past was largely overlooked amid the expectation that such profound political as well as cultural change could somehow be managed peacefully. For that matter, repeated examples of American intervention from the late nineteenth century through the Cold War in the internal affairs of other countries were conveniently ignored, as were persistent American leanings toward business, military, and political forces in those countries often hostile to genuine grass-roots democracy. Remarkably shallow and frankly unscientific premises were papered over with elaborate, self-consciously "scientific" models replete with graphs, statistics, public opinion surveys, and other seemingly objective paraphernalia. Like their conventional scientific counterparts, these social scientific experiments were designed to be repeated. But the laboratories for "modernization" theory were entire countries. More often than not, however, the experiments failed.[16]

Combined with the apparent national consensus over values and vision, these notable contributions by social scientists to public policy both at home and abroad made it far less risky than in prior eras to employ the social sciences in domestic science and technology policy. The most skeptical scientists and engineers had to concede this. Fairly or not, the social sciences had once been associated with the Great Depression as part of the failed and polarizing policies of Herbert Hoover, who was the first president to use them in the formulation of public policy, as epitomized in *Recent Social Trends in the United States* (1933).[17] That the book was published after Hoover's decisive loss to Franklin Roosevelt in his re-election bid naturally minimized not only its influence but also its pioneering analyses of topics ranging from communications to crime, from education to religion, and from recreation to taxation. By contrast, by the 1950s the social sciences were associated with ongoing national prosperity and international prestige, leading to ever greater federal funding of science and technology. In fact, the social sciences began, in the form of public opinion surveys of unprecedented accuracy, to make a case for their own importance by proving how supportive Americans generally were about that greater funding and how much of a consensus there really was about values and vision.

In a deeper sense, and in an ironic reversal of roles, the social sciences now provided intellectual legitimacy for the scientists, engineers, and politicians, who needed to convince the general public that American science and technology policy would benefit all citizens in more ways than Vannevar Bush had contended. The social sciences had themselves come to offer a supposed scientific objectivity—an unprecedented intellectual legitimacy for public policy—as reflected in the ongoing maturation of political science, sociology, and economics.

By the early 1960s, it had become an article of faith among liberal politicians, bureaucrats, and social scientists—that is, those eager to use the powers of government to effect economic and social change—that knowledge could and should be deployed to ameliorate human life and to solve those remaining problems of American and, in due course, every other "modernized" society. This belief, which dated to the Enlightenment (the so-called "Enlightenment Project"), was hardly restricted to the United States or to other Western capitalist countries. It was popular in the Soviet Union in the same period and had likewise been popular in Nazi Germany, as detailed in Jeffrey Herf's *Reactionary Modernism* (1984). This was not altogether surprising, however, insofar as there was an unacknowledged convergence of belief among many capitalists, communists, and fascists that the supremacy of the powers of rational knowledge and technical skills to improve life rested precisely on their universality and efficiency. Recall that Lenin had tried to adopt Henry Ford's assembly line techniques and Frederick Taylor's Scientific Management schemes back in the 1920s.[18]

But nowhere was this belief in the power of knowledge practiced more persistently than in the Kennedy and Johnson Administrations and in the colleges and universities where its adherents taught and wrote. As a *New York Times* writer put it about President Kennedy after the death in 2009 of the president's brother and successor as Massachusetts senator Ted Kennedy, John Kennedy "stood at the center of a new post-ideological pragmatism." President Kennedy articulated this in a 1962 speech contending that traditional ideological politics had faded and that the "most pressing government concerns were 'technical problems, administrative problems' that do not lend themselves to the great sort of passionate movements which have stirred this country so often in the past."[19]

President Kennedy and President Johnson's' "best and brightest" advisers, such as Robert McNamara, McGeorge Bundy, and Walt Rostow, are obvious examples of such true believers. McNamara's death in 2009 generated considerable reflection on his primary responsibility for directing and promoting the Vietnam War and his steadfast refusal to try to end it while still Secretary of Defense despite his mounting doubts about its likelihood of success.[20]

Apart from America's overall defeat in the Vietnam War, nothing better revealed McNamara's blind faith in the quantification of everything than his project to install a line of electronic sensors along the Ho Chi Minh Trail in Laos in 1967 and 1968 in order to try to turn the tide of the conflict in America's favor. By that time the North Vietnamese had established an elaborate system of roads and pathways through neighboring Laos to facilitate the movements of their troops and supplies. The Defense Secretary recruited a group of distinguished scientists—including some past and future Nobel Prize winners—to devise an "electronic battlefield" to detect and, ideally, destroy those roads and pathways. This largely secret group, called the Jasons, characteristically ignored critical non-quantitative contexts that doomed their highly expensive project, later derisively termed "the McNamara Line." Their electronic sensors never worked properly and could not measure, for example, the enemy's motivations and knowledge of the region.[21]

A similar blind faith was reflected in the far more protracted and, in some respects, more influential efforts of Rostow to apply his theory of "modernization" not only to peacetime conditions in the "underdeveloped" world but also to the Vietnam War. Rostow was an MIT Professor of Economic History whose 1960 book, *The Stages of Economic Growth*, was cleverly subtitled *A Non-Communist Manifesto*. Under the Kennedy Administration, Rostow was given major responsibility for taking Latin America through his five stages: from traditional society to transitional stage to take-off stage to drive to maturity stage and finally to utopia, the age of high mass-consumption. Like Karl Marx, Rostow was a true believer in the uniformity of his particular stages of development. Unlike Marx, though, he had the opportunity to apply his beliefs to real-world conditions, including the Vietnam War, his greatest challenge. In Rostow's view, Vietnam and other Communist nations had tragically bypassed the take-off stage and so must somehow start from scratch. He advocated carpet-bombing Vietnam for, in effect, its own good. As journalist Doug Saunders put it, where American General Curtis LeMay famously wanted to bomb the North Vietnamese "'back to the stone age,' Mr. Rostow was alone in wanting to bomb them ahead to the Age of High Mass-Consumption."[22]

Alas, the line of false prophets of technocracy, of arrogant "number-crunchers" from Howard Scott through McNamara, Bundy, and Rostow has obscured the largely forgotten intellectual tradition that viewed technocracy not as an opponent of progress and democracy but as a friend. This tradition includes any number of Progressive and New Deal intellectuals and reformers as well as science fiction writers. As Lewis Mumford, perhaps the leading figure in that tradition, put it so well in a 1921 review of economist and social critic Veblen's *The Engineers and the Price System*, "What matters it if industrial society is run efficiently, if it is run only further into the same blind alley in which humanity finds itself today."[23] Ironically, the first chapter of *Life in a Technocracy* is entitled "Blind Alley."

The 1960s saw yet more interesting cases: political scientists Robert Dahl and Robert Lane and nuclear engineer Alvin Weinberg. In *Who Governs? Democracy and Power in an American City* (1961) and other works, Dahl argued that pluralism was an American fact of life as much as an American political theory and that every interest group that wished to participate in politics at every level had relatively equal opportunity to do so. Given the nation's growing affluence, there was no need for alienation from politics but likewise no need for political upheaval. As Dahl insisted in *A Preface to Democratic Theory* (1956), "A central guiding thread of American constitutional development has been the evolution of a political system in which all the active and legitimate groups in the population can make themselves heard at some crucial stage in the process of decision."[24]

Lane agreed with Dahl but went further. In such writings as "The Politics of Consensus in an Age of Affluence" (1965) and "The Decline of Politics and Ideology in a Knowledgeable Society" (1966), Lane contended that traditional ideological politics would decline as that increasing national affluence made the outcomes of political struggles ever less significant and as neutral information, rational analysis, and technical skills took their place. Lane contrasted the "domain of 'pure politics' where decisions are determined by calculations of influence, power, or electoral advantage," with the emerging, and infinitely more appealing, "domain of 'pure knowledge' where decisions are determined by calculations of how to implement agreed-upon values with rationality and efficiency." Lane conceded that "there will always be politics; there will always be rationalized self-interest, mobilized by interest groups and articulated in political parties." But he fully expected that such crass "political criteria" for determining public policy would steadily give way to "more universalistic *scientific* criteria." Not laymen, much less conventional politicians, but rather "professional problem-oriented *scientists*"—and, in effect, social scientists like Lane—would now hold sway.[25] The road to utopia had been chosen.

Lane offered examples of "scientific" findings about American society by social scientists that led to the kind of public policy activism by experts that he favored: curbing infant mortality, reducing cancer in children, raising individuals and families above the subsistence level, and increasing respect for different racial, religious, and ethnic groups. Such scientific knowledge "creates a pressure for policy change with a force all its own."[26]

Weinberg went further still. In "Can Technology Replace Social Engineering?" (1966), he offered examples of how technology could readily find shortcuts, or "Quick Technological Fixes," to solve social problems that ideological politics could not or would not solve. His examples included free air-conditioners and free electricity to reduce the discomfort that in part led to summertime riots in urban ghettos; cheap computers to replace rather than retrain inadequate teachers in impoverished elementary schools; intra-uterine devices to reduce population in overpopulated countries where large families are the norm; nuclear-powered desalination to provide fresh water in needy areas where water conservation is difficult if not impossible; safer cars to reduce accidents caused by bad drivers who resisted formal driver instruction; and atomic weapons, especially hydrogen bombs, to lessen the possibility of war because of fear of mass mutual destruction. As Weinberg conceded, "Technology will never *replace* social engineering." But technology had long provided and would continue to provide the social engineer with broader options, above all, to "buy time—that precious commodity that converts violent social revolution into acceptable social evolution." Weinberg did not define the term "social engineer," but by his use of it he clearly meant the social scientist, who would work hand-in-hand with scientists, engineers, and other technical experts. Far from patronizing social engineers/social scientists, in the manner of Bush, Weinberg praised them. For social problems are not only much more complex than technological problems but are also "much harder to identify" than technological problems. "Quick Technological Fixes" thereafter became a popular term with both positive and negative connotations. They would assist and complement but not replace conventional social engineering strategies. Contrary to Weinberg, however, all these "Quick Technological Fixes" were actually not alternatives to, but rather themselves examples of, social engineering.[27]

Perhaps the supreme technological fix was President Reagan's anti-missile defense system, which was announced years after Weinberg's article appeared. This was the logical extension of other plans—and, in some cases, actual manifestations of those plans—to end some wars and prevent others: a short-cut to allegedly permanent world peace that would preclude traditional and often unreliable diplomatic efforts.

In their separate ways, Dahl, Lane, and Weinberg, among others, justified the creation of the various institutional structures that came to shape federal science and technology policy. The most important ones were the Science Advisory Committee, established by President Truman in 1951; its successors, the President's

Science Advisory Committee and the Special Assistant to the President for Science and Technology, both of which were set up by President Eisenhower in 1957 following the launching of the first artificial satellite, Sputnik I, by the Soviet Union; and the Office of Science and Technology Policy, begun by President Ford in 1976, three years after President Nixon abolished Eisenhower's creations for political reasons.

Eisenhower had already made atomic energy subject to civilian rather than military control. But now politicians, governmental bureaucrats, political scientists, and scientists and engineers could argue that science and technology were no less under the control of the American public than any other realms and that the much-heralded spin-offs to ordinary citizens from nuclear power, space-flight, and other key areas of federal science and technology funding would indeed benefit everyone in pluralist America and, in due course, elsewhere in the capitalist world. The institutional structures were now supposedly in place to lay the foundations for a veritable scientific and technological utopia in North America and Western Europe heavily influenced by wholly objective social scientists.

Equally importantly, Dahl, Lane, Weinberg, and others tempered the hostility toward politics in technocratic discourse and vision that had previously prevented the Technocrats of the 1930s and like-minded groups from being taken seriously by decision-makers. Where such leading Technocrats as Scott and Loeb had no use for politicians and for politics itself—deeming the whole enterprise messy and so morally if not literally corrupt[28]—Dahl, Lane, and Weinberg, along with Galbraith, Bell, and many others, recognized the inevitability of politics, notwithstanding fundamental consensus, and sought to integrate technical and social science expertise with political expertise. They understood that every decision in governance, no matter how seemingly technical, is to some degree a political decision and that the denial of that fact of life both by anti-political Technocrats and by similarly inclined scientists and engineers is itself a political stance. As the political theorist Franz Neumann observed, "No society in recorded history has ever been able to dispense with political power. This is as true of liberalism as of absolutism, as true of laissez faire as of an interventionist state."[29] True, the existence of that alleged post-war consensus on national values and vision certainly made the respective positions of Dahl, Lane, Weinberg, Galbraith, and Bell far more palatable than they would have been during the Great Depression, when no such consensus existed, leading to marginal disaffected groups like the Technocrats. Nor should one underestimate the skepticism about politics as insufficiently manageable and predictable that is still found among many engineers and scientists.

Still, the fundamental assumption of post-war social scientists like Dahl, Lane, Galbraith, and Bell, and of socially minded engineers like Weinberg, was that public policy both at home and abroad could be managed by the right combination of experts in various fields. This assumption was taken to an extreme by Simon Ramo, who codified it into Systems Analysis or, more accurately, Systems Engineering.

Ramo is a cofounder of TRW, a large pioneering high-tech company, and has been an adviser to several presidents and the Pentagon. Ramo did not alone devise Systems Engineering but he has advocated, practiced, and written about it more than nearly any other American. Both the modest Social Engineering at the federal level pioneered by President Hoover and the grander schemes envisioned by Weinberg were dwarfed by the *de facto* utopian vision of Ramo and his fellow true believers. Systems Engineering was not, however, limited to engineers but instead embraced like-minded social scientists. Moreover, any problems not solvable by the designated original teams of experts would by definition eventually be solved by additions to or replacements of team members, which increasingly meant more social scientists. But any problems not solvable under these conditions were by definition not genuine problems and so could be safely dismissed. Ramo and other proponents of this approach utilized the general systems theory of the 1920s but added a new twist: rather than examine the dynamics of the system or the system itself, these analysts instead focused exclusively on the final or end product. That focus enabled them to treat any element of any complicated system in a singular fashion: how did it contribute to the output and how could its contribution to the output be enhanced? Each part of any such system could therefore be looked at as a discrete element rather than, as in earlier systems, a non-detachable part of the whole. Different kinds of experts were thereby needed for each part, and social scientists were thus as invaluable as engineers and scientists. Ramo detailed his scheme in a book entitled *Cure for Chaos: Fresh Solutions to Social Problems Through the Systems Approach* (1969).[30]

Ramo's title and subtitle clearly reflected an increasing sense of social, cultural, and political upheaval in the United States and other "advanced" societies in the several years just before the book was published (and, of course, in the first few years immediately after its publication too). Like the Technocrats of the 1930s, Ramo and his fellow systems engineers had come to see their world as desperately needing the kind of order only they could provide: efficient, honest, non-ideological. In the heady atmosphere of the Kennedy and early Johnson Administrations there had been little reason to question the logic of Systems Engineering: certainly not until the growing public perception of mismanagement of the Vietnam War by the "Best and the Brightest"; and, no less important, not until the campus protests at the University of California at Berkeley and elsewhere that passionately attacked the growing impersonality of education (and, by extension, other spheres of life and work) and the bureaucratic identification of students and workers by numbers and computer punchcards. More precisely, by focusing on output and by assuming that output is an agreed-upon commodity, systems engineers such as Ramo more often distorted than resolved problems. As historian and social critic Theodore Roszak observed, "the good systems team does not include poets, painters, holy men, or social revolutionaries, who, presumably, have nothing to contribute to 'real life solutions.'"[31]

In their 1986 book entitled *TVA and the Tellico Dam, 1936–1979: A Bureaucratic Crisis in Post-Industrial America*, historians William Bruce Wheeler and Michael J. McDonald offer a provocative case study that implicitly represents the kind of challenge to public policy that is not reducible to systems analysis. In brief, beginning in 1973 a proposed TVA dam in East Tennessee was opposed by some environmentalists on the grounds that its creation would eliminate the snail darter, a tiny fish akin to the perch, allegedly found nowhere else. For several years the dam's opponents successfully stopped ongoing construction by suing under the recently enacted federal Endangered Species Act. Proponents of the dam put traditional economic, recreational, and other local benefits above the need to keep alive a species that did not, to say the least, have the romantic appeal of endangered right whales or spotted owls. If Systems Engineering can solve all public policy dilemmas, how would Ramo and his disciples have solved this one? As things turned out, the dam was finally completed in 1979, sixteen years after the TVA initially approved it, because its proponents had more political clout than its opponents. Congress exempted Tellico Dam from the Endangered Species Act and President Jimmy Carter, initially against the project, reluctantly signed the bill. Happily, the snail darter was later discovered to be alive elsewhere and so survived after Tellico Dam was built. The key issue, however, is the impoverished nature and blind faith of Ramo's utopia.

Other critics have complained that Systems Engineering not only is elitist, self-justifying, self-perpetuating, and narrowly conceived but also, and most ironically, *in*efficient, *in*adequate, and *un*scientific.[32] Certainly Systems Engineering hardly enjoys a stellar record in the field in which it was initially embraced: the military. Quite the opposite: a seemingly endless progression of poorly made weapons and vehicles, plus enormous cost overruns, have made many Americans equate military expenditures with waste and greed.

The failed "electronic battlefield" in Vietnam exemplifies this. As one scholar put it about the Jasons group who devised it, those "scientists felt a large degree of optimism over their abilities to 'solve' the problem of the Vietnam War."[33] This meant nothing less than winning the war.

Interestingly, the failure of Systems Engineering has given rise to a much broader and more sophisticated approach to solving the most intractable social problems, problems termed "wicked." The term derives from several seminal writings of the late 1960s and early 1970s on "wicked problems" by University of California at Berkeley professors C. West Churchman, Horst Rittel, and Melvin Webber. They coined the phrase to describe social problems that were extremely difficult to solve because of various complexities, changes, and contradictions. Examples include biodiversity loss, global warming, urban violence, and overpopulation. Such problems contrast with what these authors called "tame" social problems: those that were assumed to be capable of being solved by Ramo and McNamara's brand of technical, scientific, and managerial experts.

Those who deal with "wicked" social problems endorse Roszak's sarcastic criticism of "the good systems team" as being narrowly conceived. They instead seek just such persons and cite the Romantic poet Samuel Taylor Coleridge's still helpful distinction between fleeting fancy and sustained imagination: if fancy is "merely an elaboration of memory," imagination constitutes the "prime agent of all human perception."[34]

Those dealing with "wicked" social problems concede, like so many other scholarly studies have by now, that knowledge is socially constructed, but go on to acknowledge that ignorance is also socially constructed. By this, they mean that, contrary to diehard systems analysts such as Ramo and McNamara, what constitutes knowledge and ignorance heavily depends on which persons, groups, societies, and ideologies are constructing the definitions. It is not a matter of one side having more powerful computers and other electronic analytical and communications devices than another. Consequently, not arrogance and immediacy but humility and patience are crucial for any eventual success. This perspective, however, is hardly a wholesale attack on either science or objectivity. The contributors seek to "tame wicked problems" precisely by joining science with imagination, for too long wrongly deemed anti-science.

Yet, until the mid-1960s the overwhelming public faith in government on the one hand and scientific and technological advance on the other had transformed post-war science and technology policy into seemingly progressive social policy about the entire nation, not just the military establishment or the space program or the nuclear power industry. (To this degree, Senator Kilgore might have been pleased.) And, with the need to compete with the Soviet Union in science, math, and engineering education following the latter's launch in 1957 of the world's first artificial satellite, Sputnik I, science and technology policy had filtered down to the grass-roots more than at any previous time in American history, apart from "hot" wars. What has since been termed scientific and technological literacy became part of daily educational and familial conversations.

Beginning in 1959, with the publication of Englishman C. P. Snow's *The Two Cultures*, those conversations were influenced by the notion of a Western academic world bitterly divided into two camps: the sciences and the humanities. (As both a one-time scientist and a highly respected novelist, Snow himself bridged both camps, but he was, by his own account, the exception that proved the rule.) Although Snow blamed each party for ignoring the contributions of the other, he scorned "literary intellectuals" more. For they delighted in their intentional ignorance of science, where scientists more often lamented their limited familiarity with the humanities. Snow also praised scientists who, like himself, had become involved in establishing and administering public policy. (Following the Labour Party's victory in 1964, Snow became the second highest member of the newly established Ministry of Technology and the government's spokesperson for science and technology in the House of Lords. He held that post for a year and a half.) Implicit in Snow's plea for greater such involvement by more scientists was the participation of similarly minded social scientists. Like Bell, Dahl, Lane, Weinberg, and other Americans, Snow was quite optimistic about the prospect of the solution of problems at home and abroad by the application of scientific and in turn social scientific methods. He was a fervent, if unofficial, advocate of "Modernization" theory. This faith in science and technology distinguished Snow from many of his contemporaries, not least in the humanities, who lamented the decline of the British Empire and Great Britain's increasingly second-class superpower status vis-à-vis the United States.[35] As Mayer has argued, however, earlier debates between scientists and humanists in Britain were nowhere near as divisive as those generated by Snow's works and were based upon a transcendent belief in the value of both.[36]

But post-war science and technology policy was not just a reaction to the challenge of affluence or to the threat of Communism or to the need for greater scientific and technological literacy.

In 1956, William H. Whyte, Jr., published *The Organization Man*. Whyte, assistant managing editor of *Fortune*, criticized unthinking, uncritical worship of corporate organizations and pilloried the gospel of scientism, the notion that expert determinations were always non-partisan and not subject to error or debate. He railed against any organization's use of the concepts of belonging and togetherness to manipulate members and objectives, and he called on his contemporaries to challenge the status quo. Whyte conceded that the organization was here to stay, and he did not advocate nonconformity. Rather, he urged men and women to examine the premises they took for granted, to vent their individual proclivities, and to redirect their various organizations. Individualism tempered by critical thought would awaken America from its blissful organization-inspired ignorance and produce a better tomorrow.

Whyte's book drew plaudits from many corners, became an immediate best-seller, and remained popular for years. More than ever before, science and technology became a means to give flight to individual expression, which invariably had material components. Science and technology would give each American and their Western European counterparts the chance to "keep up with the Joneses," the 1950s idealized personification of unfettered opportunity.

In the late 1960s and 1970s, of course, Whyte's anti-corporate message would take on new meaning as many young Americans rejected not only the corporate ethos but also the obsession with material goods that went hand in hand with it. Yet, in some ways, Whyte's greater legacy is the early critique of expertise, and not just in corporations but throughout American and Western European life. Nowhere was expertise taken more for granted than in science and technology and, as already indicated, in the social sciences that emulated them.

Officially, it was President Eisenhower's 1961 Farewell Address that began the unraveling of the post-war consensus over science and technology policy, a consensus that fell apart over the Vietnam War, the "Star Wars" missile defense system, urban crises, environmental disasters, and the higher education–military research nexus—the focus of Eisenhower's concern. By the mid-1960s, federal support of science was being criticized as inattentive to social issues in a manner reminiscent of Senator Kilgore, but now in a climate of criticism rather than of celebration of American life. In 1968, Congress amended the NSF's chartering legislation to support more formally and more fully applied research and the social sciences, both already funded on a modest basis. The NSF even began an avowedly social scientific program on "Research Applied to National Needs." In the Reagan, Bush, and Clinton Administrations, however, socially useful research was redefined as research making high-tech America more competitive vis-à-vis other major powers, Japan above all. Ironically, Senator Kilgore's post-war dream was of a national science and technology policy and structure that would help small businesses, not giant corporations.

Yet federal policy, however supportive of the social sciences, cannot alter the sea change in recent years in public attitudes toward science and technology. The historic bedrock American faith in scientific and technological progress, and in such progress as leading directly to social progress, has clearly diminished. If it is premature to proclaim the end of the "Enlightenment Project," let alone the "end of science,"[37] the evident growth of scientific and technological pessimism has made the optimism of the late 1950s and early 1960s seem hopelessly naïve and utterly passé.[38]

Put another way, there has been a steady erosion of faith in recent decades in what psychologist Kenneth Keniston terms the "engineering algorithm": the core belief that "the relevant world can be defined as a set of problems, each of which can be solved through the application of scientific theorems and mathematical principles."[39] This belief at once underlay and justified post-war science and technology policy and the expanding role of the social sciences in applying scientific and technological advances to social policy at home and abroad. The diminution of that belief has in turn led to ever more radical positions on the nature of science itself. If, as some outside policy circles now contend, objectivity itself is socially constructed, any claims of genuine expertise, much less of genuine objectivity, are logically impossible. And no systems engineering team, no social science models, and no computer programs can change that.

A 2009 joint survey by the highly respected Pew Research Center for the People and the Press and the American Association for the Advancement of Science (the world's largest scientific organization) revealed an enormous gap between scientific beliefs and American public perceptions. And that gap surely extends beyond the United States. On the "hot-button" issues of evolution and climate change, shocking percentages of Americans reject evolution and/or global warming altogether as scientifically proved facts of life. And, where roughly fifty percent of respondents in a 1999 poll believed that scientific advances were among the nation's most important achievements, a decade later only twenty-seven percent agreed with that proposition.[40]

This declining national faith in scientific and technological progress has inevitably lessened the complementary faith in the social sciences. As social critic Kirkpatrick Sale asked in 1980 about the nation's post-World War II track record of "Quick Technological Fixes":

> Do we seem to be moving toward real and healthy solutions to our nation's crises, does the populace seem safer and healthier and happier with it all, or do we seem, somehow, to have accumulated problems instead of dispelling them and to have created a world of greater anxiety and risk and chaos than we had before? Solutions, we must remember, are very much like problems: they are rooted in people, not in technology. Schemes that try to devise miracles to bypass people, negate, deny, nullify or minimize people, will not work.[41]

Sale's critique may be excessive, but the repeated failure of the social sciences to provide lasting solutions to so many social problems has certainly contributed to that sea change in public attitudes toward science and technology. As economist Richard Nelson detailed in *The Moon and the Ghetto: An Essay on Public Policy Analysis* (1977), too many social scientists working in science and technology realms have never appreciated the gap between their elegantly rational methodologies and analyses and the messier and more complex conflicts of interest in the "real world" they seek to illuminate and to improve.

The elimination of the Office of Technology Assessment (OTA) in 1995 by the then new Republican Congressional majority exemplified that sea change. Not only was the OTA officially apolitical, but its budget was so modest that its shutdown was as much symbolic as substantive. This point was conveniently overlooked by the Republicans who killed the OTA in order, they claimed, to demonstrate their willingness to tighten Congress' own belt so as then to justify deeper budget cuts affecting ordinary citizens. Yet the end of the OTA also exemplified, contrary to Lane's 1966 analysis, the persistence of ideological politics in the very realm where "universalistic scientific criteria" applied by "professional problem-oriented scientists" and social scientists might have been expected to triumph. If anything, science and technology policy are today more political and more ideological in nature than ever before in American history.[42]

Still, it was ironic that the assault on the OTA was led by then House Speaker Newt Gingrich. Not only had Gingrich deemed himself a high-tech visionary and admirer of gurus Alvin and Heidi Toffler, but it was Alvin Toffler's bestselling *Future Shock* (1970) that, for all its flaws, made millions of readers aware of the need to anticipate the future more systematically than had ever been attempted before. The disappearance of the OTA hardly contributed to this effort. That a self-proclaimed leading policy-maker like Gingrich, with a Ph.D. in history to boot, had pushed for its disappearance appeared to make no intellectual sense. And if, in some early cases, the OTA was not strictly neutral, in virtually all of its later cases it was avowedly non-partisan and conscientiously served all its Congressional constituents. As political scientist Bruce Bimber puts it, the OTA gradually "developed a *strategy of neutrality* . . . not as a professional standard but as a political survival strategy to ward off critics." If anything, the OTA kept such a low bureaucratic profile that, according to Bimber, it failed to develop sufficient political support that might have saved it from elimination by persons with political agendas ultimately having little to do with the OTA itself, including Gingrich.[43]

Moreover, however partisan the OTA might have been perceived as being, it was set up in 1972 not to block scientific and technological developments but instead to assess their potential ramifications, positive and negative, for American society. Its creation reflected the initial wavering American faith in scientific and technological progress, for if there had been no skepticism about progress there would logically have been no reason to assess those potential ramifications. In the wake of *Future Shock*'s extraordinary popularity, the special concern at the time was preparing for the unexpected: the "effects on all sectors of a society that may occur when a [particular] technology is introduced, extended, or modified, with special emphasis on any impacts that are unintended, indirect, or delayed."[44]

In the early 1970s, though, there was still sufficient bedrock faith within both parties in government and in scientific and social scientific expertise to justify the OTA's establishment. If the future was increasingly uncertain, social scientists such as Dahl and Lane and socially oriented scientists such as Weinberg would nevertheless be able to save the day. Whatever politics lay behind the OTA's demise, its elimination did not reflect any lessening of that wavering American faith in scientific and technological progress. Quite the opposite: the subtext of the OTA's disappearance was a belated acknowledgment of this sea change.

This brings us back to Bush's *Science—The Endless Frontier*. In 1994 the Clinton Administration issued a report entitled *Science in the National Interest*. Billed as the first official presidential statement on science policy since 1979, and personally endorsed by both President Clinton and Vice President Gore, the report made a passionate case for expanded federal support of science and technology in the post-Cold War era. It was also an avowed sequel to *Science—The Endless Frontier*. The new report's first section was outright entitled "Science: The Endless Resource." The only explicit qualification the 1994 report made of its 1945 predecessor was in acknowledging that the "societal benefits" of science and technology derive from an "interdependence" of basic and applied research. "We depart here from the Vannevar Bush canon, which suggested a competition between basic and applied research" for prestige, power, and recognition. Trying to avoid Bush's hierarchy, the 1994 report characterized the contemporary science and technology relationship as "more like an ecosystem than a production line," a production line presumably exemplifying one group (scientists) controlling another (engineers and other technical experts, including social scientists) and demanding conformity by the latter to the former's conception and pace of work; or, as some historians have characterized it, the misleading assembly line model of technology in which we put science in and get technology out. That a production line might well be the crowning achievement of many engineers apparently did not occur to the report's writers. Elsewhere in the report, the common conception that Bush perpetuated of engineers merely applying what scientists discover came through, no matter how unintended this was. The report's very title slighted technology, as did its repeated paeans to the frontiers of scientific discovery but not to invention.

More precisely, one would never have gathered from *Science in the National Interest* that some of the nation's (and the world's) most significant post-war research has been and will continue to be both basic and applied, at once advancing fundamental understandings of science and helping to solve major practical problems. As political scientist Donald Stokes demonstrated in *Pasteur's Quadrant: Basic Science and Technological Innovation* (1997), it is quite possible for first-rate scientific research to be motivated by avowedly practical objectives without sacrificing contributions to scientific knowledge. Contrary to Bush's model, such linkages could enhance, not undermine, basic research, not least for those contemporary policy-makers eager—in a manner akin to Senator Kilgore—to see some fruits of government funding in the form of material improvements.[45]

Stokes rejected Bush's linear model of basic science leading to applied science and in turn to technology and then to commerce and industry, in favor of a model using the geometry of "quadrants." According to Stokes, all research falls into one of four quadrants. One quadrant, named for the theoretical physicist Niels Bohr, is for research, like Bohr's on the atom, that is exclusively basic, never applied. Another quadrant, named for the inventive genius Thomas Edison, is for research that is exclusively applied, never basic. A third quadrant, to which Stokes gives no name, is for research that does not seek to advance either basic or applied science; examples would be nineteenth-century classification projects in natural history. The fourth quadrant, named for the great French chemist and life scientist Louis Pasteur, is for Stokes the most important. For this quadrant encompasses research that, like Pasteur's, is *both* basic and applied. It advances fundamental understandings while solving significant practical problems. Pasteur's research "was motivated by the very practical objectives of improving industrial processes and public health. It led directly to applications that saved the French silk and wine industries, improved the preservation of wine and beer, and created effective vaccines."[46] But these applications were based on Pasteur's breakthroughs in developing the germ theory of disease and in establishing the field of bacteriology. Hence, Stokes' endorsement of this model of research for contemporary American scientists, engineers, and, not least, social scientists.

Most importantly, *Science in the National Interest* ignored the point made by Billington, Vincenti, and other historians of technology that engineering has significant intellectual properties of its own separate from those of science, and that the making of things by engineers requires an intellectual discipline as taxing as the making of discoveries by scientists. Significantly, Snow recognized that engineering is actually a third culture separate from both science and the humanities. In passages of *The Two Cultures* that are rarely cited, he acknowledged that scientists can be as patronizing toward engineers and other technical experts—including, implicitly, social scientists—as any self-proclaimed humanists. As Snow put it, "Pure scientists have by and large been dim-witted about engineers and applied science. They couldn't get interested. They wouldn't recognize that many of the problems were as intellectually exacting as pure problems, and that many of the solutions were as satisfying and beautiful" as those set forth by scientists. Instead, scientists invariably assumed that "applied science was an occupation for second-rate minds."[47] (Of course, engineering and technology generally are not, contrary to Snow, simply "applied science.")

Science in the National Interest touted a number of high-tech advances while ignoring any downsides. For example, it cited genetic-engineering experiments without any mention of attendant controversies; the repair of the mirror on the Hubble space telescope, which should never have been so flawed in the first place; and the satellite monitoring of the earth's ozone layer, which has been damaged by our own handiwork. And the report presumed a continuing (but, in reality, non-existent) national consensus in favor of increased federal funding for science and technology. "While we cannot foretell the outcome of fundamental research," the report conceded in a revealing comment, "we know from past experience that, in its totality, it consistently leads to dramatically valuable results for humanity." Bush could hardly have disagreed with ahistorical rhetoric like this, rhetoric antedating the wavering faith in progress that led to the creation of the OTA in the first place. But the Congressional majorities that in 1993 stopped funding the Texas-based Superconducting Super Collider and that in the past few years have sometimes threatened to stop funding the space station surely would have disagreed.[48]

Nowhere in *Science in the National Interest*, then, was there any acknowledgment of the legitimation crisis that has begun to color American science and technology policy. Whyte's early critique of scientific and social scientific expertise has by now become commonplace, as has his cry for intraorganizational individualism. In the process science and technology have steadily been reduced from the nation's principal sources of authority and the objects of unparalleled reverence and deference to those mere means of enhancing individual expression that Whyte identified in their early embodiments. Moreover, contemporary high-tech advances allow a degree of separation and distance from unwanted outside authorities undreamed of when Whyte wrote. Examples abound: from buying and selling goods and securities through the Internet to choosing from among hundreds of cable television channels through satellite dishes to seeking romance and adventure through personal websites. The fact that these and so many more activities can be carried on at home on personal computers makes them all the more appealing to those growing numbers of Americans who expect and demand insulation and protection from the world about them. Not surprisingly, their varied individual political agendas increasingly do not include taxpayer support for megaprojects such as super colliders and space stations.

For that matter, whatever appreciation follows for the scientific, technological, and social scientific advances that allow for these new living and working arrangements does not, as in the past, translate into any celebration of science or technology, much less of social science, as wonders in and of themselves. Instead, it is, to repeat, the empowerment of the individual—as seen from each individual's perspective—that is nowadays celebrated. Science, technology, and social science are praised, if at all, for their practical payoffs rather than for their cultural values. This is not exactly the world envisioned by Bell, Dahl, Galbraith, Lane, Ramo, Snow, or Weinberg—or, needless to say, by Vannevar Bush.

On Misreading Frankenstein: How Scientific and Technological Advances have Changed Traditional Criticisms of Utopianism in the Twentieth and Twenty-First Centuries

Both the Technocracy movement in its brief heyday and, for a longer period, the post-World War II beliefs and projects just described represented peaks of optimism about the probable achievement of utopia in the not too distant future. Yet neither eliminated serious criticism of the utopian prospect in America or elsewhere, especially amid the rise of left-wing and right-wing totalitarian regimes and movements throughout the world from the 1920s onward.

True, countless objections to utopianism in any serious form have been raised since Plato's *Republic* and certainly since More's *Utopia*. Utopianism has been persistently criticized as impractical, immoral, deviant, conformist, revolutionary, reactionary, stagnant, authoritarian, and libertarian. One might, then, maintain that the rejection of utopianism is as old as utopianism itself. Beyond the obvious question of whether specific utopian schemes could ever be implemented has come the traditional concern over forcing individuals, groups, and entire societies to adopt values, institutions, and ways of life that many might otherwise reject— that is, if offered a choice, given the equally persistent association of utopianism with a lack of choice.

However, for roughly a century now, there have been two main objections. First, insofar as the realization of utopia presumes human perfectibility, it is impractical. The scientifically and technologically assisted horrors of the years since World War I (the world wars, the genocides, the nuclear bombs, the environmental disasters) have rendered forlorn any hope of radical improvement in human behavior. Second, and more perversely, any scientific and technological progress has made utopia as undesirable as it has become possible. Given the human propensity toward selfish and exploitative behavior, achievement of the kind of planning and control required by utopia would inevitably result in "dystopia," or anti-utopia. The visions of Eugene Zamyatin's *We* (1920) and of the more popular Aldous Huxley's *Brave New World* (1932) and Orwell's *1984* have transformed utopia from something to be yearned for to something to be dreaded.

Yet, since the 1980s, arguments about the impossibility of changing and so improving human behavior have diminished with the ongoing development of genetic engineering. It has become increasingly apparent that our propensity toward either optimism or pessimism has much to do with our individual genetic makeup. Certainly non-genetic factors play a role, but of great importance is the nature of and extent to which our genes are connected with serotonin, a molecule that conveys messages to and from nerve cells and that affects our behavior. Experiments to determine the role of serotonin indicate that, as the phrase goes, optimists are genetically predisposed to see the world differently from pessimists and skeptics. It would surely be revealing to conduct experiments on avowed utopians or other persistently upbeat persons.

Nevertheless, as *New York Times* columnist David Brooks reminded us in 2008, "Today, if you look at people who study how genetics shape human behavior, you find a collection of anti-Frankensteins. As the research moves along, the scientists grow more modest about what we are close to knowing and achieving," contrary to earlier proclamations of the "discovery of an aggression gene, a happiness gene, or a depression gene."[49] Moreover, as the *New York Times* detailed in a 2010 article entitled "Awaiting the Genome Payoff," in the ten years since the completion of the first draft of the Human Genome Project and the identification of our roughly 22,000 human genes, few drugs have been developed. The billions spent to date by drug companies have not yielded "the cornucopia of new drugs" predicted at the outset. Yet it is much too early to despair. A number of potential drugs are in the pipeline, and the extremely complex processes just take far more time than originally anticipated.[50]

Yet according to Harvard psychologist Daniel Gilbert, whose research concentrates on the nature of happiness, humans have a general predisposition not to allow such bad things as the loss of loved ones or divorce to ruin their lives when they still enjoy relative freedom. Likewise, we are not usually transformed by good things such as winning the lottery. Paradoxically, many persons, perhaps most, are poor prognosticators of how they might react to bad or good things and commonly exaggerate the likely outcomes in both instances. When these events do occur, "most of us will return to our emotional baselines, more quickly than we'd predict. Humans are wildly resilient," Gilbert concludes. This is another example of the limited power and success of forecasting.[51] Gilbert argues that positive experiences and fulfilling relationships are far more satisfying than material wealth, no matter how seductive the latter might appear.[52]

What, however, about the prospect of changing even positively inclined human nature? On July 5, 1996, the first mammal to be cloned, a sheep named Dolly, was born in Scotland. Until Dolly, cloning was commonly thought to be an impossible biological feat. Dolly came into being by being cloned from the "stored and frozen udder cells of a sheep that had been dead for years" and so was the identical twin of that deceased and unnamed sheep. Dolly lived for six years until dying of a lung infection deemed to be unrelated to her having been cloned. She lived a happy if, for a sheep, relatively short life and, unlike many other sheep, loved the company of people. She gave birth to several lambs that were produced in the conventional manner, with a ram. There were never any plans to clone Dolly herself.[53]

The contemporary cloning of animals has obviously suggested the prospect of cloning humans in the not-too-distant future and has led to endless debates about the nature and morality of technological "progress" that rival, if not surpass, those debates of past decades regarding the use of nuclear weapons. (For that matter, witness the enormous controversies in recent years merely about the possible use of stem cells to develop cures for some major diseases.)

For years now mice have been created to be research tools. But mice are quite different genetically from humans and so do not provide adequate models for investigating diseases, for instance. Recently, however, biotechnology has created the first generation of genetically modified monkeys that are much closer to humans and that are capable of passing on genetic attributes to their offspring. That in turn makes them far better subjects than mice for testing vaccines for such diseases as Parkinson's and Huntington's.[54]

Meanwhile, current capabilities to determine an individual's genetic susceptibility to certain life-threatening ailments, and to investigate possible cures for certain diseases, have themselves already generated discussions and disagreements. In fact, many companies now offer genetic tests "that claim to tell people what foods they should eat to live longer and what cosmetics they should use." Yet many of these tests have never been scientifically validated and have often provided erroneous findings, with sometimes tragic results.[55] Less controversially, cancer is being detected and treated earlier and more successfully than ever before with the development of such tools as virtual colonoscopies, nanotechnology, and genomic profiling.[56] There are also new online dating services that claim to utilize knowledge about certain groups of genes to increase the knowledge of and, ideally, the attractiveness toward, potential partners.[57]

Related to this has been the development of robotics, not just as the traditional replacements for humans for various tasks that are painful or dangerous but also as a means to try to understand and perhaps alter human behavior itself. In the former realm, e-commerce companies are increasingly using "autonomous robots" made in Massachusetts to fulfill online orders for any number of leading companies. These robots can handle loads of up to three thousand pounds and can work around the clock, save when their batteries need to be recharged. In the latter realm, Boston-area scientists have created a four-foot-tall moonfaced robot named Nexi with "expressive eyebrows, dexterous mechanical hands, and a face that can flick from boredom to happiness."

Nexi's behavior can be controlled by her creators to avoid the "subtle gestures" and the "unintentional mimicry" that inevitably affect humans' interactions with fellow humans as they decide whether or not to become or remain friends. Removing those factors may illuminate the complex ways by which well-meaning people seek to survive and flourish in the world—certainly a crucial basis of nearly every utopian project.[58]

Still, humans are in no danger of being replaced by robots in areas outside manufacturing with repetitive tasks. It will require enormous advances to design robots that can match humans in grasping objects and in moving about easily. Contrary to what one might imagine, the challenges here are far greater than those of overcoming "artificial intelligence hurdles like speaking and hearing." Robots currently cannot generally do more than one task at a time and, if the "tiniest task is introduced," they invariably fail. Designing robots that can fold laundry, cook, or wash dishes will require new software that "mimics perception" and motion in humans—such software is nowhere on the horizon.[59] So, the traditional utopian expectations about robots' likeliest capabilities must be completely revised.

Though not the same as genetic engineering, the extraordinary success, beginning in 1978, of in vitro fertilization (IVF) in helping millions of infertile couples to have children has been part of the "reconceptualization" of creating life through non-traditional means. The awarding of the 2010 Nobel Prize in Medicine to British biologist Robert Edwards for his efforts here represented the highest official approval of the technique by which eggs are removed from a woman, fertilized outside her body, and then implanted into her womb. As of 2011 the prospects for infertile couples having healthy babies after IVF cycles are the same as those for fertile couples trying to conceive.[60]

Still, we are a long way from designing chromosomes. Not long ago prominent venture capitalist and scientist Craig Venter announced that his team had created the first "synthetic cell." However, in terms of his "declared goals of making fuel from carbon dioxide and creating new medicines and new sources of food," it was a major but not a monumental accomplishment. What was synthesized was not a completely new chromosome that could do "wonderful new things" but an exact copy of the chromosome that "causes mastitis in goats." Yet this "humble circular" chromosome itself contains 1,080,000 letters of the four-letter genetic alphabet that must be read in the precise sequence in order to do its job. For three months Venter's team struggled to determine why things went wrong, only to discover after all that time that one letter was out of line. Once the error was finally corrected, the reproduction process went on and on for about a billion times![61]

Mary Shelley's *Frankenstein* (1818) has been repeatedly invoked as an alleged denunciation of genetic engineering (though the term was, of course, unfamiliar to the author). Insofar as the book remains a staple of countless college courses in any number of disciplines, it is timely to reappraise it.

Recall that the novel did not carry Shelley's name until it had become popular a few years after its initial publication. This was because, to repeat, few male readers (and perhaps few female readers) would have thought a woman capable of such provocative and penetrating writing. Many readers attributed the book to Shelley's already famous husband, the poet Percy Shelley, who helped her with the composition but who did not actually write it.

Initial reviews were either mixed or negative. But eventually the novel became wildly popular if, as noted below, either unread or misread by those who popularized it in plays and later movies. It is nearly impossible today to separate the novel from the grotesque distortion provided by Boris Karloff in the 1931 film: "the flat head, the rectangular face, the bolted neck, and the criminal brain."[62]

Shelley's actual story of *Frankenstein* is that of a talented scientist, Victor Frankenstein, who grew up in a well-to-do and loving Geneva family but who became obsessed with the prospect of creating life by unconventional means. Using animal and human body parts dug from graves, Victor created a grotesque being that was eight feet tall simply because larger body parts were easier to work with. He never considered how it might be received by the outside world, nor did he bother giving it a name, contrary to the many misrepresentations of the book in popular culture. Also contrary to conventional wisdom, what Victor accomplished

Figure 5.5 Mary Shelley's *Frankenstein* (1818) has become ever more influential over time as the possibility of biotechnological developments leading to the creation of human life by non-traditional means looms. This cartoon from *Punch* (May 20, 1882) is called "The Irish Frankenstein." The creature in the book was never named, but he steadily became symbolic of scientific and technological problems that seemed to be out of mankind's control.

was not a primitive form of genetic engineering but rather one of *physiological* engineering. Like many of her contemporaries, Shelley was fascinated by contemporary reports of corpses being temporarily revived by electrical charges and by speculations over the potential uses of both electricity and chemistry to create new life forms.

Victor sought fame, regardless of the consequences, but ultimately lost everything, including the lives of his brother, best friend, and wife. Paradoxically, at first, his creature was infinitely more sensitive, caring, and compassionate than Victor himself. What led Victor astray was his failure to divulge his experiments to anyone else, his growing detachment from his loving family and friends, and his immediate abandonment of, and refusal to take responsibility for, his creation and its actions.

But, also contrary to most popular culture treatments, *Frankenstein* is a warning against such mistakes, *not* a wholesale condemnation of research, not a sort of Luddite "machine breaker" tract advocating the destruction of scientific research laboratories. Nor is its message akin to the controversial ten-year moratorium on all scientific research proposed by Britain's Bishop of Ripon in 1927. Only if experiments prove harmful to society should they stop or be stopped. Otherwise, Shelley actually argues, such experiments should be undertaken and continued, but with close technical and moral supervision. The potential and unanticipated consequences of researchers' efforts should also be considered from day one as far as is possible. Such cautions would also apply to research on genetically altered food, often termed "Frankenfood" by critics.[63]

Cautions have also been applied to contemporary efforts by well-meaning parents of high school students who are pressured to achieve more than is humanly possible in order to enhance their admission prospects at the most prestigious colleges and universities. One critic of such excesses calls this the crusade to create "Frankenstudents."[64]

Moreover, Victor is hardly the "mad scientist" that he is commonly portrayed as being in most popular culture treatments. Had Shelley deemed him mad—as opposed to completely rational but enormously self-centered—she would have lacked the moral authority to insist upon scientists' responsibility for their own actions. The ethical challenges that engaged Shelley nearly two centuries ago make *Frankenstein* more timely than ever.

True, Nathaniel Hawthorne and other American writers have portrayed outright "mad" scientists whose behavior is akin to Victor's.[65] But they do not deny their madness and proclaim their sanity, as Victor does: "Remember, I am not recording the vision of a madman," Victor tells us fairly early in the book. Nor do they deny the selfishness of their endeavors, as Victor does in his dying moments: "During these last days I have been occupied in examining my past conduct; nor do I find it blamable." To other seekers of knowledge—especially the Arctic explorer Robert Walton, who plucked Victor from the ice and has been recording his life story—Victor states:

> Farewell, Walton! Seek happiness in tranquility and avoid ambition, even if it be the apparently innocent one of distinguishing yourself in science and discoveries. Yet why do I say this? I have myself been blasted in these hopes, yet another may succeed.[66]

For that matter, Victor's intended usurpation of women's unique reproductive role is no less outrageous than his abandonment of his male creature. It epitomizes his self-centeredness. His usurpation of female procreation constitutes a threat to women far greater than any presented by his creature. At one point, he begins to make a female companion for his creature but later changes his mind and destroys the experiment. His justification in his dying moments is typical:

> I created a rational creature and was bound towards him to assure, as far as was in my power, his happiness and well-being. This was my duty, but there was another still paramount to that. My duties toward the beings of my own species had greater claims to my attention because they included a greater proportion of happiness or misery. Urged by this view, I refused, and I did right in refusing, to create a companion for the first creature. He showed unparalleled malignity and selfishness in evil; he destroyed my friends .... I am only induced by reason and virtue.[67]

Notes

1 See especially Kenneth M. Roemer, *The Obsolete Necessity: America in Utopian Writings, 1888–1900* (Kent, OH: Kent State University Press, 1976), 9–12.
2 For an example of the difficulties I encountered in attempting to learn more about the female author of a related utopian work published under a pseudonym, see Howard P. Segal, "The First Feminist Technological Utopia: Mary E. Bradley Lane's Mizora (1890)," in *Future*

Imperfect: The Mixed Blessings of Technology in America (Amherst, MA: University of Massachusetts Press, 1994), ch. 9.

3   See Segal, *Future Imperfect*, ch. 9.

4   Howard P. Segal, *Technological Utopianism in American Culture*, 2nd edn. (Syracuse, NY: Syracuse University Press, 2005 [1985]), 209 n. 58.

5   For elaboration of the discussion about Technocracy in this and the following paragraphs, see my new introduction to the reprint of Harold Loeb, *Life in a Technocracy: What It Might Be Like* (Syracuse, NY: Syracuse University Press, 1996 [1933]).

6   "Technocracy—Bloom, Blight, or Bunk?" *Literary Digest*, 114 (December 31, 1932), 5.

7   Thorstein Veblen, *The Engineers and the Price System* (New York: Viking, 1933), 135.

8   Anna-K. Mayer, "Reluctant Technocrats: Science Promotion in the Neglect-of-Science Debate of 1916–1918," *History of Science*, 43 (2005), 139–159.

9   See Frederic Cople Jaher, *Doubters and Dissenters: Cataclysmic Thought in America, 1885–1918* (New York: Free Press, 1964).

10 Vannevar Bush, Science—*The Endless Frontier: A Report to the President on a Program for Postwar Scientific Research* (Washington, DC: National Science Foundation, 1990 [1945]), 12.

11 On the unsuccessful efforts of some leading American social scientists to include the social sciences in the newly established National Science Foundation, see David Paul Haney, *The Americanization of Social Science: Intellectuals and Public Responsibility in the Postwar United States* (Philadelphia, PA: Temple University Press, 2008).

12 Daniel J. Kevles, "Principles and Politics in Federal R&D Policy, 1945–1990: An Appreciation of the Bush Report," in Bush, *The Endless Frontier*, xi.

13 On Bush's life and work, see G. Pascal Zachary, *Endless Frontier: Vannevar Bush, Engineer of the American Century* (New York: Free Press, 1997).

14 Bush quoted by John Brandl in the latter's review of Donald E. Stokes, *Pasteur's Quadrant: Basic Science and Technological Innovation* (Washington, DC: Brookings Institution Press, 1997), in *Journal of Policy Analysis and Management*, 17 (Fall 1998), 734.

15 Two works recast the origins of the National Science Foundation and the conflict between Bush and Kilgore in more complex and more historical perspective. See Daniel Lee Kleinman, *Politics On the Endless Frontier: Postwar Research Policy in the United States* (Durham, NC: Duke

University Press, 1995) and David M. Hart, *Forged Consensus: Science, Technology, and Economic Policy in the United States, 1921–1953* (Princeton, NJ: Princeton University Press, 1998). Their scope and analyses are by no means identical, but each is an excellent study.

16 See the many examples of these studies in the self-congratulatory report of Princeton University's Center of International Studies, *A Record of Twenty Years, 1951–1971* (Princeton, NJ: Woodrow Wilson School of Public and International Affairs, 1971). See my critique of "Modernization" theory in Segal, *Future Imperfect*, ch. 4.

17 See Barry D. Karl, "Presidential Planning and Social Science Research: Mr. Hoover's Experts," *Perspectives in American History*, 3 (1969) 347–409.

18 See Charles S. Maier, "Between Taylorism and Technocracy: European Ideologies and the Vision of Industrial Productivity in the 1920s," *Journal of Contemporary History*, 5 (1970), 27–61.

19 Sam Tanenhaus, "The Roar of the Liberal," *New York Times*, Week in Review, August 30, 2009, 4. Ironically, the article illuminated how Ted Kennedy's embrace of liberal causes never wavered, while his older brothers John and Robert both became less ideological and more pragmatic in their public policies.

20 See, for example, obituaries by Tim Weiner, *New York Times*, July 6, 2009, A1; and by Tomas Lippman, *Washington Post*, July 7, 2009, A1.

21 See Peter Brush, "The Story Behind the McNamara Line," *Vietnam Magazine*, February 1996, 18–24; Christopher P. Twomey, "The McNamara Line and the Turning Point for Civilian Scientist-Advisers in American Defense Policy, 1966–1968," *Minerva*, 37 (Autumn 1999), 235–258; and Seymour J. Deitchman, "The 'Electronic Battlefield' in the Vietnam War," *Journal of Military History*, 72 (July 2008), 869–887.

22 Doug Saunders, "Reckoning: The Father of 'Bombing for Progress' Dies A Timely Death," *(Toronto) Globe and Mail*, February 22, 2003, F3.

23 On that more progressive intellectual tradition, see Andrew Ross, *Strange Weather: Culture, Science, and Technology in the Age of Limits* (New York: Verso, 1991), 7. Lewis Mumford's review is in his "If Engineers Were Kings," *The Freeman*, 4 (November 23, 1921), 262.

24 Robert A. Dahl, *A Preface to Democratic Theory* (Chicago, IL: University of Chicago Press, 1956), 137.

25 Robert E. Lane, "The Decline of Politics and Ideology in a Knowledgeable Society," *American Sociological Review*, 31 (October 1966), 657–659; emphasis added. See also Lane, "The Politics of Consensus in an Age of Affluence," *American Political Science Review*, 59 (December 1965), 874–895. See also Haney, *The Americanization of Social*

Science, which is an illuminating study of the efforts by post-World War II sociologists to become avowedly scientific and the price paid in terms of reduced dialogue with the public and the ironic trivialization of sociology in the public mind.

26 Lane, "The Decline of Politics," 661.

27 Alvin M. Weinberg, "Can Technology Replace Social Engineering?" *University of Chicago Magazine*, 59 (October 1966), 6–10, reprinted in *Technology and the Future*, ed. Albert H. Teich, 7th edn. (New York: St. Martin's, 1997), 56, 64 (emphasis in original).

28 See Loeb, *Life in a Technocracy*, ch. 4 and new introduction by Segal.

29 Franz Neumann, *The Democratic and the Authoritarian State: Essays in Political and Legal Theory*, ed. Herbert Marcuse (New York: Free Press, 1964), 8.

30 See Simon Ramo, *Cure for Chaos: Fresh Solutions to Social Problems Through the Systems Approach* (New York: McKay, 1969). See also Ramo, *What's Wrong with Our Technological Society—And How to Fix It* (New York: McGraw-Hill, 1983).

31 Theodore Roszak, *Where the Wasteland Ends: Politics and Transcendence in Postindustrial Society* (Garden City, NY: Doubleday, 1972), 36.

32 See Ida R. Hoos, *Systems Analysis in Public Policy: A Critique*, 2nd edn. (Berkeley and Los Angeles, CA: University of California Press, 1983).

33 Twomey, "The McNamara Line," 256.

34 Valerie A. Brown, John A. Harris, and Jacqueline Y. Russell, eds. *Tackling Wicked Problems: Through the Transdisciplinary Imagination* (Washington, DC, and London: Earthscan/James and James, 2010), 10. This is the best book on the topic.

35 On the controversy and its aftermath, see Stefan Collini's introduction to C. P. Snow, *The Two Cultures* (New York and Cambridge: Cambridge University Press, 1993) and Guy Ortolano, *The Two Cultures Controversy: Science, Literature, and Cultural Politics in Postwar Britain* (New York and Cambridge: Cambridge University Press, 2009). On the traditional reluctance of engineers to become involved in both politics and public policy, see Howard P. Segal, "The Third Culture: C. P. Snow Revisited," *Technology and Society Magazine*, 15 (Summer 1996), 29–32. The Technocrats are an obvious exception, but not a complete exception, for two of their principal leaders—Scott and Loeb—were themselves not engineers, as detailed in Segal's new introduction to *Life in a Technocracy*.

36 See Mayer, "Reluctant Technocrats."

37 On controversies over science in recent years see, for example, Gerald Holton, *Science and Anti-Science* (Cambridge, MA: Harvard University

Press, 1993); Paul R. Gross and Norman Levitt, *Higher Superstition: The Academic Left and its Quarrels with Science* (Baltimore, MD: Johns Hopkins University Press, 1994); Andrew Ross, ed., *Science Wars* (Durham, NC: Duke University Press, 1996); and John Horgan, *The End of Science: Facing the Limits of Knowledge in the Twilight of the Scientific Age* (Reading, MA: Addison-Wesley, 1996).

38   See Yaron Ezrahi, Everett Mendelsohn, and Howard P. Segal, eds., *Technology, Pessimism, and Postmodernism* (Amherst, MA: University of Massachusetts Press, 1995 [1994]).

39   Kenneth Keniston, "Trouble in the Temple: The Erosion of the Engineering Algorithm," unpublished paper, 1992.

40   See Scott Shane, "Views of Scientists and Public in Conflict, Survey Finds," *New York Times*, July 10, 2009, A16.

41   Kirkpatrick Sale, "My Turn: The 'Miracle' of Technofix," *Newsweek*, 25 (June 23, 1980), 12.

42   On this development, see Yaron Ezrahi, "Technology and the Illusion of the Escape from Politics," in Ezrahi, *Technology, Pessimism, and Postmodernism*, 29–37. See also Ezrahi, *The Descent of Icarus: Science and the Transformation of Contemporary Democracy* (Cambridge, MA: Harvard University Press, 1990).

43   Bruce Bimber, *The Politics of Expertise in Congress: The Rise and Fall of the Office of Technology Assessment* (Albany, NY: State University of New York Press, 1996), 51 (emphasis in original). Bimber readily concedes that the OTA "was highly politicized in its first half-dozen years of operation. It was widely viewed as dedicated to a narrow set of political interests, and its technical credibility suffered as a result. But the OTA evolved over time to be less *politicized*" (20; emphasis in original), though some other scholars believe it was no less politicized at the end than at the beginning. The OTA was perceived by many Republicans as an invention of liberal Democrats. To these Republicans, the OTA was anything but non-partisan in its analyses, contrary to its explicit mission. To them, the OTA routinely favored one outcome in its evaluations—that desired by liberal Democrats— rather than simply presenting all possible options, as the OTA was mandated to do. In the process, those Republicans charged, the OTA repeatedly misused the social sciences despite a pretense of objectivity and expertise. The new majority's willingness to eliminate the OTA was therefore considerably more than a self-righteous budgetary cutback.

44   Edward W. Lawless, *Technology and Social Shock* (New Brunswick, NJ: Rutgers University Press, 1977), 5. On the attempted application of

technology assessment to history, see Howard P. Segal, "Assessing Retrospective Technology Assessment: A Review of the Literature," *Technology in Society*, 4 (Fall 1982), 231–246.

45 See, for example, United States Representative Vernon Ehlers, "Congress, Science, and the Two Cultures," *University of Michigan Research News*, 49 (1998), 22–23. Representative Ehlers of Michigan is the first research physicist ever elected to Congress and is a former professor and chair of physics at Calvin College in Grand Rapids, Michigan. First elected to the House of Representatives in a special election in 1993, he won re-election to eight full terms but decided to retire at the end of his eighth term in 2010.

46 M. Granger Morgan, review of Stokes, *Pasteur's Quadrant*, in *IEEE Spectrum*, 36 (January 1999), 12.

47 Snow, *The Two Cultures*, 32. See also Henry Petroski, *The Essential Engineer: Why Science Alone Will Not Solve Our Global Problems* (New York: Knopf, 2010), ch. 11.

48 See, for example, Daniel J. Kevles, *The Physicists: The History of a Scientific Community in Modern America* (Cambridge, MA: Harvard University Press, 1995 [1977]), ix–xlii.

49 See "Psychology: Sunny Side Up: Optimism, it Seems, is in the Genes," *The Economist*, 390 (February 28, 2009), 85; and David Brooks, "The Luxurious Growth: What Our Genes Don't Tell Us," *New York Times*, July 15, 2008, A19. See also the letters in response to Brooks' column, *New York Times*, July 17, 2008, A22; and Margaret Wente, "Optimism Is Highly Overrated," *Globe and Mail* (Toronto), May 16, 2009, A21.

50 Andrew Pollack, "Awaiting the Genome Payoff," *New York Times*, June 15, 2010, B1, B5 (the quotation comes from B5). See also Christopher Westphal, "Biotechnology's New Frontier," *Boston Globe*, June 14, 2010, A11; and Carolyn Johnson, "Born to Age Gracefully: Genes Hold Clues on Who May Live Long and Prosper," *Boston Globe*, July 2, 2010, A1, A8.

51 Daniel Gilbert quoted in Claudia Dreifus, "A Conversation with Daniel Gilbert," *New York Times*, April 22, 2008, D2. See also Gwynne Dyer's cynical "Usefulness of World Map of Happiness in Question," *Bangor Daily News*, June 8, 2010, A7.

52 See the confirming comments of Martin Seligman, a University of Pennsylvania psychology professor known as the father of "positive psychology," as summarized in his interview with Karen Weintraub, *Boston Globe*, June 6, 2011, G23. But see also the qualifications of the obsessive "pursuit of happiness" as noted in Deborah Kotz, "Daily

Dose: New Study Sheds Light On 'Dark Side of Happiness,'" *Boston Globe*, May 23, 2011, 11. See also Lauran Neergaard, Associated Press, "Pessimism Can Block Medical Treatments," *Bangor Daily News*, March 1, 2011, D1; and Mark J. Penn, "The Pessimism Index," *Time*, 178 (July 11, 2011), 36–37.

53 See Gina Kolata, "First Mammal Clone Dies; Dolly Made Science History," *New York Times*, February 15, 2003, A4.

54 See Rob Stein, "Glowing Monkeys Raise Ethics Concerns," *Washington Post*, reprinted in *Boston Globe*, May 28, 2009, A7.

55 See Rob Stein, *Washington Post*, "Mix-ups Spur Calls for Regulation of Genetic Test Kits," *Boston Globe*, July 19, 2010, A8.

56 See Francis S. Collins, "The Cancer You Can Beat," *Parade*, June 20, 2010, 8, 10.

57 See Sally McGrane, "Social Norms: Online Dating and Genetics," *Time*, 173 (June 29, 2009), 47.

58 Scott Kirsner, "Innovation Economy: Kiva, The Warehouse Robot Company," *Boston Sunday Globe*, November 28, 2010, G1, G4; and Carolyn Y. Johnson, "Robots May Furnish Lesson in Human Trust," *Boston Globe*, July 15, 2010, A1, A6. See also Peter W. Singer, "The Unmanned Mission," *Fortune*, 161 (March 1, 2010), S2; Associated Press, "Robot Performs Wedding Ceremony in Tokyo," *Boston Globe*, May 17, 2010, A3; and Kirsner, "You, Robot," *Boston Sunday Globe*, May 30, 2010, G1, G4. Interestingly, Ramo has recently argued that robots could and should replace humans as much as possible in future space landings on Mars and elsewhere. See Simon Ramo, "Too Big a Step for Mankind," *Los Angeles Times*, April 26, 2010, A15.

59 John Markoff, "Race to Build a Robot More Like Us," *Science Times*, *New York Times*, July 12, 2011, D1.

60 See Karl Ritter, Associated Press, "Nobel Prize in Medicine Goes to In Vitro Fertilization Pioneer," *Boston Globe*, October 5, 2010, A4; and Nicholas Wade, "In Vitro Fertilization Pioneer Wins Nobel Prize," *New York Times*, October 5, 2010, A1, A3.

61 Quoted by Gwynne Dyer in his "A Long Way from Designing Chromosomes," *Bangor Daily News*, May 25, 2010, A7.

62 Review by Deborah D. Rogers of Audrey A. Fisch, *Frankenstein: Icon of Modern Culture* (Hastings: Helm Information, 2009), in *Times Higher Education* (London), 1912 (September 3, 2009), 49. Fisch's book illuminates, in reviewer Rogers' words, the novel's "extra-textual life" and the "over-the-top permutations of the Frankenstein franchise in various genres" (3) around the world and down to the

present. A recent example is Alicia Chang, "Scientists Try to Envision Impact of a Frankenstorm," *Boston Globe*, January 25, 2010, A2.

63   The best edition of Mary Shelley's *Frankenstein* that has no text full of accompanying materials is published by Signet (New York: Signet Classics, 1963); an excellent afterword by Harold Bloom was added in 1965; an equally fine new foreword by Walter James Miller first appeared in 2000. An edition with some notes is published by Penguin (New York: Penguin Classics, 1992), ed. Maurice Hindle. Two editions with extensive notes, biographical information, and commentaries are published by Bedford (Boston, MA and New York: Bedford Books of St. Martin's, 2000), ed. Johanna M. Smith; and by Broadview (Peterborough, ON: Broadview, 2003), eds. D. L. Macdonald and Kathleen Scherf.

64   See Joan Wickersham, "The Myth of the Frankenstudent," *Boston Globe*, April 15, 2010, A17.

65   See Taylor Stoehr, *Hawthorne's Mad Scientists: Pseudoscience and Social Science in Nineteenth-Century Life and Letters* (Hamden, CT: Shoe String Press, 1978); and Glen Scott Allen, *Master Mechanics and Wicked Wizards: Images of the American Scientist as Hero and Villain from Colonial Times to the Present* (Amherst, MA: University of Massachusetts Press, 2009). Allen does also treat Victor as outright "mad," arguing— wrongly, I believe—that, whatever Shelley's portrayal in her novel, popular culture's misrepresentation is more important.

66   Mary Shelley, *Frankenstein* (New York: Signet Classics, 2000), 37, 193, 193. This is the same text as mentioned in note 63 but with different pagination.

67   Shelley, *Frankenstein*, 193.

Chapter 6

Utopia Reconsidered

The Growing Retreat from Space Exploration and Other Megaprojects

Nothing is more indicative of the fading of scientific and technological utopian fantasies from the sensibilities of ordinary Americans (and most other people) than the relatively muted response
on the twenty-fifth anniversary of the first moon landing of 1969.
In 1994 there was hardly the euphoria that had characterized
similar major anniversary celebrations involving New York City's
Brooklyn Bridge, the completion of the first transcontinental
railroad at Promontory, Utah, the first coast-to-coast telephone
hookup, or the first Ford Motor Model T automobile (though the
2007 Model T centennial was severely reduced from original plans
because of the threat of bankruptcy facing Ford Motor Company
and, for that matter, the possible collapse of the entire American
auto industry). By 1994 it had become painfully clear to most
people that, contrary to centuries of utopian dreams, the moon
landing had not changed the world. Like utopian communities,
utopian writings, and world's fairs, moon landings could not bring
about lasting peace on an international or merely national scale.
Nor, as a result, has there persisted in recent decades the uncritical
zeal for further space exploration and the possible colonization
of space that was commonplace before 1969. For that matter, the
Apollo program was popular with the American public only in the

Utopias: A Brief History from Ancient Writings to Virtual Communities,
First Edition. Howard P. Segal.
© 2012 Howard P. Segal. Published 2012 by Blackwell Publishing Ltd.

context of the Cold War and not for the sake of space exploration. Recently released declassified tapes stored at the John F. Kennedy Library in Boston reveal the president's own doubts about the value of a moon landing megaproject months before his assassination.[1]

Certainly the two fatal space shuttle disasters of 1986 ("Challenger") and 2003 ("Columbia") severely damaged public confidence in the space program overall. The specific causes differed, but in both cases prior warnings about possible catastrophes were largely ignored by NASA. The 1986 tragedy reflected NASA's efforts to have a non-professional (a "teacher in space") on board the "Challenger" in order both to demonstrate the vehicle's alleged safety and to enhance NASA's (and, no less importantly, President Ronald Reagan's) often negative relationships with educators at all levels.[2]

True, the George W. Bush Administration revived the mission to Mars project, but it didn't go much beyond a rhetorical commitment. Some cynics dismissed this as a public relations stunt to deflect growing opposition to the Iraq War. And that same administration ended the space shuttle mission. Meanwhile, the fortieth anniversary in 2009 of the first moon landing did generate some enthusiasm for future space travel to Mars and for space colonies. The Apollo 11 crew was honored by President Barack Obama, among others, even as he eliminated a program to return Americans to the moon by 2020 and proposed ending all manned space missions unless funded by the private sector. He did, however, continue his predecessor's plans for a new American spaceship, the Orion, that could be used for deep space exploration far from the earth.[3]

The ever-expanding list of products either generated or designed outright by NASA is promoted in, among other places, *Spinoff*, a journal of commercialized NASA science and technology. These products include, besides the MRIs, lasers, smoke detectors, and dustbusters noted earlier, viscoelastic foam used in Tempur-Pedic mattresses and pillows, Eagle Eyes powerful sunglasses, Zen strong fragrances, "thermally adaptive" materials for "cool" sports socks and dog jackets, and extremely streamlined Olympic swimsuits.[4]

Most recently, a Japanese astronaut wore the same underwear for his entire month-long stay at the space station and returned to earth without any complaints about foul smells from his fellow space travelers. The Japanese-made garments, called J-Wear, also include pants, shirts, and socks. They are "anti-bacterial, water-absorbent, [and] odor-eliminating" garments that, equally significantly, are also "anti-static and flame retardant." Furthermore, being made of cotton and polyester, they are seamless and lighter than the usual space wear. Ordinarily, space station residents simply ditch their dirty clothes and add them to the garbage that is placed on unneeded cargo ships and then sent into the atmosphere to be burned up.[5]

Yet much of the 2009 celebration was a simultaneous lamentation for the absence since those heady days of 1969 of the grass-roots national and international fascination with space. It had by then become a truism that the Apollo and later space projects were primarily responses to the Soviet threat of continuing to "outclass" the United States in space and to the ongoing fear of Soviet use of space for strategic purposes. Not until the final moon landing, in 1972, did an actual scientist (Harrison Schmidt, a geologist) walk on that surface.

Instead, there was considerably more grass-roots skepticism about the value of these megaprojects in view of more pressing needs on earth. Meanwhile, some conspiracy theorists still maintained that the original moon landing had been faked and that NASA's failure to retain some crucial television footage only confirmed that fraud perpetuated upon the entire world. (Whether they would have preferred a "real-life" landing was not clear.) For the fortieth anniversary, however, NASA unveiled the start of an improved version of the footage that might quell some doubts when completed.

The same skepticism, of course, applies to other megaprojects such as the so-called "Star Wars" anti-missile defense system and the Superconducting Super Collider in Texas, though it should be said that the latter project has been abandoned while the missile defense project lives on despite having cost more than one hundred billion dollars. H. Bruce Franklin's pioneering *War Stars: The Superweapon and the American Imagination* (1988; revised and expanded in 2008) has traced Americans' fascination (and some-times obsession) with this and earlier weapons allegedly intended to prevent or end wars back to inventor Robert Fulton. Fulton, of course, helped to invent the steamboat but also contributed to early versions of both submarines and "torpedoes" (really mines). As Franklin shows, the road from poison gas to atomic bombs to lasers in outer space is fairly straight, with Thomas Edison's envisioned atomic ray beams and General Billy Mitchell's envisioned fleet of airplanes to bomb civilians coming in-between. As Franklin discovered, the one-time actor Ronald Reagan had starred in a 1940 movie in which his character, a Secret Service agent, used a ray machine to destroy a spy's airplane. This role may well have generated his passion for the formally entitled Strategic Defense Initiative.[6]

In 2008, the twenty-fifth anniversary of the speech by President Reagan that announced that Strategic Defense Initiative was also noted with restrained celebrations. Since 1985 some 120 billion dollars has been spent on this enterprise, despite it never having been tested. So many technical obstacles remain that it might prove impossible ever to perform tests. Yet in its final year the George W. Bush Administration spent another twelve billion dollars on it. What has also aroused intense criticism has been the legitimate concern about the inadequate funding of security measures against terrorist weapons on earth that might be sneaked into our harbors, for example. America's post-9/11 world has not yet faced up to more banal challenges than attacks from space.[7]

Nuclear Power: Its Rise, Fall, and Possible Revival—Maine Yankee as a Case Study

The history of Maine's only nuclear power plant, Maine Yankee, is a superb case study of the rise and fall and possible renewal of the nuclear power industry in the United States in the second half of the twentieth century. Maine Yankee was the nation's thirtieth nuclear power plant when it opened in 1972. The plant was located on an eight-hundred-acre tract six miles from the center of Wiscasset, a town of over 3,600 whose motto has long been, of all things, "the prettiest village in Maine." The town has handsome old sea captains' houses and other remnants from its rich maritime history, and for local citizens the plant did not seem an affront to its charm. Far from it: the plant's overall popularity during most of its years of operation before it closed in 1996 cannot be disputed.

The plant was built between 1968 and 1972 at a cost of 231 million dollars and was granted a forty-year license. The plant's largest shareholder was Maine Yankee Power Company.[8] The company chose Wiscasset for several reasons: its sufficient land area, its proximity to fresh water and to the ocean, its nearby railroad and highway routes, its nearness to electrical load centers and to transmission lines, its excellent bedrock for foundations, and its "favorable geologic, hydrologic, seismologic, and meteorological characteristics."[9]

The Wiscasset facility was one of several nuclear power plants built by the Maine Yankee Atomic Power Company, which was established in 1954 after President Dwight Eisenhower signed the amended Atomic Energy Act that, for the first time, allowed private companies to build atomic facilities. The legislation was part of Eisenhower's "Atoms for Peace" policy, which was designed to ameliorate national anxiety over atomic power, which dated back to the dropping of atomic bombs over Hiroshima and Nagasaki. Moreover, a peaceful civilian role for atomic power shrewdly offset Cold War tensions repeatedly raised by Eisenhower's Secretary of State, John Foster Dulles, whose combative rhetoric suggested the likelihood of nuclear war against the Soviet Union in the not too distant future. Further contributing to the "Atoms for Peace" proposal was the allure of "electrical power too cheap to meter," as promised by Atomic Energy Commission chairman Lewis Strauss in the early 1950s.[10]

Among the brochures published by Maine Yankee Atomic Power was one entitled "The Atom, Electricity, and You!" Similar publications could be found elsewhere in America in this period. The publication's cartoons feature "the Fosters," as a stereotypical white middle-class family consisting of a father, mother, son, and daughter. The Fosters respond to an invitation from the electric company to attend a presentation on "The Atom, Electricity, and You—Today's Greatest Exhibit." The meeting's speaker, John Blaine, summarizes various electrically powered appliances that have vastly improved Americans' lives. Blaine informs the audience that families are "using more electricity than ever before," but that the cost per kilowatt hour is dropping. However, Blaine goes on to explain that generating sufficient water power to meet this growing demand for electricity would be much too expensive, and using more coal and oil to manufacture electricity would likewise prove costly. The practical alternative is nuclear energy: "the miracle product of the splitting of the atom."[11]

Blaine then explains the workings of a nuclear power plant. He doesn't mention safety concerns because, presumably, there are none. "And get this: there are no storage problems when this wonderful fuel is used. Plants no longer must store reserve coal or tanks of oil." As for "what happens when the fuel is used up," Blaine responds that it would never be completely exhausted. The fuel rods in the center of the assembly would give out first, and rods from the outer regions would be "moved in turn towards the center."[12]

Regarding any "danger from radiation in the vicinity" of a plant, Blaine reassures his audience that "there's considerably *less* radiation from such a plant than from the radium on the dial of your wristwatch." Every day, moreover, people are exposed to radiation "in mountain vacation areas and jet flights, for example," and those exposures are often "far greater than radiation from nuclear plants—and they don't cause the slightest harm."[13]

Waxing slightly historical about radiation, Blaine reminds his audience that "man's been living with [it] for quite a few years now, with *no* problems whatsoever," drawing attention to atomic submarines and atomic ships as well as the sixteen existing nuclear power plants. The electric power companies "are very conscious of radiation problems—and have successfully *solved* them."[14]

Not surprisingly, given the trouble-free history of nuclear power in America, "many more nuclear generating plants will be built!" Furthermore, Blaine reminded readers, once nuclear fuel is no longer needed for plant operations, it could be used for other purposes such as medicine, industry, and space travel. Ordinary citizens could look forward to "nuclear-powered airplanes, auto-mobiles, trains—and just about anything and everything that moves under its own power." The nation has "entered the *nuclear age* that will make our living *easier* and more *productive*!" The Foster family thanks Blaine for his uplifting presentation and concludes that "one thing's sure—it's going to be a *great* thing for all of us!"[15]

Over its lifetime, the single-unit 900 megawatt plant was Maine's largest generator of electricity, producing about 119 billion kilowatt hours.[16] Maine Yankee contributed twelve million dollars in property taxes to Wiscasset. That in turn cut ordinary residents' property taxes by ninety percent. In addition, the plant's workers (480 full-timers when it closed) spread their incomes through the community. Not surprisingly, the town was able to dramatically improve its schools, parks, and roads, to expand its fire and police departments, to build a new cutting-edge community center, and to provide a free ambulance service—to the envy of nearby communities with traditional property tax bases. As local resident John Chester put it, "It was like living in fairyland. Everything you wanted, you got." Or, in the words of Judy Flanagan, a member of Wiscasset's board of selectmen, "We called it the golden goose."[17]

The majority of the residents of Vernon, Vermont, the site of the still-operational Vermont Yankee Nuclear Plant, held a similarly positive attitude after it opened in 1972. The town of 1,200 also enjoyed property tax reductions and municipal improvements. Yet, within the first twenty months of its operation, numerous faulty parts problems, outages, and minor accidents closed the plant down seventeen times. Such difficulties did not plague Maine Yankee during most of its years of operation. Such difficulties were, however, increasingly common among the first generations of plants. Yet town official Erma Puffer, like many other Vernon residents, dismissed concerns over nuclear waste: "if the Good Lord is smart enough to let them build a nuclear plant, He's smart enough to give them a way to get rid of the waste." Significantly, in both communities residents appeared to be quite familiar with the complexities of nuclear power "because of extensive media coverage and well-organized public relations campaigns by the power companies."[18]

Nothing, perhaps, is more reflective of Wiscasset's official warm embrace of Maine Yankee than the latter's inclusion in the fifth edition of a brochure entitled "Wiscasset Invites You," which appeared shortly after the plant opened. The publication, intended for prospective businesspeople, home buyers, and tourists, touted Wiscasset as "a town where a great historical past truly blends with a promising future." After a summary of the community's history and descriptions of some of its municipal buildings, the brochure discussed Maine Yankee as just another part of the community.[19] After the Maine Yankee pages came sections on transportation, schools, municipal improvements, churches, the library, art galleries, and historical points of interest. What is revealing about these topics is the inclusion of Maine Yankee as a fully integrated feature of the community rather than, as one might have expected, an industrial concern discussed somewhat apart from the conventional institutions and structures one finds in most old Maine communities. It is the very banality of this order of topics that reinforces the notion of Maine Yankee's warm embrace by Wiscasset as just another part of the community.[20]

In these respects, Maine Yankee and its sister plants were widely viewed as veritable scientific and technological utopias, especially in their early years, when nuclear power was widely touted throughout the world as a safe, efficient, and inexpensive alternative to conventional energy sources such as coal and oil. In those days, there were still echoes of the kinds of genuinely utopian visions held out for nuclear power in the 1950s and 1960s, as outlined in Stephen Del Sesto's now classic 1986 article, "Wasn't the Future of Nuclear Engineering Wonderful?" These claims included a variety of domestic uses: nuclear explosions for quick excavating irrigation projects; individually operated nuclear-powered cars, and, yes, airplanes for easier transportation in big cities; employment of nuclear-powered rocket ships for space exploration and travel; nuclear-powered medical devices to cure cancer, heart disease, arthritis, and other life-threatening ailments; and nuclear mechanisms to transform deserts into agricultural gardens and so end world hunger.[21]

Nevertheless, concern about nuclear power was rising during Maine Yankee's early years. As early as 1977, at the bequest of parents of schoolchildren, Wiscasset formed a committee to come up with a town evacuation plan in case of a serious accident at Maine Yankee. This concern peaked during the potential meltdown at Three Mile Island near Harrisburg, Pennsylvania, in 1979, and the actual meltdown at Chernobyl in the Ukraine in 1986.[22]

In the aftermath of Three Mile Island, opponents managed to launch an official state referendum on Maine Yankee's continued operation in 1980 and again in 1982. Both lost, as did a third and final referendum in 1987 following the Chernobyl disaster. Yet the 1980 referendum was the first anywhere in the United States to challenge an existing nuclear power plant. Two years earlier voters in Montana—then one of sixteen states without a nuclear power plant—had voted to ban the construction of all such plants. The 1980 referendum in Maine failed by a margin of 230,000 to 160,000. Amazingly, more than half of Maine's eligible voters cast ballots. During the early 1980s, opposition throughout New England generated anti-nuclear positions based on cost, safety, and environmental concerns.[23]

All three referenda in Maine garnered more than forty percent of the vote in favor of closing the plant down. Not surprisingly, defenders of Maine Yankee criticized these exercises in democracy on the grounds that they asked ordinary citizens to vote on highly technical matters about which they had no expertise. Yet, in so much as Wiscasset residents knew a lot about nuclear power, and Maine voters had access to comparable information through the campaign literature, this complaint seems anti-democratic and technocratic. As public access to information has exploded, thanks to electronic devices, it would not be surprising to see future referenda on nuclear power and other controversial scientific and technological issues such as cloning.[24]

Raymond Shadis, spokesman for the anti-nuclear Friends of the Coast-Opposing Nuclear Pollution, cynically called Wiscasset's attitude toward Maine Yankee a "cargo cult"—the anthropological term invoked to characterize a group's willingness to worship a god in return for its "bounty." Thus, others' characterization of the plant as a veritable utopia was for Shadis and his fellow critics the very opposite: the plant was an anti-utopia, or dystopia. Residents of

Vernon, Vermont, simultaneously attributed opposition to Vermont Yankee to those "from away," be they recent arrivals in town or city folks. This naturally reduced the legitimacy of the critiques, regardless of actual facts and figures. (Shadis, however, lived on a farm in Edgecomb, only two miles from Maine Yankee.)[25]

In fact, Maine Yankee's opponents ultimately, if indirectly, prevailed years later when the plant's owners decided to close it down for financial and safety reasons—reasons espoused by the opponents years before. In 1994 officials discovered cracks in the plant's steam generator tubes, and the repairs required a year-long shutdown. In 1996 the plant was closed again, and in the following year its owners concluded that the recent passage of Maine's electric restructuring and deregulation legislation made it impossible to operate at a profit, as its monopoly status had been ended. Cheaper electricity could now flow across the state's borders.[26]

In 1997 the Nuclear Regulatory Commission (NRC) cited Maine Yankee among the country's worst run nuclear plants. All of these developments led to the company's decision to close the plant, unless a buyer could be found. That decision was greeted enthusiastically by most residents of the adjoining areas.[27]

Not surprisingly, there were no buyers. Officials hoped to dismantle the plant for use elsewhere, but they found no takers for this approach either. Once the decision to close had been made, an eight-year five-hundred-million-dollar decommissioning process began in 1997.[28] In terms of both safety and budget, this process has gone very well. In 2000 workers began gutting some of the plant's structures; in 2003 the plant's reactor section was put on a barge and shipped to a secure waste facility in Barnwell, South Carolina. On September 17, 2004, the plant's containment building was demolished by explosives, the first such demolition in the history of nuclear power. At 150 feet tall, the dome was too large to be taken apart mechanically. A local newspaper reported that there were approximately 400 people present and that "the mood on site ... was much like a wake before a funeral," though both friends and foes alike "burst into applause."[29]

Longtime critics of Maine Yankee such as *Boston Globe* columnist David Nyhan had predicted a dismal scenario that would only confirm that it had been a mistake to build the plant in the first place. Nyhan extended his pessimism to the Seabrook Station nuclear plant in New Hampshire that had finally opened in 1990. "Now Seabrook is a Wiscasset in waiting," Nyhan concluded, "like 100 other nuclear dinosaurs whose deadly tails will threaten our offspring a thousand generations hence." Where Maine Yankee was built within budget and on time, Seabrook was completed years behind schedule and billions of dollars over budget. For those reasons the planned two reactors were scaled back to one—and that cost 6.6 billion dollars. More protests surrounded the plant than any other in the region and, for that matter, perhaps the whole of the United States.[30]

But Nyhan may have been unduly pessimistic about Maine Yankee, at least in terms of safety. The removal of radioactive material continued until 2005, when grass was planted over the area's eight hundred acres. With so much accomplished, the NRC then amended Maine Yankee's license, reducing the amount of land under license to the twelve-acre independent Spent Fuel Storage Installation on Bailey Point Peninsula in Wiscasset.[31]

Maine Yankee's remaining task was to store and eventually dispose of the 1,434 spent fuel rods temporarily locked away on Bailey Point in sixty-four airtight canisters housed in concrete casks. These rods will remain toxic for thousands of years. Because of long-unresolved political issues surrounding the designated Yucca Mountain storage facility in Nevada, one hundred miles from Las Vegas, the storage process could take years, possibly decades.[32]

The decision to close the plant prompted a variety of proposals for redeveloping the site (apart from the area containing the spent fuel rods). None, however, materialized. In 2006 a company called National Resources of Greenwich, Connecticut, purchased the plant site along with a 431-acre buffer zone. The company has two projects underway: on the buffer zone there will be "an office and technology park," while the power plant "eyesore is being turned into eye candy—an old-fashioned waterfront village" to be filled with fine restaurants, microbreweries, upscale "stores, art galleries, condominiums, and cottages, and 281 slips for those who wish to park their boats in the river." The state-of-the-art marina will include a repair and retrofit yard and storage facilities, and will be open to vessels of all sizes. This Point East Maritime Village will be a tribute to both a former Wiscasset summer colony and the town's maritime past.[33]

In recent years proponents of wind, water, and solar power have certainly demonstrated the practicality of those alternative energy sources. Wind power has become particularly popular for appropriate areas. A 2010 study by a General Electric subsidiary concluded that New England has sufficiently strong land and ocean winds to enable the region to obtain twenty-four percent of its total annual electricity needs by 2020, provided that vastly expanded wind energy projects increase by forty-four fold over the present capacity, and at a cost of from nineteen to twenty-five billion dollars for new transmission lines and wind farms. If, at this point, New England generates 270 megawatts of wind power—with one megawatt powering 750 to 1000 homes—it would be necessary to build enough additional turbines to reach possibly twelve thousand megawatts. One proposal would harness the exceptional power of high-altitude winds through lightweight flying and floating turbines.[34] "Utopian" might well apply here to both the vision and its actual prospects for realization. These alternative energy proponents have not, moreover, persuaded a majority of Americans that any (or, for that matter, all three) could possibly substitute traditional energy sources or replace nuclear power.

Moreover, strong opposition to wind power has developed, particularly on the part of residents of generally rural areas who have come to detest both the aesthetics and the noise of large wind turbines within sight of their formerly pristine and quiet residences. Proposals for offshore wind turbines in places such as Massachusetts' Nantucket Sound have also generated enormous opposition. Cape Wind, as this first proposed American off-shore wind farm is called, needs huge private financing and, for that to happen, needs to enlist sufficient customers. Rhetorical commitments to green energy are increasingly undermined by the realization that wind energy may not constitute the panacea it has been touted to be. For that matter, the actual costs to ratepayers of wind energy megaprojects such as Cape Wind's 130 turbines have been calculated by skeptics to be considerably higher than originally contended. Meanwhile, federal law requires that the key tax credits that have prompted much wind energy discussion and would-be construction here and elsewhere in America be utilized soon or expire. European examples have largely confirmed these dystopian expectations: a total of 948 offshore wind turbines have been "clearly recognized in Europe as the technology with the greatest cost." They exist primarily because of "widespread public opposition to siting windmills on land." Denmark has been the foremost European country to invest in wind turbines but has wound up importing as much coal as ever while not reducing its carbon dioxide emissions. Great Britain, however, opened the world's largest offshore wind farm in 2010, seven miles off the southeast coast. The one hundred turbines, each up to 380 feet tall and collectively taking up the space of four thousand football fields, are intended to provide power for some two hundred thousand homes. At present, Britain ranks only twenty-fifth out of the twenty-seven European Union nations in terms of the percentage of its energy derived from renewable sources. This project is intended to begin to change that.[35]

No less a power than the Pentagon has come to oppose wind turbines in large, sparse areas such as California's Mojave Desert, which is used for experiments. The turbines' blades can wreak havoc with radar systems in being indistinguishable from airplanes, in creating blackout zones where airplanes disappear from radar, and, when clustered together, in appearing similar to storms on radar and thus affecting weather analysis.[36]

In the years since Maine Yankee closed down, there has been a resurgence of interest in the United States in nuclear power to offset the environmental damages and financial costs associated with coal and oil production.[37] The George W. Bush Administration made the revival of nuclear power a component of its energy policy, and fears of nuclear power accidents have diminished in many quarters. In 2010, President Obama authorized loan guarantees for two large reactors in Georgia and additional loans for new reactors elsewhere. Yet new plants "remain insanely expensive to build." Much cheaper alternative "mini-plants" that could power a moderate-sized town are being developed by some American and Japanese companies. Each entire plant, says one of those companies, "including the reactor and protective cabinet, will be about the size of a hot tub—eight feet tall by five feet wide"—and might be available very soon. They would be buried at least fifteen feet underground. Still, how safe they would be remains the subject of debate.[38]

France's nuclear industry has been tremendously successful in terms of productive capacity, with fifty-eight plants providing nearly eighty percent of that nation's electricity. But, despite this success, Electricité de France has been plagued by financial problems that have been compounded with the increased cost of storing radioactive material. Meanwhile, Japan relies on nuclear power for nearly thirty-five percent of its electricity and opened eight new plants in just the two years before the March 2011 disaster at the Fukushima Daiichi plant, caused by a huge earthquake and subsequent tsunami. The cores of three of the plant's six reactors eventually melted down, with roughly one sixth of the radiation emitted by the Chernobyl meltdown spewing out. As with Chernobyl and Three Mile Island, so with Fukushima: inadequate staff training and failure to anticipate worst-case scenarios were crucial factors. Once the toll of dead and missing mounted, Japan scrapped its plan to increase its reliance on nuclear power to fifty percent by 2030.[39]

More distressing for the worldwide future of nuclear power, however, was the 2011 decision by Germany, the world's fourth largest economy and fourth largest user of nuclear power, to phase out all seventeen of its nuclear power plants by 2022. This was a direct result of the Japanese reactor disaster. Back in 1997, though, Germany and other European Union countries had agreed to have twelve percent of their electricity needs provided by renewable sources by 2010. Germany's 2010 level was thirteen percent. It now hopes to raise the level to eighty percent by 2050. Interestingly, no other European country has taken this same complete path away from nuclear power.[40]

Despite the virtual shutdown of America's nuclear power industry in recent decades in terms of new construction, nuclear power still generates about twenty percent of the United States' electricity. There are currently 104 nuclear power reactors in operation in the United States, the last one coming online in 1996, its construction having begun back in 1973. Most were designed and licensed to last for forty years. But their expected replacement by newer reactors never happened, thanks to Three Mile Island and the unsustainable cost of constructing those successor reactors. Instead, sixty-six reactors have been relicensed for another twenty years while renewal applications for another sixteen reactors are being reviewed. Of those 104 reactors, eighty-two are over twenty-five years old. In order to overcome the various structural and operational challenges of maintaining aging reactors, the NRC has repeatedly lowered safety margins. A 2011 Associated Press investigation revealed the inadequacies of this process and the dangers posed by the lowered standards. It discovered that radioactive tritium, a form of hydrogen, has increasingly leaked from all but one quarter of the nation's commercial nuclear power plants, sometimes into groundwater sites used by the public. Any exposure to radioactivity heightens the chance of developing cancer.[41]

To make matters worse, the earthquake that struck the eastern United States on August 23, 2011, the strongest ever recorded in that region, indicated that a quarter of America's reactors need modifications to withstand any future such shocks, let alone a stronger earthquake. Yet the NRC does not routinely require plants to review their seismic risks as they seek to renew their operating licenses for an additional twenty years.[42]

Nevertheless, twenty-one companies now expect to seek permission to build thirty-four new plants, ranging in location from New York to Texas to Idaho, and factories are being built in Indiana and Louisiana to manufacture plant parts. Much of the renewed interest derives from the Energy Policy Act of 2005, which "is stuffed with generous subsidies for nuclear power and other alternatives to fossil fuels." As the head of General Electric, Jeffrey Immelt, has argued, "it's hard to believe simultaneously in energy security and reduction of greenhouse gas emissions without believing in nuclear power."[43]

Increasing numbers of environmentalists are conceding this point, among them the famous Stewart Brand, creator of *The Whole Earth Catalog*. Brand confessed to his traditional opponents: "I'm sorry. I was wrong, you were right. I'm sorry." Brand has nevertheless maintained his utopian propensities despite this change of heart and has embraced a decentralized corporate vision of information technologies and computer networks that nicely complements those of capitalist leaders such as Immelt. Fred Turner has called Brand's ideological position "digital utopianism."[44]

Ironically, the preponderance of aging plants is a barrier to nuclear power's resurgence in the United States. In order to maintain a twenty percent share in electricity generation, replacement plants will have to be built fairly soon. There are also such mundane challenges as the rising cost of steel and concrete and the diminished number of qualified welders.[45]

Some advocates for an American "nuclear renaissance" believe that increasing the capacity and/or the operating life of existing plants is the most practical measure and certainly a complement to the building of any new plants. As of 2004, eight years after the last new plant had been completed, this process had increased the output of the nation's nuclear power plants "by the equivalent of twenty-four new plants."[46]

Meanwhile, in Vermont, perhaps the most environmentally conscious of all fifty states, opponents of Vermont Yankee want to shut it down because of safety concerns. In 2007 the plant's cooling tower collapsed, the apparent result of rotting wooden timbers that had not been properly inspected. No radioactivity was released, but this accident took place just as the plant's owners had applied to the NRC for a twenty-year extension of its license beyond its 2012 expiration date. That twenty-year extension was later granted by the NRC, but both the governor and the state are fighting it. Yet Vermont Yankee provides a third of the state's electricity generation, and the same dilemma that converted Stewart Brand confronts Vermont's residents. As a *New York Times* reporter noted recently, at present Vermont has "only one commercial wind farm, eleven turbines along a mountain ridge. They have less than one percent of the capacity of Vermont Yankee," itself a relatively small nuclear power plant.[47] Should we be surprised that Maine Yankee's most passionate defenders have made the same point in denouncing that plant's closure?

Admittedly, the possibility of another nuclear power plant catastrophe or, perhaps worse, a terrorist attack on a safely operating plant cannot be ruled out. But retrospective analysis of the Three Mile Island disaster reveals a personnel and a public relations failure rather than a nuclear catastrophe akin to Chernobyl. Confirming the arguments made by the fictional John Blaine quoted above, the radiation exposure "even in the most extreme cases" was less than what "anyone living in the area receives from natural sources."[48]

Equally importantly, the decline of the nation's nuclear power industry preceded, and so was not caused by, Three Mile Island. Whereas in 1974 President Richard Nixon predicted that there would be one thousand commercial nuclear reactors by the end of the twentieth century, "only 250 were ever ordered, only 170 filed for permits, [and] just 130 opened." The causes of this decline included unexpected building delays and shutdowns, high costs, high interest rates, protests, and, unexpectedly, reduced electricity demand. In sum, Three Mile Island "didn't kill the nuclear dream" but instead was "just another nail in the coffin."[49]

It has by now become the conventional wisdom that nuclear power's coffin also contained the remains of self-proclaimed "experts" in the field, whose overly optimistic scenarios received richly deserved burials. Meanwhile, the three referenda on Maine Yankee in the 1980s are often characterized as demonstrating the superior common-sense wisdom of ordinary citizens—not least, tough-minded, skeptical Mainers who could cut through the baseless promises of persistently cheap and effective power held out by those often arrogant experts. But this picture is too simplistic.

As historian Brian Balogh demonstrated in his 1991 *Chain Reaction: Expert Debate and Public Participation in American Commercial Nuclear Power, 1945–1975*, the fading of these experts' luster steadily gave rise to the arrival of other experts. The latter's ranks included not only other engineers and scientists without the common ties to the nuclear power industry and government regulatory agencies but also "competing" experts in biology, economics, environmental studies, and public health. Alas, this "counter" expertise did not usually lead to improved public policy formulations or legislation or regulation. Far from it. The naïve traditional expectations of eventual consensus among experts, comparable to the naïve one-time expectations of nuclear power being "too cheap to meter," fell apart amid debate and dissent. In addition, the collapse of communism and of the Soviet Union in the late 1980s and early 1990s undermined the historic reliance in the United States upon "national security" concerns as a means of imposing consensus. Moreover, the steady fading of the luster and influence of the physicists and other nuclear power experts associated with the Manhattan Project also undermined that once bedrock faith in experts in this area.[50]

Growing public skepticism, protest, and opposition, as with Maine Yankee, must be placed in this more complex context. Critical though it surely was, public dissent alone did not turn the tide against nuclear power and its once untouchable decision-makers. As one reviewer phrases Balogh's argument, "the result was a political Catch-22. Experts were always in demand for their authority, but the more they became involved the less creditable they seemed. Nevertheless, no substitute for expertise has yet been found."[51] Instead, the political considerations that had always been critical to the nation's nuclear power, far from diminishing, remained as powerful as ever.

This is not to suggest that Maine Yankee should have remained open in the face of the technical, environmental, and financial challenges that confronted its owners and operators in its final years of operation. It is, however, to suggest that, just as Maine Yankee was hardly a genuine technological utopia at any time, neither was it ever a full-fledged technological dystopia. Rather, its history reflects both the positive and negative aspects of nuclear power, not just in New England but throughout the country. The utopian promotional rhetoric of the plant's early years must therefore be appreciated as more than fantasy and naïveté, as having some "core" truth to it. Like all serious utopian schemes, as noted at the outset, the vision of Maine Yankee and of its peer plants in New England and elsewhere must be played back to illuminate the society and the culture that produced it: an America ambivalent about "atoms for peace" and about science and technology's promise and peril.

However, lessons from Maine Yankee *are* being discussed in Maine itself, and by proponents of a new nuclear plant in, of all places, Wiscasset and possibly elsewhere in the state. In addition to the familiar arguments that nuclear power is environmentally friendly, that Maine "is at the end of all fossil fuel pipelines" and so will always be paying more than most other states, and that renewables such as solar, wind, wood, biomass, and tidal power can never provide more than a small fraction of the state's energy needs, the traditional stumbling blocks of nuclear waste storage and of reactor rod reprocessing have been partially removed. France in particular has been a pioneer in these areas, and its nuclear plants have convincing safety records. Today's nuclear power plants require less potentially fallible mechanisms. In addition, the 2005 Energy Policy Act allows for streamlining of the application process for new plants, and plants can now be built much more quickly than decades ago. In these ways, Maine Yankee may be a form of "living history."[52]

The Declining Belief in Inventors, Engineers, and Scientists as Heroes; in Experts as Unbiased; and in Science and Technology as Social Panaceas

The growing retreat from such megaprojects as nuclear power plants extends to a declining belief in inventors, engineers, and scientists as heroes; in experts as wholly objective; and, most broadly, in science and technology in general as social panaceas. Until recent decades America's heroes were not limited to sports and entertainment figures, as they are today, but instead encompassed engineers, scientists, and especially inventors. Eli Whitney, Alexander Graham Bell, Thomas Edison, George Westinghouse, George Eastman, and Henry Ford were household names, revered as much for their (presumably) noble character, wisdom, and vision as for their actual inventions. Their opinions and ideas about many issues quite beyond the realm of their technical and managerial skills were routinely sought. For that matter, reverential "major motion pictures" were made about both Bell and Edison. By contrast, few inventors are well known today, much less sought after for advice outside their areas of technical expertise. Most famous these days is Bill Gates, though naturally his fame derives far more from his fabulous wealth than from his technical contributions to what became Microsoft. Those persons who really were responsible for important inventions often remain in comparative obscurity. How many Americans know about Jack Kilby, the co-inventor of the integrated circuit—and later the pocket calculator—who was awarded the 2000 Nobel Prize for Physics for the former?[53] It would not be much of a challenge to elevate him to overnight celebrity status in the manner, common today, of infinitely less accomplished persons in countless realms. (Robert Noyce also invented the integrated circuit but worked separately from Kilby; however, because he was already dead, he was ineligible for the prize.)

There is, however, a bit of historical reverence in Silicon Valley for the three garages in which three major high-tech companies began: Hewlett-Packard (William Hewlett and David Packard, starting in 1938), Apple (Steve Jobs and Steve Wozniak, starting in 1976), and Google (Sergey Brin and Larry Page, starting in 1998). None is open to the public, but all are popular brief stopping places for contemporary geek tours.[54]

More generally, there is a declining confidence in scientific and technological panaceas—not simply a declining faith in utopia. This was a process that began in Europe during World War I as Victorian confidence and complacency were shattered by the tragic futility of trench warfare and by the use of terrible new weapons of mass destruction such as machine guns, tanks, airplanes, and poison gas.

That same kind of declining confidence in scientific and technological panaceas also reflects the growing acknowledgment in the United States from the 1960s onward of (1) endless science- and technology-related environmental crises; (2) repeated disappointments over nuclear power and other alleged scientific and technological panaceas; and (3) distrust of both public officials and technical experts growing out of the Vietnam War and the Watergate scandal of the 1970s. These developments would likely have diminished the optimism of ordinary citizens even if some form of genetic engineering for humans were by now a fact of life rather than just a prospect. Friedel's monumental and generally positive *A Culture of Improvement*, noted at the outset, nevertheless ends with two darker chapters on the world wars and eugenics ("The Corruption of Improvement") and on environmental challenges and dilemmas of genetic engineering ("Improvement's End").

The first two points hardly need elaboration, but the third does. Since the 1960s there has been a waning perception of "experts" as presumably objective analysts and a growing sense that they are paid partisans of any cause that will hire them. As noted, some experts in the 1960s and 1970s advocated such short-term "techno-fixes" as air-conditioners and free electricity to cool urban ghettoes and prevent violence, and drugs to reduce anxieties. They would substitute these for genuine solutions to long-term problems such as poverty, racial inequality, crime, and mental illness. Moreover, both the Vietnam War and the Watergate scandal permanently undermined Americans' traditional faith in the honesty and integrity of their leaders and simultaneously in those leaders' ability to employ experts who really knew more than ordinary citizens. The commonplace conservative denigration of "big government," of the strategy of attacking problems by "throwing money at them," is certainly disingenuous in many respects. Yet it does epitomize the change from Franklin Roosevelt's New Deal and Lyndon Johnson's Great Society to the vastly diminished contemporary American faith in government's ability to use science and technology to solve major social, economic, and cultural problems. The recent turn to high tech as a means of fulfilling personal hopes and dreams is the logical consequence. Insofar as experts are relied upon, it is a matter of consumers' demands and expectations, not their blind trust.[55]

Simultaneously, and in some respects related, have been the powerful historical, philosophical, and political critiques of the very notion of scientific objectivity and the rise of the basic argument that truth is therefore relative. That position remains fiercely contested, but it is significant that the debates evoked by Snow's 1959 lecture and its subsequent published versions have been equaled by the controversies generated by the so-called "Science Wars" of the late 1990s. By that point the sanctity—and veracity—of the presuppositions and methods of traditional science that Snow and his contemporaries in science and technology took for granted had been profoundly challenged. These controversies were especially fueled by the publication of physicist Alan Sokal's hoax article in the journal *Social Text* in 1996 and Sokal's acknowledgment in the journal *Lingua Franca* of the article as a highly sophisticated parody of "post-modern" skepticism and relativism. Entitled "Transgressing the Boundaries: Towards a Transformative Hermeneutics of Quantum Gravity," the article was intended to embarrass the avant-garde editors who had accepted it and, more importantly, to demonstrate the alleged intellectual poverty of those who rejected the historic hegemony of Enlightenment philosophies and models of inquiry. By contrast, Sokal was defending the Scientific Revolution and the positivist method.[56]

Contemporary Prophets for Profit: The Rise and Partial Fall of Professional Forecasters

The utopian claims of the 1960s and 1970s of systems "experts" such as Ramo to be able to solve *all* problems certainly ring hollow in light of the cosmic failures of the "Best and the Brightest" in Vietnam. So, too, do the failures of other experts in such realms as environmental protection and nuclear power to achieve promised goals safely and efficiently.[57] For that matter, predictions of an ever growing population in the developing world are now recognized as outdated, in favor of a far more complex picture.[58] These dismal records have in turn led to a declining faith in forecasting as a serious intellectual and moral enterprise—just as, paradoxically, forecasting has become a highly profitable industry.

A revealing footnote here is the failure of the otherwise brilliant scientists and engineers who invented computers during and after World War II to anticipate the evolution of the computers of their day. Interviews, memoirs, and other accounts from pioneers such as John Mauchly and John Von Neumann reveal no expectations of significant changes from the handful of room-sized behemoths—operated by skilled programmers and dependent on vacuum tubes that constantly needed to be replaced— that were to be used only by the largest national and international institutions to solve the most complex quantitative problems. They were generally unable to "step outside the box" in speculating about computers' future. Yet, within a few decades, ever smaller and ever more powerful computers requiring little operational expertise had become embedded almost everywhere in the world. What should we conclude about this inability to predict? And is this inability necessarily a bad thing?[59]

Once, forecasting was the province of people who, regardless of their particular strategies, had a genuine hope of improving the world, or at least a small part of it.[60] Now it has become an almost purely commercial enterprise intended only to make money. If, as John Kenneth Galbraith often quipped (as previously noted), economists make forecasts not because they know but because they are asked, self-proclaimed visionaries seduce a culture that, beneath its surface sophistication, seeks simple, reassuring answers to complex, unsettling questions. Traditional utopians (and anti-utopians) who cared about the future, no matter how they might have foreseen it, have been replaced by another sort: men and women who care primarily about getting rich by playing off anxieties over the future. This represents a profound and troubling change.

It is indicative of such pecuniary motivations that prominent forecasters such as Michael Dertouzos, Bill Gates, John Naisbitt and Patricia Aburdene, Nicholas Negroponte, Virginia Postrel, and Alvin and Heidi Toffler rarely if ever offer explanations when their predictions turn out to have been erroneous. Instead, they point to developments they could not possibly have foreseen or simply ignore their mistakes altogether. To take a highly significant example, Negroponte has for years now been promoting the production of a one-hundred-dollar laptop for children that would supposedly transform the lives of and educate millions of impoverished souls. Genuinely committed to this non-profit crusade, called "One Laptop per Child," he has raised huge sums of money but has been defeated by the impossibility of meeting that low cost per computer. Unexpectedly high expenses for the original laptop resulted from too many moving parts; too many features needed to "withstand glaring sun, blowing sand, and spotty access to electricity"; and customized keyboards for countries not using the Latin alphabet. Negroponte has consequently dropped the laptop in favor of a "tablet design" that, he claims, will not cost over one hundred dollars. So much for his earlier predictions. Meanwhile, a small New York firm has produced a one-hundred-dollar Sylvania netbook that is about the same size and weight as a hardback book but is not an especially good or useful computer overall.[61]

It is tempting to dismiss the Tofflers and Naisbitt and Aburdene as intellectual lightweights not worthy of serious investigation. But the fact that they are taken *very* seriously by millions of admirers— including leaders in business, government, and education—makes them worthy of mention. Interestingly, where utopias have often been associated with marginal members of society, all eight of the people mentioned above are (or were, in the case of Dertouzos, who died in 2001) greatly respected.

By contrast, the last major visionary who, as noted, was not "in it for the money" was Buckminster Fuller. If it is true that Fuller endured decades of indifference and sometimes ridicule before he obtained respect, influence, relative affluence, and a devoted following, it is *not* true that he contemplated suicide on Chicago's lakefront in 1927 at age thirty-two. In the story repeated by most of his biographers and others (including the curators of the 2008 New York and 2009 Chicago Fuller exhibits discussed in Chapter 8), Fuller was so beset by business failures and by the tragic death of his young daughter five years earlier that he allegedly thought about ending his life. But this story has a happy ending, for he allegedly instead resolved to follow an inner voice telling him that his mission to improve humankind had just begun. Yet research in the archives of Fuller's papers suggests that this supposedly pivotal episode never happened; that Fuller was nowhere as suicidal as he later claimed; and that he was far more distressed by the collapse of an extra-marital relationship in 1931. Still, this apparently invented suicide attempt enabled Fuller to initiate his greatest achievement: inventing himself.[62]

Admittedly, Fuller was similar to the contemporary high-tech prophets in his reluctance to concede mistakes. Nor was he above making up numbers in purported proof of his assertions. So he is hardly beyond criticism. Yet he was certainly different from today's prophets, who provide no genuine moral critique and who make no serious effort to alter society for higher purposes.

True, there are exceptions, notably Gates, whose admirable philanthropic enterprises led to him being chosen (along with his wife Melinda and the rock star Bono) as *Time* magazine's 2005 "People of the Year." But none of the others have any of the sense of social responsibility that Fuller had, or that most of the other people mentioned in this chapter had.[63] (As noted earlier, the same distinction can be applied to earlier versus recent world's fairs.)

Moreover, as varied as high-tech visions are, they make the same three basic claims about the future. First, science and technology will make the West and eventually the entire world healthier, happier, more efficient, more productive, and more democratic than ever before. Second, present-day advances dwarf all prior scientific and technological advances in their extraordinary speed and impact, including the English Industrial Revolution that began in the 1750s and spread throughout the world. Third, comparisons with all prior scientific and technological revolutions can therefore be ignored, so profoundly different will the future be from the past. History no longer matters. Not surprisingly, old-fashioned and simple-minded technological determinism pervades such books as Toffler's *Future Shock* (1970), Gates' *The Road Ahead* (1995), and Negroponte's *Being Digital* (1995). Fuller was hardly a professional historian, but he did understand that his was not the first techno-logical utopian vision in all history (though, in his own mind, it was surely the best).

It is so seductive, if so simplistic, to assume that high tech transforms everything in its path and that the twenty-first century will therefore reflect the globalization of culture as well as tech-nology. Yet historians and other scholars of technology know otherwise.[64] It is not enough to dress up various high-tech items to look old in order to pay minimal respect to the past: for instance, "full-size jukeboxes that are really $4,000 iPod docks and manual typewriters reconfigured to work as U.S.B. keyboards."[65] True, though, these retro designs may appeal to those who are intimidated by the latest gadgets or who seek some measure of permanence for items that otherwise may seem destined for only a short stay before becoming outdated.

Yet history in *some* form still repeatedly crops up in the works of these contemporary prophets. For instance, *Future Shock* suggests creating simulated medieval villages as shields against the shock of the new, thereby implying that the Middle Ages was a period of stagnation when it was actually a time of enormous technological achievement. Dertouzos's *What Will Be* (1997) envisions flying a virtual "histori-copter" to visit the past, but for what purpose is hardly clear. Postrel's *The Future and its Enemies* (1998) does concede that "history matters," but it matters largely as a point of comparison with the far more impressive future. By contrast, earlier visionaries as far back as More, Andreae, Campanella, and Bacon took history seriously. So, too, did the European and American imperialists, who argued that non-Western societies provided historical markers against which to measure Western progress. Equally significant, where the 1939–1940 World of Tomorrow world's fair looked twenty years hence to 1960 for the realization of utopia, the proponents of high-tech utopias anticipate almost *immediate* fulfillment. The metaphor of the "wave of the future" that these visions repeatedly invoke compels our attention; one either goes along with such a wave or one drowns. Although Fuller entitled his 1969 book in terms of a similar choice—*Utopia or Oblivion*—he certainly had an understanding of history.

The traumatic experiences of those who lived through the English Industrial Revolution are well-known and need not be detailed. Those who prospered as well as those who did not had their lives and their livelihoods transformed.[66] But consider that increasingly common claim about the allegedly unprecedented speed of change today. Enda Duffy's book, *The Speed Handbook: Velocity, Pleasure, Modernism* (2009), implicitly challenges that position. Duffy's starting point is Huxley's 1931 essay entitled "Wanted, a New Pleasure." The essay claimed that "Speed ... provides the one genuinely modern pleasure." Duffy extends that observation to a remarkable range of twentieth-century phenomena: American and European novels, paintings, posters, photographs, films, advertising, and news reports. He contends that the prevailing negative connotation of speed in relation to clocks, schedules, and Frederick Taylor's stopwatch Scientific Management was gradually "rerouted into the excessive speed of individual pleasure."[67]

The automobile was not the only invention to provide that pleasurable experience, but it transcended all others, allowing people "to feel modernity in their bones."[68] Duffy suggests (somewhat unconvincingly) that, as European colonial empires declined, experiencing speed at home replaced thrilling adventure abroad. These "speed demons" of roughly a century ago hardly saw themselves as leading slow-paced lives. The key point is how the world was perceived by ordinary people then as much as now. Unlike those ahistorical high-tech prophets, Duffy properly respects and reads the past in its own complex terms.

To be sure, people who rode and witnessed early-nineteenth-century railroads made similar statements about their own pace of change. Yet Duffy convincingly interprets a representative painting of early railroads, J. M. W. Turner's "Rain, Steam, and Speed—The Great Western Railway" (1844), as a "passive experience—as passengers borne along" in a train even as that train "literally vaporizes the landscape through which it cuts."[69]

By 1908 things had changed. Duffy contrasts such passivity with Jacques-Henri Lartigue's 1908 photograph of a racing car driver entitled "November 9, Road from Nice to Peira-Cava." The camera suffers from "technological inadequacy" in trying to capture the object's speed. Yet that forces a focus on the driver. The flash in his eye resonates fear. Unlike railroad passengers, the driver must be alert as he tries to control the situation. The possibility of accidents and deaths became one of the automobile's thrills.[70]

Speed rewarded citizens depending upon their geographical location, income, and, being a predominantly male province, gender. Speed also necessitated governmental controls in the form of highway construction, traffic regulations, and drivers' licenses. Yet Duffy fails to appreciate the inability of many auto and other workers, including those in Detroit, to afford Henry Ford's Model T, the cheapest American car through to the early 1920s. These workers presumably never experienced speed first-hand. Meanwhile, for many twentieth-century workers, speed remained associated primarily with Taylor's stopwatches and other non-pleasurable methods of control. This qualification has parallels with those contemporary claims of the supposed universality of high-tech's transforming effects—a very dubious stance.

In their common ignorance of history, these high-tech prophets (and others too) rarely evidence any appreciation of the extreme difficulty, if not the utter impossibility, of predicting major developments that are more than mere extrapolations from the present to the future. A prime example is from the year 1984, when the longtime president of the World Future Society, the respected head of this otherwise serious and worthwhile organization, criticized George Orwell's classic dystopia, *1984*, insofar as Orwell failed to predict the world more accurately from the vantage point of 1949. This leading professional prognosticator actually composed a scorecard evaluating Orwell's record.[71] He completely misunderstood what compelled Orwell to write about Big Brother: *not* to describe the future but *precisely to prevent* it from coming about. And he failed to recognize that Orwell's target was as much his own day—specifically, authoritarian British and Russian socialists and communists—as it was 1984. Far from being displeased over his predictive failings, Orwell would surely have been delighted by the degree to which the real world of 1984 did *not* resemble his nightmare world. He would just as surely have been dismayed by the ways in which the real world of 1984 *did* resemble *1984* and by the repeated invocation through to today of Big Brother and Doublespeak by critics of totalitarianism.

The temptation of several high-tech visionaries to compose similar scorecards is not surprising, and not just because of the unprecedented availability of electronically generated data and analysis. Our alleged ability to quantify everything, as epitomized respectively by McNamara and Ramo, is seductive. Yet it remains dismaying that such additional classic dystopias as Huxley's *Brave New World* and Zamyatin's *We* are also largely ignored by the very persons who might temper their own romantic dreams of prediction if they had read and understood these works.

Tellingly, in November 2008, during a visit to the London School of Economics, Queen Elizabeth asked why few if any economists had foreseen the recent economic crisis. On July 22, 2009, two British professors answered her in a widely cited letter. Not long after, however, ten prominent British economists criticized that letter for failing to address how the narrowly technical, heavily quantitative methods commonly used in contemporary economics precluded looking at a larger picture that might have provided some warnings of the pending crisis.[72]

More than most of their predecessors, high-tech visions are especially revealing of more-mainstream beliefs just because they are often so bold, so unqualified, so brazen. Nevertheless, as much as these high-tech utopian visions increasingly pervade and affect our contemporary culture and our discourse, they do not shape most Americans' views of science and technology or of the future. Technological determinism does not work here any more than it has elsewhere. As indicated, the majority of Americans today are more mature and less naïve than earlier generations, who, to use the tagline of the old General Electric advertisements, believed that "Progress is our most important product."[73] Besides the obvious examples of nuclear power, oil drilling (both on land and on the sea), space exploration, and genetic engineering there are such relatively mundane concerns as cell phones reducing drivers' attention and intruding into pristine wilderness, e-mail reducing proper grammatical usage, and the supposedly paperless office generating ever more paper. More important, for instance, is the question of prolonging life in modern hospitals by various mechanical means that often undermine the quality and comfort of patients' final days. Other case studies of this growing ambivalence about contemporary technology can be found in Edward Tenner's *Why Things Bite Back: Technology and the Revenge of Unintended Consequences* (1996). A healthy skepticism about unadulterated technological advance might actually represent another form of progress.

Paradoxically, some of these high-tech visionaries may not be quite as confident about the future as they profess to be. With the Tofflers, more than with anyone else, one finds growing doubts in their later writings about future glories, but always subject to more hopeful outcomes if readers still follow their jargon-laden analyses and prescriptions. What I wrote in 1994 about their outlook still applies:

> The ongoing, generally positive powershift throughout the world toward knowledge economies, decentralized governments, and participatory democracies is [in their view] increasingly threatened

by the possible rise of one or more racist, tribal (read nationalist), eco-fascist, or fundamentalist states all too ready to suppress human rights, freedom of religion, and, not least, private property.[74]

One cannot deny the accuracy of some of this in the years since, though many others have said much the same.

For other high-tech prophets, such as Naisbitt and Aburdene, any potentially negative developments are either dismissed outright or relegated to the province of "naysayers." Yet the greater the gap between prophecy and fulfillment, the more passionate the rhetoric about high-tech utopia somehow remaining just within our grasp. This becomes clear from a close reading of their *Megatrends* (1982) and their *Megatrends 2000* (1990).[75]

It is as important to determine the sources of these prophets' popularity as it is to analyze their respective visions. In many respects they are the high-tech successors to earlier advocates of American "positive thinking" dating back to Benjamin Franklin, continuing with Dale Carnegie and Norman Vincent Peale, and leading to such contemporaries as Oprah Winfrey, Stephen Covey, Robert Schuller, and the *Chicken Soup for the Soul* authors. Their popularity reveals a good deal about Americans' and others' apparent obsession with the future and about the reasons why so many feel compelled to try to uncover the future. That obsession in turn reflects a mixture of optimism and anxiety, an ambivalence about that future that at once compels so many to seek reassurance from the alleged experts. Barbara Ehrenreich's recent *Bright-sided: How the Relentless Promotion of Positive Thinking has Undermined America* (*Smile or Die: How Positive Thinking Fooled America and the World*) illuminates the negative consequences of these upbeat crusades.

Where a century ago Henry Adams was a minority voice questioning science and technology's relentless advance, critiques of modern science and technology on comparable grounds are by now becoming routine. Among many other works, Nye's *America as Second Creation* calls for new values for our time. He seeks selective, sustainable scientific and technological development and renewal of the non-quantitative social, cultural, and psychological measures of the "good life" long relegated to the sidelines in serious discussions of "progress." The conservationist Sierra Club's motto applies to Nye and to like-minded others: "Not blind opposition to progress, but opposition to blind progress."

Post-colonial Critiques of Western Science and Technology as Measures of "Progress"

A complementary critique of the utopian assumptions of Western science and technology derives from the growing "post-colonial studies" field that has emerged in recent decades. It is increasingly common for historians and other scholars to argue that Western science and technology, the commonly deployed measures of "progress" possibly leading to utopia, were utilized by European colonial powers to dominate their empires not only materially and financially (rather familiar themes) but also culturally and psychologically. The traditional condescension toward non-Western science and technology invariably reflects ignorance of the achievements in Arab lands and in China, among many other places, in the centuries before colonial empires began. Yet, as Michael Adas demonstrates in his *Machines as the Measure of Men: Science, Technology, and Ideologies of Western Dominance* (1989), the story is more complicated. Until the English Industrial Revolution of the mid-eighteenth century, Western ethnocentrism (that is, the assumption that Western culture and Western values were ipso facto superior to those everywhere else in the world, much of it known indiscriminately as "the Orient") rested primarily on cultural constructions of race, religion, customs, aesthetics, and other non-material phenomena. But this changed, as per Adas' title, once knowledge of Western machinery and technologies of communication and transportation reached colonial lands. Racism and other cultural constructions no longer determined the hierarchy of nations and civilizations. Now advancing technology (or, rather, the lack thereof) became the measure—a "concrete" manifestation, so to speak—of native inferiority.[76]

The same held true for the imperialists' scientific discoveries, despite greater difficulty in making those achievements visible to and understood by non-scientists. The most profound measure of

Western superiority became its growing control over nature and its mastery of nature's secrets. This manifested itself scientifically in the development of such fields as tropical medicine and ethno-psychiatry.[77] It became the famous "white man's burden" to utilize Western technology and science in order to uplift and civilize the needy colonials. Hence the moral justification for all of those technological and scientific advances. By comparison, Chinese gunpowder, printing, and textile and porcelain products, along with African stone structures (especially in what is today Zimbabwe), for example, hardly rose to those levels of excellence leading to utopia. There was no prospect, in the eyes of Westerners, for anything remotely utopian within their overseas colonies.

Unexpectedly, as Adas also shows, World War I undermined the hitherto uncritical faith of many Asians and Africans in Western technology and science, just as, as noted, it did for the European nations directly involved in the conflict (as noted). Victorian confidence and complacency were shattered by the unprecedented tragedy of futile trench warfare and by the use of terrible weapons such as machine guns, tanks, airplanes, and poison gas. So much for Western manifestations of "progress," which in the post-war decades was reflected in the often ambivalent attitude of non-Western intellectuals and politicians: conflicting desires to embrace these supposedly universal emblems of achievement and so be citizens of the world versus nationalist hostility toward such means of cultural and psychological subjugation. Still, regardless of the post-war disagreements about what constituted "progress," centuries-old racial categories designed by Westerners steadily diminished in respectability insofar as the "measure of men" (and of women, whom Adas largely ignores) had instead become technological and scientific. A notable exception was Japan, which, having escaped colonization and having become a world power early in the twentieth century, never relinquished its old attitudes about racial supremacy and homogeneity.[78]

Interestingly, in recent years there have been controversies about the alleged African origins of Western (especially Greek) science and technology and condemnations of the supposed Western theft of these intellectual and material treasures (despite that post-World War I skepticism about modern developments). But such attempted revisionism had been decisively refuted, especially in Mary Lefkowitz's superb *Not Out of Africa: How Afrocentrism Became an Excuse to Teach Myth as History* (1996).

Meanwhile, in a throwback to that skepticism about Western science, South Africa's President Thabo Mbeki (born in 1942), the successor to Nelson Mandela and the nation's second black president, set back his country's response to its widespread AIDS epidemic during his administration. Mbeki repeatedly questioned what was the scientific consensus on the causes and treatment of AIDS, condemning these as remnants of Western colonial oppression, and simultaneously insisted on the use instead of traditional African medical remedies. The latter failed and caused many unnecessary deaths and endless misery to countless numbers of his fellow South Africans. One might term this situation a real-life dystopia.

Utopian Visions in India   Somewhat more compelling than Afrocentrism are the arguments of serious scholars such as Gyan Prakash in *Another Reason: Science and the Imagination of Modern India* (1999). Prakash illuminates how Indian elites under British rule appropriated Western science and technology as key components of their utopian vision of a modernized India that they would create and rule. In the process, they translated those phenomena into distinctly Indian intellectual discourses and thereby undermined the very universality of science and technology that they simultaneously espoused. Just as the British touted such new or improved technologies as the telegraph, the railroad, and public works such as canal, irrigation, sanitation, medical, postal, and information-collection systems as instruments of progress for its entire colonial empire, so these Indian elites envisioned taking them over, unifying the "Jewel of the Crown," and promoting nationalism and eventual independence. There were those who claimed that, with "aircraft and even nuclear power back in ancient times," India had constituted a veritable technological utopia that would eventually be restored and then surpassed. Others contended that Hinduism, the religion of most Indians, was originally far more rationalistic and scientific than it had become over the centuries. Many scientists, engineers, and religious figures further maintained that India "was the original home of science" and technology but that, "unlike the West, it had never separated [them] from religious life." They went so far as to charge that Europeans had borrowed scientific and technical knowledge—for that matter, the fundamental ideas of reason and rationality—from Indians without acknowledgment. Such arguments were intended to turn the European colonizers into the real subordinates and thereby eradicate the European racism used to brand Indians and other Asians and of course all Africans as biological as well as cultural inferiors. Indian elites thereby positioned themselves to become the foremost nationalists as the country struggled for independence.[79] The fact that Western science and technology alike were hardly monolithic and were themselves frequently aligned with religion was conveniently overlooked.

A more traditional account of India since independence in 1947, Ainslie Embree's *Utopias in Conflict: Religion and Nationalism in Modern India* (1990), concentrates on the ideological and physical conflicts between its Hindus, Muslims, and Sikhs that still persist today. Embree argues that the religious-political movements aimed at enhancing indigenous power are struggles in the name of modernity, not attempts to return to an alleged golden age, as so commonly claimed. Relying heavily on modern technology, "these visions of a good society, or blueprints of the future, are integral components of the vitality and creativity of contemporary Indian life."[80] Like Prakash, but less explicitly, Embree suggests that India's own version of modernity differed significantly from that of its colonial rulers. Under the post-World War II leadership of Jawaharlal Nehru, India outpaced other "underdeveloped" or "Third World" nations in selectively embracing Western and sometimes Soviet technology and values in the name of maintaining neutrality amid the Cold War. India's growth in recent years as a center of global high tech only reinforces these utopian sentiments.[81]

It should not, however, be forgotten that, like China, Japan, and other Asian countries, India had its backward-looking utopian elements. Literary works describing Hindu paradises akin to the Garden of Eden were common in the nineteenth and early twentieth centuries, and a few elevated women to the equals, if not the superiors, of men. Most important, though, was the pre-industrial vision of the founder of Indian independence, Mohandas Gandhi (1869–1948), whose commitment to a Hindu golden age constituted his vision for modern India. Gandhi wished to keep small communities, but less class- and caste-ridden communities than in his day, as the principal form of Indian life and culture. He stressed simplicity and collective self-sufficiency.[82]

Notes

1   See Nelson Hernandez, *Washington Post*, "As NASA Marks Anniversary of Apollo 11, It Looks to Future," *Boston Sunday Globe*, July 19, 2009, A10; and Carolyn Y. Johnson, "JFK Had Doubts About Moon Landing," *Boston Globe*, May 25, 2011, B1, B4.

2   See Constance Penley, NASA/TREK: Popular Science and Sex in America (New York: Verso, 1997).

3   See Louis Friedman, "NASA's Down-to-Earth Woes," *Bangor Daily News*, March 24, 2010, A5; Joshua Green, "Takeoff: With the Shuttle Program Ending Next Year, What Will Be the New Face of NASA?" *Boston Globe*, July 8, 2010, A13; Seth Borenstein, "Moon Landing Still a Measure of Success: Forty Years Later, Audacity of Feat Unmatched," *Bangor Daily News*, July 20, 2010, A1, A2; Bill Wrobel, "New Era of Space Discovery Begins," *Bangor Daily News*, June 9, 2011, A7; "A Long Overdue, But Bittersweet End to NASA's Shuttle Program," Editorial, *Boston Globe*, July 8, 2011, A12; and Gareth Cook, "A Space for Robots: US Can Lead in Daring Missions—Without Humans," *Boston Sunday Globe*, July 10, 2011, K11.

4   "Products Designed by NASA," *Washington Post*, reprinted in *Bangor Daily News*, July 22, 2009, A5.

5   Marcia Dunn, Associated Press, "Japanese Astronaut Tests New High-Tech Undies," *Bangor Daily News*, July 31, 2009, C9.

6   See H. Bruce Franklin, *War Stars: The Superweapon and the American Imagination*, 2nd edn. (Amherst: University of Massachusetts Press, 2008 [1988]).

7   "Star Wars" continues to be a possible megaproject in one form or another and is commonly understood in its basic structure and operation. On its historical background, see Franklin, *War Stars*. Concerning the twenty-fifth anniversary of President Reagan's

speech, see John Tierney and Stephen Flynn, "Misguided Missile Defense," *Boston Globe*, March 28, 2008, A11. On the far less familiar supercollider, see Daniel J. Kevles, *The Physicists: The History of a Scientific Community in Modern America* (Cambridge, MA: Harvard University Press, 1995 [1977]), preface.

 8   Other owners included North East Utilities and New England Electric System, both at twenty percent; Bangor Hydro Electric at seven percent; and Maine Public Service Company at five percent. The remaining ten percent was shared between six other New England utility firms.

 9   "Maine Yankee Facts" (Augusta: Maine Yankee Atomic Power Company, circa 1971), 1. From the collections of the Maine State Museum, Augusta.

10   Lewis Strauss quoted in Brian Balogh, *Chain Reaction: Expert Debate and Public Participation in American Commercial Nuclear Power, 1945–1975* (New York: Cambridge University Press, 1991), 113. The same claim was made in the 1930s by those advocating rural electrification, especially but not exclusively in the Tennessee Valley Authority. Maine Yankee Atomic Electric Power's first plant, which opened in 1960, was Yankee Atomic at Rowe, Massachusetts; it closed in 1992. In 1968 came Connecticut Yankee in Haddam Neck, which closed in 1996. Millstone 1 in Waterford, Connecticut, opened in 1970 and closed in 1998; Millstone 2 and Millstone 3 started in 1975 and 1986, respectively, and continue to operate, as do Pilgrim in Plymouth, Massachusetts; Seabrook in New Hampshire; and Vermont Yankee in Vernon, Vermont.

11   "The Atom, Electricity, and You!" (Augusta: Maine Yankee Atomic Power Company, circa 1968), 1. From the collections of the Maine State Museum, Augusta. There is no publication date, but the cartoons that comprise most of the brochure have a 1968 copyright date. Although the company is listed as the *de facto* publisher, the contents suggest a generic publication applicable to all nuclear power construction and operation companies of the era. Only three pages are not generic in nature and lack cartoons.

12   "The Atom, Electricity, and You!" 3.

13   "The Atom, Electricity, and You!" 6, 7.

14   "The Atom, Electricity, and You!" 10.

15   "The Atom, Electricity, and You!" 11, 13, 15; emphasis added.

16   Richard C. Hill, unpublished letter to the *Bangor Daily News*, January 7, 2008, in reply to Ernie Hilton, "Nuclear Power Not the Solution," *Bangor Daily News*, January 7, 2008, A7.

17   John Chester quoted in Carey Goldberg, "In a Post-Nuclear Town, Some Adjustments Hurt," *New York Times*, July 14, 1998, 14; Judy Flanagan quoted in Ann S. Kim, "Maine Yankee's Dome Coming Down This Week," *Maine Sunday Telegram*, September 12, 2004, A14. Those who worked at Maine Yankee were satisfied with their jobs and employment conditions. Engineer Bryan Selee recounted in Kim's article that a job there "was a good job to have, good benefits, the job security was there." He met his wife at the plant, and his father, stepmother, and father-in-law worked there. Selee believed that opponents often lacked sufficient understanding of the competence and concern of the staff. See also "Maine's Nuclear Plant, Age Five, Is Accident Free," Nashua, New Hampshire, *Telegraph*, December 29, 1977, 13.

18   All quotations are from Warren E. Leary, Associated Press, "Vermont Nuclear Plant, Despite Problems, Brings Prosperity to Town," Newport (Rhode Island) *Daily News*, May 8, 1974, 31; other papers carrying shorter versions of the same Associated Press article include the Portsmouth, New Hampshire *Portsmouth Herald* (April 29, 1974) and the Nashua, New Hampshire *Telegraph* (May 1, 1974). Still, "did you ever buy a car that operated 100 per cent effectively when you got it?" asked town official Erma Puffer. Similar sentiments might have arisen in Wiscasset had Maine Yankee experienced comparable challenges in its initial years, and certainly Maine Yankee had like-minded defenders years later, when serious problems did arise.

19   "Wiscasset Invites You," 5th edn. (Wiscasset: no publisher, no date), 5. From the collections of the Maine State Museum, Augusta.

20   A similar optimism can be found in the undated brochure published by Maine Yankee for its Energy Information Center. "If you live in Maine, chances are you use electricity from Maine Yankee every day," the brochure states. Maine Yankee was not only the state's single largest source of electricity but also "the nation's third most productive nuclear plant"—however one measures that. On December 28, 1977, Maine Yankee Power Company held a party celebrating the fact that the plant's first five years of operation had been accident-free. The plant had produced almost twenty-three billion kilowatt hours of electricity without any environmental problems, saving Maine consumers "some $150 million over five years because it replaced about 40 million barrels of high-priced fuel oil." Yet officials feared that any proposals for other nuclear power plants in the state would be met by strong opposition. "If you want to build a nuclear plant," warned company president Elwin Thurlow, "you will have to

spend $50 to $75 million before you know whether the government will let you build the plant." Thurlow blamed President Jimmy Carter, who, ironically, proclaimed himself an expert in nuclear engineering on the grounds of his undergraduate studies at the United States Naval Academy.

21 See Steven Del Sesto, "Wasn't the Future of Nuclear Engineering Wonderful?" in *Imagining Tomorrow: History, Technology, and the American Future*, ed. Joseph J. Corn (Cambridge: MIT Press, 1986), 58–76.

22 On Three Mile Island, see the following still-important accounts: John L. Campbell, *Collapse of an Industry: Nuclear Power and the Contradictions of U. S. Policy* (Ithaca: Cornell University Press, 1988); and Edward J. Walsh, *Democracy in the Shadows: Citizen Mobilization in the Wake of the Accident at Three Mile Island* (Westport: Greenwood Press, 1988). See also the fine summary in David Whitford, "Going Nuclear," *Fortune*, 156 (August 6, 2007), 42–54. By contrast, Joseph G. Morone and Edward J. Woodhouse, *The Demise of Nuclear Energy? Lessons for Democratic Control of Technology* (New Haven: Yale University Press, 1989) attributes the demise of nuclear energy in the United States in the wake of Three Mile Island and less serious malfunctions elsewhere to the wrong choice of reactors. For them, a "technical fix" would have solved all problems. They thereby overlook the various non-technological forces—political, economic, social, and cultural— that helped to shape the nation's nuclear power development. Concerning the twenty-fifth anniversary of Chernobyl, see Natalya Vasilyeva, "Legacy of Chernobyl Is Neglected, Activists Say," *Boston Globe*, April 26, 2011, A5.

23 Threats of a referendum a year or two earlier were dropped when proposals for a second plant on Sears Island were abandoned. See, for example, "AEC Environmental Ruling Could Stop Yankee Plant," *Daily Kennebec Journal*, September 2, 1971. On the 1982 referendum, see Michael Harris, "Maine Vote May Pull Plug on Nuclear Power Station," *Toronto Globe and Mail*, November 1, 1982, 10.

24 On the 1980 referendum, see Michael Knight, "Maine Votes to Keep its Nuclear Plant," *New York Times*, September 23, 1980, A1; and "Yankee, Yes," *Time*, October 6, 1980, 29. The margin of victory in 1982 was smaller: fifty-six percent to forty-four percent. On this opposition, see Jerry Ackerman, "Nuclear Power Pulling Up Short: After 20 Years in the Fast Lane, It's Hobbled by Cost, Safety Concerns, and Conservation," *Boston Globe*, March 24, 1982, 2. In defense of experts' hegemony, even after Three Mile Island, see James J. Duderstadt and Chihiro Kikuchi, *Nuclear Power: Technology on Trial*

(Ann Arbor: University of Michigan Press, 1979), viii, 194–197; the authors were University of Michigan professors of nuclear engineering at the time.

25 Raymond Shadis quoted in Goldberg, "In a Post-Nuclear Town."

26 Some of these problems would surely have been discovered in due course, but an anonymous letter sent in 1995 by someone claiming to be an employee with extensive inside knowledge triggered safety inspections by the NRC. The letter alleged that "engineers manipulated computer simulations and codes to hide potentially serious deficiencies in the reactor's emergency-cooling system." The writer contended that the faulty data and simulations demonstrated that the plant could safely operate at higher power outputs—outputs requiring increased license power levels—when in fact that was a risky strategy. See Peter N. Spotts, "Federal Probe of Maine Nuclear Plant," *Christian Science Monitor*, December 12, 1995, 4.

27 Colin Woodard, "Nuclear Power: Yankee Yanked," *The Bulletin of the Atomic Scientists*, 53 (November/December 1997), 11. See also Peter Pochina and Tux Turkel, "Is Maine Yankee Worth Repairing?" *Maine Sunday Telegram*, February 9, 1997, 1A, 6A, 7A. Commission investigations confirmed these allegations and blamed them, along with other safety and maintenance problems, "on the 'lack of a questioning culture' among managers, who placed cost savings ahead of safety improvements."

28 On efforts to sell or reuse Maine Yankee, see Tux Turkel, "Maine Yankee Fails to Find a Buyer," *Portland Press Herald*, June 2, 1998, 1C; and Associated Press, "Effort to Reuse Yankee Site Stalls," *Bangor Daily News*, August 5, 2002, B1, B5. For background on the decision to close the plant, see Carroll R. Lee et al., *Report of the Special Committee to the Maine Yankee Board of Directors*, July 30, 1997.

29 Quoted in Charlotte Boynton, "Maine Yankee Dome Toppled," *Boothbay Register*, September 23, 2004. See also Leanne M. Robicheau, "Power Switch: Yankee Dome Leveled," *Bangor Daily News*, Saturday–Sunday, September 18–19, 2004, A1, A9. When longtime plant opponent Shadis conceded in 1998, the rancor steadily diminished. No less importantly, Maine Yankee became more open than ever before in making its files accessible to the public. See Goldberg, "In a Post-Nuclear Town." By contrast, as reported by Evan Halper, "Maine Yankee Opponents Get Few Answers to Questions" (*Maine Times*, May 2, 1996, 8–9) prior to the plant's closing. Halper's title said it all.

30   David Nyhan, "Maine Yankee's Nuclear Albatross," *Boston Globe*, August 22, 1997, A23. See also Walter Griffin, "N-Plant Safety Tops Concerns; Residents Question Waste Monitoring," *Bangor Daily News*, November 7, 1997, 1, on the NRC's scheduling only one public hearing on the plant's decommissioning process—a process then expected to take a decade to complete. See Stephanie Plasse, "Community Profile: Seabrook, N.H., A Community with a Major Contrast," *Boston Globe*, July 24, 1993, 39; Randi Goldberg, Associated Press, "Years Don't Erase 'Line in the Sand' at Seabrook," *Maine Sunday Telegram*, April 20, 1997, 14B; Charles Stein, "Economic Life," *Boston Sunday Globe*, November 10, 2002, C1; Beth Daley, "Water Weakened Seabrook Tunnel," *Boston Globe*, May 30, 2011, A1, A9; and esp. Henry F. Bedford, *Seabrook Station: Citizen Politics and Nuclear Power* (Amherst: University of Massachusetts Press, 1990). See also Hilton, "Nuclear Power," which focuses on Seabrook, and Hill's unpublished response (see note 16).

31   On the considerable accomplishments to date in Maine Yankee's complex decommissioning process, see The Maine Yankee Decommissioning Advisory Panel's February 2005 report, *A Model for Public Participation in Nuclear Projects: A Report By the Maine Yankee Community Advisory Panel on Decommissioning*, http://www.maineyankee.com/ public/cap%20final.pdf. See also two related reports on the decommissioning process worldwide: *Decommissioning Nuclear Facilities* and *World Nuclear Association: Decommissioning: An Overview*, both available at http://www.world-nuclear.org/info.

32   Many residents of Nevada, and most of its top officials, now oppose ever using that locale. Largely for political reasons, the Obama Administration scrapped the Yucca Mountain plan in its first year in office. The license is now officially in limbo, while the project's cost over thirty years has risen to more than fifteen billion dollars. Everyone involved in this issue throughout the nation agrees that a second such site must be found and opened to accommodate the metric tons now being stored in temporary facilities in Maine and elsewhere—an amount that already exceeds the seventy thousand metric tons designated for Yucca Mountain. In Maine's case, the storage casks have been licensed for twenty years and, by the end of 2007, the costs totaled over 189 million dollars. A new federal panel, the Blue Ribbon Commission on America's Nuclear Future, is attempting to devise proposals, but everyone also concedes that it could take years to develop a safe disposal facility elsewhere. See Tux Turkel, *Portland Press Herald*, "Yankee's Radioactive Legacy Still

Haunts Wiscasset," *Bangor Daily News*, August 11, 2010, B5; Robert Knox, "Plymouth: Nuclear Waste to Linger," *Boston Globe*, South Edition, October 3, 2010, regarding its Pilgrim plant; and Matthew Daly and Dina Cappiello, Associated Press, "Inquiry Faults NRC Chief Over Yucca Site," *Boston Globe*, June 11, 2011, A8.

33   See, for example, Charlotte Boynton, "Ship Demolition Proposed for Maine Yankee Site," *Boothbay Register*, August 14, 2003, 1; and Ellen F. Kratz, "The Brave New World of Recycled Real Estate," *Fortune*, 153 (March 6, 2006), 176.

34   See Jay Lindsay, Associated Press, "GE Study Looks at New England Wind," *Bangor Daily News*, December 18–19, 2010, C1, C5; and Lindsay, "Seeking Cheap Power, Firms Look to the Sky," *Portland Press Herald*, May 30, 2011, A2. See also Lindsay, "Wanted: Buyer for Controversial Cape Wind," *Bangor Daily News*, December 21, 2010, B3.

35   Quotations from Manfred Raschke, an energy consultant currently in Massachusetts but with vast experience in Europe, in *Boston Globe*, August 9, 2010, A10. See also the varied positions found in Jonathan Carter, "Mountaintop Wind Power Is Not Green: High Elevation Wind Farms are the Antithesis of 'Going Green,'" *Bangor Metro*, Opinion, March 2010, 65; Tom Keane, "Memo to Cape Wind Foes: Enough Already," *Boston Globe Magazine*, May 23, 2010, 6; Tom Walsh, "Get Facts on Wind Turbines," *Bangor Daily News*, June 28, 2010, A5; Tux Turkel, "Poll: Mainers Strongly Back Wind Power," *Bangor Daily News*, June 30, 2010, A5; Peter Vigue, "Wind Power 'No-Impact' Standard at Odds with Law," *Bangor Daily News*, July 16, 2010, A11; David G. Tuerck and Jonathan Haughton, "The Great Wind Power Bait and Switch," *Boston Globe*, July 28, 2010, A11; Heather Steeves, "Grievances Aired Over Wind Turbines," *Bangor Daily News*, August 21–22, 2010, B1, B5; Clyde MacDonald, "Maine's Rush to Develop Wind Power is Ill-advised," *Bangor Daily News*, September 9, 2010, A7; Abigail Curtis, "Consultant: Turbine Noise Exceeds Limit," *Bangor Daily News*, September 13, 2010, B1, B6; Associated Press, "World's Largest Offshore Wind Farm Opens," *Boston Globe*, September 24, 2010, A3; Matt Wickenheiser, "Wind Project May Aid Maine," *Bangor Daily News*, October 13, 2010, A1, A2; Bill Trotter, "Offshore Wind Research Aired at Conference," *Bangor Daily News*, October 20, 2010, B1, B4; Turkel, "Wind Power Foes Target First Wind," *Bangor Daily News*, November 15, 2010, B1, B5; Erin Ailworth, "The Year's Top Business Stories: A Mighty Wind," *Boston Sunday Globe*, Money and Careers, December 26, 2010, G1; Wickenheiser, "Turbine Total

Slashed in Highland Wind Project," *Bangor Daily News*, December 29, 2010, A1, C5; CBC News, "Wind Turbine Flicker Upsets Neighbours", January 21, 2011, http://www.cbc.ca (concerning Summerside, Prince Edward Island); Jamison Cocklin, "LePage Advisers Skeptical of $20 Billion Wind Project," *Bangor Daily News*, June 1, 2011, A1, C5; Wickenheiser, "US Energy Official, Researchers Visit Offshore Wind Turbine Site," *Bangor Daily News*, June 14, 2011, A1, A3; Wickenheiser, "Maine's Efforts in Offshore Wind Detailed at Conference," *Bangor Daily News*, June 15, 2011, A6; Norman Laberge, "Make an Investment in Energy from the Tides, Wind," *Bangor Daily News*, June 17, 2011, A9; Turkel, "Nowhere's Special: Fishing Interests in Remote Washington County Fear the Sight of Wind Turbines will Ruin the Escape They Offer," *Portland Press Herald*, June 26, 2011, 1; Carter, "It's Time to Halt Wind Projects," *Bangor Daily News*, July 14, 2011, A5; Glenn Adams, "Maine Wind Projects Humming Along," *Bangor Daily News*, July 25, 2011, A6; Turkel, "Tribes: Wind Plan May Interfere with Sacred Ceremonies," *Portland Press Herald*, July 26, 2011, A1, A10; and Lisa Pohlmann and Ted Koffman, "The Importance of Carefully Developed Wind Energy," *Bangor Daily News*, September 3–4, 2011, A7.

36 See Leora Broydo Vestel, *New York Times*, "Pentagon Emerges as Foe of Wind Power," *Boston Globe*, August 27, 2010, B9.

37 An analysis of global-warming-type pollution in Maine between 1990 and 2004 concluded that it had increased by twenty-four percent, thanks in part to expanded use of natural gas to make the electricity that replaced the power generated by Maine Yankee until it closed. State fossil fuel consumption was the principal basis on which the study was conducted. See "Report: Maine's CO2 Output Rose 24 Percent Over 15 Years," *Portland Press Herald*, April 13, 2007, B2.

38 See Brian Dumaine, "Nukes in My Backyard," *Fortune*, 161 (March 22, 2010), 36.

39 See Gabrielle Hecht, *The Radiance of France: Nuclear Power and National Identity After World War II* (Cambridge: MIT Press, 1998); Michael Bess, *The Light-Green Society: Ecology and Technological Modernity in France, 1960–2000* (Chicago: University of Chicago Press, 2003), 102; and Steve Crouse, "Nuclear Power is the Answer to Our Energy Needs," *Bangor Daily News*, June 26–27, 2010, A11. On Japan, see Hiroko Tabuchi, "A Stricken Japan Ponders its New Normal," *New York Times*, May 12, 2011, B1, B7; and Associated Press, "Japan's ex-PM Feared Worst in Crisis," Boston Globe, September 8, 2011, A3.

40 See Judy Dempsey and Jack Ewing, "In Reversal, Germany Announces Plans to Close All Nuclear Plants by 2022," *New York Times*, May 31, 2011, A4.

41 See Jeff Donn, Associated Press, "As Nuclear Plants Age, NRC Loosens Safety Regulations," *Boston Globe*, June 20, 2011, A2; and Donn, Associated Press, "Report: 75% of US Nuke Sites Have Leaked Tritium," *Bangor Daily News*, June 21, 2011, A1, A4.

42 See Dina Cappiello and Jeff Donn, Associated Press, "Quake Risk to US Reactors Worse than Once Thought," *Boston Globe*, September 2, 2011, A7.

43 These figures and the quotations come from Whitford, "Going Nuclear," 45, 45–46. See also Matthew L. Wald, "After 35-Year Lull, Nuclear Power May Be in Early Stages of a Revival," *New York Times*, October 24, 2008, B3; and Elizabeth Spiers, "The Case for Nukes," *Fortune*, 157 (June 9, 2008), 22.

44 Steward Brand quoted in Whitford, "Going Nuclear," 54. See Fred Turner, *From Counterculture to Cyberculture: Stewart Brand, the Whole Earth Network, and the Rise of Digital Utopianism* (Chicago: University of Chicago Press, 2006).

45 See Whitford, "Going Nuclear," 48.

46 One possible new—or, more precisely, partially new—plant could be the presently dismantled Unit 2 of Seabrook Station. Although there are no plans to reopen Unit 2, opponents of any revival have made their concerns amply known. At the fortieth anniversary of the Seacoast Anti-Pollution League in 2008, they contended that nuclear power remains obsolete and that renewable energy is still the wave of the future. They note that "FPL Energy, owner and operator of Seabrook Station, is the largest provider of wind energy and has the largest solar fields in the country." So why not use that expertise instead? Associated Press, "Group Pushes Renewable Energy," *Maine Sunday Telegram*, June 1, 2008, B3. Concerning Seabrook's request for an operating license extension twenty years before its original one is due to expire, see Mary Daly, "Nuclear Agency is Urged Not to Hurry Relicensing," *Boston Globe*, June 13, 2011, B6.

47 Kate Galbraith, "Climate Enters Debate Over Nuclear Power: Alternatives Have Their Problems," *New York Times*, May 30, 2008, C4. See also Matthew Wald, "Vermont Nuclear Reactor Is Purchased by Entergy," *New York Times*, August 16, 2001, C4; Beth Daley, "Nuclear Plans Stir Concern in Vermont," *Boston Globe*, October 12, 2004, A12; Associated Press, "Vermont Yankee Clears Hurdle in Bid to Extend License Twenty Years," *Bangor Daily News*, April 2, 2007, B5; Ross

Sneyd, Associated Press, "Report: Vermont Nuclear Waste Highest Per Capita in Nation," *Bangor Daily News*, Saturday–Sunday, May 19–20, 2007, C6; Dave Gram, Associated Press, "Vermont Yankee Closer to License Extension," *Bangor Daily News*, February 26, 2008, B6; Daley, "Leaks Imperil Nuclear Industry: Vermont Yankee Among Troubled," *Boston Globe*, January 31, 2010, A1, A10; Lisa Rathke, Associated Press, "Mishaps Close Two Nuclear Plants," *Boston Globe*, November 9, 2010, B15; Wilson Ring, Associated Press, "Vermont N-plant to Refuel Despite Uncertainty," *Bangor Daily News*, July 26, 2011, B4; and Gram, Associated Press, "Vermont Yankee Bid to Stay Open Denied," *Boston Globe*, July 19, 2011, B3.

48   Since Three Mile Island, technical training has vastly improved. But Whitford, "Going Nuclear," 48–49, 52, discusses a potentially greater disaster than Three Mile Island, at Ohio's Davis-Besse plant, that resulted from inept maintenance and inspection. Fortunately, critical repairs were belatedly made just in time. Quotation in Whitford, "Going Nuclear," 46.

49   Whitford, "Going Nuclear," 46.

50   See, for example, Kevles, *The Physicists*, chs. 20–25 and preface.

51   Bruce J. Dierenfield, review of Balogh, *Chain Reaction* in *American Historical Review*, 98 (February 1993), 270.

52   Richard de Grasse, "Why Not Nuclear for Wiscasset?" *Bangor Daily News*, November 26, 2007, A7; and Bob Walker, "Nuclear Energy Can Help Power Maine's Future," *Bangor Daily News*, October 17, 2007, A7.

53   See especially T. R. Reid, *The Chip: How Two Americans Invented the Microchip and Launched a Revolution*, 2nd edn. (New York: Random House, 2001). Robert Noyce also invented the integrated circuit but worked separately from Kilby; because he had died by 2000, he was ineligible for the prize.

54   See Jane Margolies, "California: Follow the Spirits," *New York Times*, Travel, July 4, 2010, TR 6.

55   See the interesting advice to then President-elect Obama by Elaine Kamarck ("Look to the Internet to Fight Poverty," *Boston Globe*, November 29, 2008, A11) as reflecting more modest expectations for cutting-edge technology to solve massive social problems—to "fight" but not eliminate poverty in America. But see also George Will's critique of Obama's Wilsonian great expectations: "American Politics Caught Between Madison, Wilson," *Bangor Daily News*, June 5, 2010, A7.

56   See the review of Ortolano, *Two Cultures Controversy* by Patricia Waugh, *Reviews in History* 849, http://www.history.ac.uk/

reviews/review/849. See also the references in Chapter 5, notes 34 and 35.

57 See Simon Ramo, *Cure for Chaos: Fresh Solutions to Social Problems Through the Systems Approach* (New York: McKay, 1969) and David Halberstam, *The Best and the Brightest* (New York: Random House, 1972).

58 See Charles P. McQuaid, "Squirrel Chatter II: The Population Bust," Annual Report, *Columbia Acorn Family of Funds*, December 31, 2008, 3–5.

59 See Paul Ceruzzi, "An Unforeseen Revolution: Computers and Expectations, 1935–1985," in *Imagining Tomorrow*, ed. Corn, 188–201.

60 For many excellent examples, see I. F. Clarke, *The Pattern of Expectation, 1644–2001* (New York: Basic Books, 1979).

61 See Jessica Mintz, Associated Press, "One Laptop Shifts Focus to Producing Low-Cost Tablet PCs," *Boston Globe*, May 28, 2010, B8. On the mixed results of the introduction of laptops to a few classes in the State of Maine, see Karen Kusiak, "Students, Laptops, and School Achievement: Identity Construction in One-to-One Classrooms," unpublished Ed.D. dissertation, University of Maine, 2011. See also Christopher Cousins, "Powerful Tool or Waste of Money? Fans, Critics, Students Share Views on Maine's School Laptop Program," *Bangor Daily News*, May 27, 2011, A1, A5. On the one-hundred-dollar Sylvania netbook, see Hiawatha Bray, "Tech Lab: $100 Netbook Not Quite a Prescription for Success," *Boston Globe* (September 23, 2010), B1, B11.

62 See James Sterngold, "The Love Song of R. Buckminster Fuller," *New York Times*, Architecture, June 15, 2008, 26; and Howard P. Segal, "Getting Bucky Fuller Right: A Review Essay," *Technology and Culture*, 51 (October 2010), 1006–1009.

63 For an early analysis of just the Tofflers, and Naisbitt and Aburdene, see Segal, *Future Imperfect*, ch. 12. See the excellent analysis of these and other of the prophets I mention plus a few others I don't mention in Merav Katz-Kimchi, "The Rise of the Internet in America: Myths, Metaphors, and Discourses, 1993–2000," unpublished Ph.D. dissertation, Bar Illan University (Israel), 2008. Katz-Kimchi offers illuminating distinctions between older and contemporary technological utopians. Although the Tofflers began writing before contemporary information technology became commonplace, their later works do take those developments into account. Fuller's own later years and growing fame were tarnished by a failure to recognize that the world had changed, as evidenced by questions about his ready acceptance of the Pentagon's use of giant helicopters in the Vietnam War—a war he

didn't endorse—because they might later be employed to transport and deposit ever-larger geodesic domes elsewhere in the world, and for non-military purposes.

64 See Merritt Roe Smith and Leo Marx, eds., *Does Technology Drive History?* (Cambridge: MIT Press, 1994).

65 Roy Furchgott, "High-Tech Electronics Dressed Up to Look Old," *New York Times*, December 23, 2010, B6.

66 See the pertinent works cited in Chapter 3, note 5.

67 Enda Duffy, *The Speed Handbook: Velocity, Pleasure, Modernism* (Durham: Duke University Press, 2009), 5.

68 Duffy, *The Speed Handbook*, 4.

69 Duffy, *The Speed Handbook*, 11.

70 Duffy, *The Speed Handbook*, 13. Duffy further contrasts these two works with a 1915 avant-garde lithograph by Francis Picabia called "Portrait of a Young American Woman in a State of Nudity." The nude has become a spark plug critical to automobiles' speed. The tender female body is now "wholly technologized" and "floating upright in total blankness" (13). Unlike the painting or the photograph, there is no connection to any actual landscape or space. Also unlike them, the "for-ever" (14) printed on the object's side disconnects it from real time. The image could be from a sales catalog of auto parts and reflects the consumer culture that steadily made speed into just another commodity.

71 This critique of Orwell by Edward Cornish appeared in the *New York Times*, January 1, 1984. See also Cornish, *Futuring: The Exploration of the Future* (Bethesda: World Future Society, 2004), 281, where he correctly revises his views and states that *1984* was more of a satire than a scientific prediction. Yet in *Futuring* (150), Cornish implicitly criticizes Orwell for anticipating atomic wars that never occurred. On the contemporary challenge of prediction, see Richard A. Posner, "When it Comes to Disaster, Never Say Never," *Bangor Daily News*, June 14, 2010, A7.

72 See e-mail from Geoffrey M. Hodgson, August 16, 2009, http://www.feed-charity.org/user/image/queen2009b.

73 On General Electric's later corporate slogans, see Stuart Elliott, "G. E. to Spend $100 Million Promoting Itself as Innovative," *New York Times*, January 16, 2003, C1, C8.

74 Segal, *Future Imperfect*, 172.

75 See Segal, *Future Imperfect*, 173–177.

76 Michael Adas, *Machines as the Measure of Men: Science, Technology, and Ideologies of Western Dominance* (Ithaca: Cornell University Press,

1989). The classic discussion of Western attitudes toward the East—that is, "orientalism"—is Edward W. Said, *Orientalism* (New York: Random House, 1978).

77 See William E. Burns, *Knowledge and Power: Science in World History* (Upper Saddle River: Pearson, 2011), 15–16, ch. 4.

78 See Adas, *Machines as the Measure*. As various reviews of Adas have noted, he fails to recognize the role women played in measuring societies' qualities; fails to devote sufficient attention to medicine, geology, zoology, and botany; fails to acknowledge both anti-imperialists in Europe and North America and critics of technological and scientific advance on both continents; fails to concede that some colonial powers such as the Netherlands and Portugal were not technologically or scientifically advanced; and fails to distinguish the modest power of early-nineteenth-century machines as measures of human achievement from the greater power of late-nineteenth-century machines.

79 Sanjay Seth, review of Gyan Prakash, *Another Reason: Science and the Imagination of Modern India* (Princeton: Princeton University Press, 1999), in *Postcolonial Studies*, 4 (November 2001), 385; and Prakash, *Another Reason*, 230. As several other reviews of Prakash have noted, he ignores the Muslims, who constituted one-third of British India's population and who had governed India for seven centuries before the British.

80 Ainslie T. Embree, *Utopias in Conflict: Religion and Nationalism in Modern India* (Berkeley: University of California Press, 1990), xi, 12–14, 16–18, 129–132.

81 See, for example, Robert Weisman, "High-Tech Talent Flows Back to India," *Boston Globe*, August 8, 2005, A9; Associated Press, "Boom Time in India: Stock Market Surges as Foreign Investment Leaps in Retooled Economy," *Boston Globe*, September 1, 2005, E2; Fareed Zakaria, "The New India: Asia's Other Powerhouse Steps Out," *Newsweek*, 147 (March 6, 2006), 32–34; Vikas Bajaj, "Cultivating a Market in India: Wal-Mart Nurtures Suppliers as It Lays Plans for Expansion," *New York Times*, April 13, 2010, 1, 3; and Erika Kinetz, "India Builds $35 Tablet Computer," Associated Press, *Bangor Daily News*, July 24–25, 2010, C1, C6.

82 See Richard G. Fox, *Ghandian: Experiments With Culture* (Boston: Beacon, 1989) and Lyman Tower Sargent, *Utopianism: A Very Short Introduction* (New York: Oxford University Press, 2010), 72–74.

Chapter 7

The Resurgence of Utopianism
The Future is Now

It is certainly too early to write off the failures outlined here of scientific and technological utopias, ranging from nuclear power to systems analysis, as permanently doomed. They may be revived and may someday flourish again. For now, let us consider other avowedly utopian crusades.

The Major Contemporary Utopians and Their Basic Beliefs

Despite the influence of those dystopias, and in the face of enormous ambivalence over genetic engineering, there still exist influential pockets of scientific and technological utopianism. These include prominent contemporary forecasters such as Dertouzos, Gates, Naisbitt and Aburdene, Negroponte, Postrel, and the Tofflers. "High tech" characterizes these contemporary utopians and their visions. "High tech" is broadly conceived as virtually all post-World War II technological and scientific developments, but especially information technology—particularly computers, satellites, the Internet, and the World Wide Web—and biotechnology.[1] Without high tech, these utopian visions would be utterly unrealistic; with high tech, they seem quite possible.

Utopias: A Brief History from Ancient Writings to Virtual Communities,
First Edition. Howard P. Segal.
© 2012 Howard P. Segal. Published 2012 by Blackwell Publishing Ltd.

More generally, according to countless newspapers and magazines, television and radio programs, opinion surveys, and, not least, websites and Internet discussions, much of the world has for years now been experiencing "techno-mania" of an unprecedented intensity. Not only are endless high-tech advances all the rage, but those advances—especially computers, the Internet, the Web, cell phones, Skype, iPods, iPhones, and, most recently, iPads—are rapidly transforming the world, and generally for the better. By the time of his death in 2011, Apple Computer co-founder Steve Jobs had become the foremost promoter of "techno-mania," though hardly the only one.[2]

We are given to believe that Americans have never seen so much scientific and technological change in so short a time and have rarely been so optimistic about the future. Because of the contemporary "global economy"—also endlessly cited as supposedly unique—what happens in the United States eventually happens in the rest of the world too.

Divine Aspirations According to the historian David F. Noble in his *The Religion of Technology: The Divinity of Man and the Spirit of Invention* (1997), there are four research areas in which certain scientists, engineers, and others are currently engaged that would grant humans the sort of powers that rival those of God or the gods: nuclear weaponry, space flight, artificial intelligence, and, not surprisingly, genetic engineering. Moreover, these are being conducted with little or no regard for morality or social responsibility. All of these scientific and technological pioneers avowedly link their achievements with the recovery of human divinity, lost after Adam's fall. They wish to transcend earthly boundaries through space flight and to exercise God-like powers of artificial intelligence and genetic engineering. Safe, efficient, and comparatively cheap nuclear power stations are their envisioned principal energy sources.[3]

To these envisioned powers we must now add contemporary megaprojects intended to reduce, if not eliminate, global climate change. Historian James Fleming has analyzed this revived faith in "techno-fixes," which makes the "Star Wars" anti-missile defense system seem modest by comparison. There are historical precedents for such present-day geo-engineering schemes dating back to American experiments in the 1940s. For that matter, over a century earlier, in 1839, America's first meteorologist, James Espy, suggested lighting fires along the Appalachians to try to produce rainfall on the East coast. Present-day schemes would shade the planet by launching a solar shield into orbit or suck carbon dioxide out of the air with hundreds of thousands of giant artificial trees. These megaprojects, moreover, are hardly limited to the United States. In 2008, shortly before the Beijing Olympics began, China had 30,000 artillerists shooting chemicals at clouds of pollution to produce rainfall, and similar Chinese efforts have continued since. In all cases it is impossible to determine the consequences for the earth for either the actual or the imagined experiments.[4]

These scientific and technological elites, says Noble, are overwhelmingly male and aggressively masculine in their culture and values. For that matter, in the spirit of Victor Frankenstein, the ultimate dream of many of Noble's visionaries is the creation through genetic engineering of a womanless world—the culmination of centuries of mistreatment of women in general and of female engineers and scientists in particular.[5] Such schemes go beyond the eugenics crusades of many "reformers" in both Europe and America in the nineteenth and twentieth centuries that culminated in Nazism's quest for a pure Aryan race—but not, of course, one of men alone.

The Absence of Historical Context   History can therefore be ignored, so profoundly different will the future be from the past. History no longer matters.[6] One might, of course, suggest that our ahistorical contemporary visionaries have embraced a watered-down version of Francis Fukuyama's still controversial *The End of History and the Last Man* (1992), but there is no evidence of that kind of sophisticated argument in any of their writings.

Consequently, few if any of the high-tech zealots of our own day have ever considered the possibility that, far from being original, their crusades fit squarely within a rich Western tradition of scientific and technological utopianism. It is not likely that very many of them realize how old-fashioned they really are when celebrating science and technology's prospects for transforming the United States and, in due course, the world. Because of their historical ignorance, they can naïvely lay claim to originality when, in truth, they are not original at all. Take, for example, the remarkably similar paeans to the wonders of the Internet as a vehicle for promoting democracy that were expressed in the 1990s by then Speaker of the House Newt Gingrich and then Vice President Al Gore. Despite their sharp political differences on other matters, each waxed eloquent on the relationship of the Internet to the march of freedom. They both loved to describe the ongoing "information superhighway" they were helping to construct. *The Net Delusion: The Dark Side of Internet Freedom* (2011) by Evgeny Morozov destroys this fantasy with its analysis of how such autocratic regimes as China, Iran, and Venezuela use the Internet not merely to identify dissidents but also to promote their own official views as alternatives and, furthermore, cynically offer benign Western television programs and movies on the Internet to distract otherwise unhappy citizens.

Not only was the high-tech zealots' rhetoric naïve, it was also virtually identical to what thousands of American and European technological enthusiasts had said and believed in the nineteenth and early twentieth centuries about the liberating power of transportation and communications systems, from canals to railroads to clipper ships to steamboats, and from telegraphs to telephones to radios. They had repeatedly argued that the growth of science and technology and the growth of democracy were reciprocal—that each bolstered the other in the most banal but most common of ways. Thus, the United States, for a time the world's only democracy, welcomed skilled and creative foreigners who, regardless of socio-economic status, invented, built, and manufactured countless "labor-saving" machines. Usually from modest backgrounds, such persons could not find similar opportunities in elitist, class-ridden European countries. Simultaneously, the nation's transportation and communications systems promoted democracy: diverse sorts of passengers traveled together and diverse messages were delivered to diverse audiences. This was the start of the kind of "diversity" so many Americans debate—if not celebrate—today. (Of course, non-whites were ordinarily excluded from this mixing, while any variety of accommodations separated the wealthier passengers from the less well-off and frequently separated men and women.) Meanwhile, the upbeat content of messages and programs marking the opening or expansion of those transportation and communications systems was viewed as reinforcing the techno-logy–democracy ties.[7]

Equally significantly, as historian Ann Blair has detailed in her pathbreaking *Too Much to Know: Managing Scholarly Information Before the Modern Age* (2010), the assumption that "information overload" is a purely late-twentieth- and twenty-first-century challenge is historical nonsense. Once Gutenberg's fifteenth-cen-tury invention of the printing press became a fact of European life, at least for the educated elite, thousands of books became available for reading and possible purchase, and the initial rejoicing at such abundant intellectual riches eventually turned to despair. Blair quotes Erasmus, the eminent humanist of the early sixteenth century, asking whether there is "anywhere on earth exempt from these swarms of new books"? Practical solutions included pioneer-ing public libraries, bibliographies of supposedly all books, books advising on note-taking, outlines and alphabetical indexes as substitutes for reading whole books, larger encyclopedias than ever before for the same purpose, and even "slips of paper for cutting and pasting information from manuscripts and printed matter—a technique that, centuries later, would become essential to modern word processing."[8]

No less important was the absence from the thoughts of the visionaries discussed by Noble, the promoters of the dot-com "revolution," and the political opportunists such as Gingrich and Gore of any sense that the scientific and technological achieve-ments of the twentieth century invariably brought mixed bles-sings: whether automobiles or airplanes or nuclear power plants or, not least, moon landings. Far from so-called "techno-mania" being unprecedented in the 1990s and 2000s, the historical record demonstrates that Americans today are far more ambivalent about the relationship between science and technology and progress than ever before, notwithstanding Nye's significant findings on skepticism about scientific and technological "progress" early in American history.

A 1995 Maine Humanities Council video entitled "Modern Times in Maine and America, 1890–1930" brings this out in its interviews with several elderly Mainers. They recalled how the introduction of cars for middle-class consumers, of "talking pictures," of radios, and of comparatively tall buildings in Maine's cities profoundly altered their sense of space and time, also describing how they felt ever more in tune with more populated parts of the nation and the world. They knew that America was changing, and they felt that no less intensely than do ordinary citizens in our day. But they also lamented the loss of traditional personal contacts and of smaller-scale living and working arrangements.

Playing on this ambivalence, in 2009 the makers of the popular American cereal Post Shredded Wheat promoted its basically unchanged product in print ads proclaiming "Beware of New: Being new is not always a good thing." The ads mentioned the familiar theme of there often being less rather than more time available in contemporary workplaces, notwithstanding the various technologies that were supposed to bring about more free time. By contrast, Post Shredded Wheat has apparently remained largely the same since its origins in 1892.[9]

One small but revealing confirmation of this ahistorical or antihistorical trend is the increasing claim of writers on various topics—from history to sports—that one particular year or sports event transformed the nation or perhaps the world. True, one purpose here is to promote books. But the remarkable arrogance in setting up a single year or event bespeaks that fundamental resistance to making serious comparisons with the past. Recent books include Mark Bowden's *The Best Game Ever: Giants vs. Colts, 1958, and the Birth of the Modern NFL* (National Football League); Howard Bryant's *The Last Hero: A Life of Henry Aaron*; David Maraniss' *Rome 1960: The Olympics that Changed the World*; and, boldest of all, Fred Kaplan's *1959: The Year that Changed Everything*. Or, as a *Boston Globe* columnist wrote in 2005, "This has to be the Golden Age of Apocalyptic Presentiments. The death of newspapers. The death of glaciers. An *Atlantic Monthly* writer recently speculated on the death of death" because of healthy habits.[10]

Ironically, a genuine and profound change in the common conceptualization of technology has not been sufficiently appreciated. Whereas throughout most of the twentieth century science and technology were commonly conceived as the solution to widely acknowledged large-scale problems such as poverty, education, irrigation, and water and electrical power, in recent decades science and technology have increasingly come to be viewed as the fulfillment on a small scale of individual needs and desires, ranging from birth control pills to online college degrees to virtual travel to cyberspace relationships. High tech enhances individual sanctity and provides choices in an ever more digitized, programmable world. If one major aspect of high tech is that machines tend to shrink exactly as their power increases—thereby reversing the tradition of bigger being more powerful—another major aspect is the consumer mentality that asks what a specific item will do for oneself rather than for society. Granted, America's consumer culture can be traced back to at least the late nineteenth century,[11] but its pervasiveness and power have expanded along with high tech. Here, then, is a complete reversal of President John F. Kennedy's famous 1961 inaugural address, asking not what one's country could do for you but what you could do for your country. Victor Frankenstein would certainly embrace this contemporary ethos. Insofar as scientific and technical experts are relied upon, it is a matter of consumers' demands and expectations, not their blind trust. The ramifications for utopianism are extraordinary attention to material goods and to high-tech versions of "the good life."[12]

For example, Hewlett-Packard has for decades now been a major player in Silicon Valley and elsewhere. Its principal tagline for print, television, and online advertisements was for a long time "Everything is Possible," but was later changed to "The Future is Here and It Feels Great. It's Called the Touchsmart PC." What could be clearer? Similarly, the tagline for most Microsoft advertisements in the same venues is "Your potential. Our passion." And that for Time Warner Cable advertisements is "The

Power of You." There are no qualifications for any of these campaigns.

Social Media: Utopia at One's Fingertips

"Social media" are cutting-edge communications devices such as cell phones, iPads, iPods, YouTube, Facebook, text messaging, Twitter, and Wikipedia, the online encyclopedia open to and editable by all. Both text messages and Twitter are limited to 140 characters and usually include abbreviations and other "revisions" of whatever languages are being used.

The growth of social media in the past few years has been remarkable. At the outset, the principal question was "What are you doing?" This reflected the sheer thrill of instant contact and the ability to know what one's family and friends were up to without the relative intrusiveness of cell phones. Once texting, Twitter, YouTube, and Facebook had taken hold around the globe, they became increasingly valuable sources of serious information for news organizations, for businesses, and for governments. In 2010 Facebook surpassed Google as the United States' most visited website, with 8.9 percent of all American website visits versus Google's 7.2 percent. Facebook had reached more than 500 million users.[13] Not surprisingly, perhaps, *Time* magazine's 2010/2011 Person of the Year was Facebook's founder, Mark Zuckerberg.

Now, the new question was "What's happening?" Despite their respective drawbacks, social media continue to promote utopian expectations of instant and ever growing communities, including Wikipedia's volunteer communities. Not just consumers but corporate executives themselves seek vastly expanded social interactions for their devices and enterprises. In almost all cases one finds a shallow utopian faith in the processes of connecting and sharing as supposed means to individual and collective fulfillment with minimal regard for the downsides suggested above. As Deborah Rogers has observed, "social websites maintain their optimism, even when the party's over. You may be dead, but ... Facebook allows us to continue our relationships with the deceased." It is extremely hard to delete one's own account entirely. Revealingly, those who believe things have gone too far have formed their own dissenting Facebook and other online sites. Meanwhile, Wikipedia is tightening its standards of accuracy even while being challenged by some in the East for adhering to biased Western means of verifying facts.[14]

The darker sides of social media are ever more prevalent. Cell phone use and texting while driving are by now painfully familiar as causes of many auto accidents. So, too, are the dystopian invasions of privacy, from sending provocative photos that damage reputations to providing inaccurate and bigoted information for Wikipedia entries. Yet the ability to generate immediate information and photos of, say, auto and other accidents and of political protests cannot be ignored. Meanwhile, prominent psychologist Sherry Turkle's *Alone Together: Why We Expect More from Technology and Less from Each Other* (2011) paints a predominantly negative portrait of social media as leading many of us away from the solitude and intimacy that, she claims, we actually seek.

No less importantly, the communications company Skype has also become exceedingly popular as a generally free (as of 2011) means of consumers using computers as telephones to communicate across long distances. "Skype me" is now a favorite phrase. The company began in 2003 as an online alternative to conventional telephone companies, with their usually high rates.[15]

Recent and Contemporary Utopian Communities

Before we look at cyberspace communities, it is important to recognize the persistence of "conventional" utopian communities into the late-twentieth- and early-twenty-first centuries. Recall that, despite the considerable number of Shaker communities and the enormous sales of *Looking Backward*, both expressions of utopianism proved unable to translate their models of utopian society into vehicles for widespread social change. By contrast, more recent communities (those of the 1960s and 1970s) functioned at least as attempted escapes from the "real world." Many of these later utopian communities, moreover, have been much more critical of the science and technology of their own day than were their predecessors. Often, though, this hostility toward science and technology was quite selective, as exemplified by the cave in Wales inhabited for a while by some of actress Elizabeth Taylor's children. Inside their supposedly "primitive" home was the then latest in music recording and performance equipment. These modern cave dwellers apparently saw no contradiction between their wanting to escape urban industrial life and the cutting-edge technology they placed inside their "simpler" life residence.

More interesting, but of no longer duration, was Drop City, a community established in the hills of southern Colorado in the late 1960s and inspired by the work of R. Buckminster Fuller. Singled out by the media as "exemplary" of the contemporary counterculture, Drop City became known for its dome style of architecture. Drop City integrated Fuller's principles and methods with low-cost local materials such as "sheet metal hacked off of junked car roofs" and lumber scraps. The name derived from the founders having literally dropped objects from the roof of a Lawrence, Kansas, loft onto the street below. This was their brand of conceptual artwork. Whereas, despite these noisy origins, the four original settlers—all university students interested in especially art and film—wanted a cheap, quiet, and sustainable place in which to pursue their own interests, the media's relentless coverage and its search for weirdness among the inhabitants prompted those four to depart in 1968, but attracted others. However, the newcomers were usually transient hippies, and Drop City was eventually vacated. As of 2011, most of the property has been developed commercially. The last of the "iconic domes" was removed in the late 1990s.[16]

Fuller was a notable, if only partial, exception to that commonplace gap in American history between those who write seriously and significantly about utopia and those who attempt to build it. True, Fuller did not establish actual communities. But he invented enough actual components of potential communities to distinguish himself from virtually all other American utopians: his Dymaxion Car, Dymaxion House, Dymaxion Bathroom, Dymaxion Air-Ocean Map, and of course his geodesic dome. In all, Fuller received patents for twenty-eight inventions, a remarkable achievement in itself. Moreover, Fuller proposed land-based cities covered by geodesic domes, tetrahedronal cities floating on the sea, and cloud-structure spheres floating in air. Fuller was a *de facto* architect long before he got a license, and that only an honorary one, in his late sixties.[17]

Since many prior communitarians had been no more specific in their plans than was Fuller, his legitimate place in the story of utopia is not undermined simply because he provided a mere scaffolding rather than detailed blueprints. In fact, by designing artifacts that could be moved and replicated, Fuller readily met a principal challenge facing most earlier (and later) communitarians: how to promote one's vision beyond its base camp, so to speak. Beside the Shakers, few other utopian communities created even a second site.

Outside the United States and Europe, utopian communities persist, as they have for centuries—as with, for instance, Buddhist monasteries and their Hindu equivalents in China, India, Japan, and Southeast Asia. There are also various secular utopian communities in these nations and regions, such as those influenced in Japan by both Robert Owen and the Garden City movement. Some of these Asian communities have also sprung up in the West and have often been characterized, whether positively or negatively, as cults—most famously the Hare Krishnas, officially known as the International Society for Krishna Consciousness. Their dancing and chanting in colorful garb in cities have become familiar sights.[18]

Israeli Kibbutzim   Paradoxically, high tech has at once helped to save and helped to undermine the small Israeli communal societies called the kibbutzim. The word is Hebrew and means "group" or "gathering." Originating in 1910, when the land was under British rule, the early kibbutzim were both predominantly agricultural and avowedly socialist. They were established by European Jews seeking alternatives to overcrowded industrial cities that often restricted Jews' geographical and occupational mobility. Most early kibbutzim disavowed traditional family structures as "bourgeois" and developed communal childrearing practices. Yet the socialist rhetoric of gender equality rarely trickled down to the actual allocations of political power and of domestic responsibilities. Decades before the establishment of Israel in 1948, most kibbutz members dreamed of an eventual Jewish state that would include their land.[19]

The kibbutzim long concentrated on draining swamps, on transforming deserts into fertile farmland, and on introducing new crops and modern methods of cattle and poultry breeding. Yet achieving these goals eventually required the development of agricultural machinery, the popularity of which led to the establishment of many small businesses. Later came other industrial enterprises—for example, small firms with assembly lines for making laminated windshields for automobiles—and, in recent decades, various high-tech enterprises in these still largely rural sites. Only about thirty percent of total kibbutz production is presently agricultural; the rest is industrial. Still, the kibbutzim grow forty percent of Israel's agricultural produce as well as providing ten percent of its industrial output and seven percent of its exports.

Kibbutz membership ranges from fewer than a hundred to more than a thousand. But growing numbers live in towns and cities and commute to and from their work on the kibbutz (likewise, numerous other members work outside the kibbutz and commute daily from and to their kibbutz residences). Today there are nearly three hundred kibbutzim scattered throughout Israel and integrated with one another to varying degrees economically, politically, and ideologically. Still, the kibbutzim have traditionally seen themselves not as mere escapist retreats from urban civilization but as utopian alternatives that should be emulated throughout Israel. If the kibbutzim have never represented more than seven percent of the Israeli population and have usually constituted less than two percent (as currently), or about 120,000 people presently, that small percentage has routinely "played a role in the nation's life out of all proportion to their numbers," whether in politics or in culture or, not least, in the military.[20] This leadership role has sometimes created resentment on the part of other Israelis.

Nevertheless, the overall future of Israel's kibbutzim is quite uncertain. The biggest challenge derives from the ongoing transformation of the overall Israeli economy from predominantly socialist to predominantly capitalist and the inevitable reduction, in the once-avowedly-socialist kibbutzim, of the belief in and practice of shared property and wealth, the core of their utopian vision. The very success of small kibbutzim industries, both high-tech and more traditional, has in many cases led to a competitive free-market capitalist spirit. This has manifested itself in, among other ways, ending financial equality among members (including paying them different wages), allowing them to own private property; outsourcing legal matters beyond the scope of most Israeli lawyers to American law firms; outsourcing tracts of land to private developers for various purposes, including shopping malls; and changing guesthouses where visitors once worked alongside regular kibbutz members into conventional hotels where they can instead relax and enjoy the surroundings. Ironically, a typical dilemma is whether to allow for the purchase of cars by individual members at times of their own choosing, where in the past all cars were communally owned and were bought only with communal approval. Some defenders of change contend that "many high-tech industries thrive on teamwork."[21] They believe that competition can enhance rather than undermine cooperation in the capitalist workplace. Such beliefs have not been common-place aspects of utopian visions.[22]

Cyberspace Communities   When virtual communities began in the mid-1990s, "chats" with others various distances away were limited in scope and content. There was only modest opportunity to develop a so-called "second life" (as most explicitly manifested in the simulation of that name) online. But that steadily changed, and ongoing contemporary virtual communities have been around for years, with members, often from throughout the world, having become close friends—regardless of whether they have ever actually met. As an ironic result, the virtual cyberspace communities that have come about through the Internet and the Web face many of the same obstacles as their "real world" pre-decessors—their utopian rhetoric notwithstanding. If, on the one hand, the sheer numbers of cyberspace communities and com-munitarians likely dwarf the number of utopians of any prior period, on the other hand the general absence of face-to-face meetings makes the establishment of long-lasting cyberspace communities more challenging than for their "grounded" predecessors. Although it is too early to know for sure, it might turn out to be easier to effect lasting relationships between individuals online than to create less intimate but obviously larger communities based on political or religious or cultural or other commonalities. It is increasingly common for persons who seek companionship online to try to live together and, in many cases, ultimately to marry. The traditional reasons for drawing people together to live in utopian communities—a charismatic leader, for example, or an idyllic setting, or a social experiment like Shaker celibacy or Oneida open marriage—might well fail in virtual worlds. Moreover, without denying the countless positive intellectual, social, political, and personal connections that *have* been brought about in cyberspace, the pervasive anxieties over psychological and intellectual seduction by electronic communications at the cost of traditional social interactions also cannot be ignored.[23]

For philosopher Hubert Dreyfus, among others, the prospect of a predominantly online life is a dismal one. His position is an extreme one, but his passionate critique is worth summarizing: "we will largely lose our sense of relevance, our ability to acquire skills, our sense of resistant reality, our ability to make maximally meaningful commitments, and the embodied moods that give life serious meaning."[24] Although Dreyfus collapses the mere use of the Internet in daily life with a total immersion in it at the expense of ordinary existence, this dystopian scenario is useful to ponder. The most supposedly successful cyberspace community would clearly not meet with his approval.

The Star Trek Empire: Science Fiction Becomes Less Escapist

Historically, as noted, utopias have differed from science fiction in their basic concern for changing rather than abandoning or ignoring non-utopian communities and societies, where science fiction has consisted primarily of escapist fantasies about exploration to distant lands or below the earth or in outer space. In recent decades, though, as also noted, science fiction has become ever more engaged with the "real world" it would supposedly either transform or escape.

This growth of science fiction in the United States and elsewhere as a serious intellectual phenomenon can be attributed in considerable part to the remarkable popularity of *Star Trek*, an American science fiction entertainment series that has become a most lucrative and multi-faceted media franchise. *Star Trek* was created by Gene Roddenberry and originated as a 1966 television series that was dropped after three seasons with modest viewership. Its final episode of the third season was aired only weeks before the first moon landing. Passionate fan enthusiasm, however, eventually brought about its revival and renewal in other forms: a total of six television series comprising 726 episodes; eleven feature films; multiple computer and video games; hundreds of spin-off novels; untold video productions; a cookbook; and, as the supreme confirmations of having arrived, two year-long exhibits at the Smithsonian's National Air and Space Museum in Washington, DC (the nation's most popular museum) in 1992 and in 1997–1998, and a themed attraction in Las Vegas in 1998. No less importantly, *Star Trek* has become a cult—albeit generally harmless—with countless fans of, by now, varying ages, who dress up for openings of various productions and attend countless conventions. Several terms from *Star Trek* have become part of pop culture: "Beam me up," "Warp factor 10," "Set phasers on stun," and "I canna change the laws of physics, Cap'n."[25]

Apart from its remarkable number of manifestations, *Star Trek* is significant because of its utopian message of the nature of transformed humanity and a vastly enlarged universe of which they are now an integral part. For public relations purposes, Roddenberry marketed his proposal as an otherwise conventional Western, but one set in outer space. In truth, he patterned it after Jonathan Swift's *Gulliver's Travels*, with each episode appearing as both an intriguing suspense story and a morality tale. Once *Star Trek* had achieved lasting popularity, his implicit purpose became explicit, and without apology. He wanted his epitaph to be "He loved humanity"—not exactly profound, but ultimately ideal for pop culture audiences over the years.

In the *Star Trek* cosmos humans developed "warp drive," or a "faster-than-light mode of space travel following a nuclear war and a post-apocalyptic period in the mid-twenty-first century." This technological achievement was noticed by the Vulcans, aliens more advanced than earthlings who then made contact with their earthly inferiors. The Vulcans helped humans to improve themselves by overcoming many earthly weaknesses and bad habits and then creating a "quasi-utopian society" in which humans rejected material wealth as the principal measure of the good life and substituted exploration and knowledge. Humans later joined the Vulcans and other "sentient species of the galaxy" to form the United Federation of Planets. Humans and aliens serve in the Federation's "Starfleet" and deal with challenges that, as per Roddenberry's plan, reflect real-world earthly dilemmas of his day and later, the specifics changing with the years. Even a debate as to whether an android could be a sentient being or a discussion about the seemingly bizarre mating rituals of aliens reflected an embrace of what would later be termed "diversity" and acceptance of differences between humans. In Roddenberry's 1960s formulation, the issues being faced were racial, gender, religious, and class conflicts; imperialism; and war and peace.[26]

Star Trek's *Enterprise* (no pun intended—the name of the spaceship) also helped to change the image of "geeks" from completely negative to ever more positive. If those who dress up as Trekkies might still seem weird, the respect accorded to dot-com innovators—especially those who, as epitomized by Bill Gates and the late Steve Jobs, became extremely wealthy—has generated unprecedented respect, and sometimes outright envy, from those who are not as gifted in science, engineering, mathematics, and business. Meanwhile, the 1984 movie *Revenge of the Nerds*, without glamorizing either the term or the almost cartoonishly nerdy characters, started a trend toward greater respect and affection. The freshman college nerds portrayed in the movie enjoyed a modest eventual triumph against their athletic tormentors.[27]

Recall popular movies about inventors and scientists screwing up: for example, *The Nutty Professor* (remake of 1963 original),

Ghost Busters (1984), *The Mosquito Coast* (1986), *Honey, I Shrunk the Kids* (1989), *Honey, I Blew Up the Kid* (1992), and *Flubber* (1997; remake of 1961's *The Absent-Minded Professor*). But these no longer represent mainstream opinion of such persons. Nowadays dreams of scientific and technological utopias rest on the talents of geeks and nerds.

Where other science fiction films, including the very popular *Star Wars* films, equaled or surpassed *Star Trek* in terms of glitzy settings and visual effects, *Star Trek* surpassed them all in its messages and its values. Several of its fictional scientific advances, moreover, have been praised by physicist Stephen Hawking, Apple Computer co-founder Stephen Wozniak, and Pulitzer Prize fiction winner Michael Chabon. As Hawking put it in a 1995 foreword to Lawrence Krauss' *The Physics of Star Trek*, "There is a two-way trade between science fiction and fiction. Science fiction suggests ideas that scientists incorporate into their theories, but sometimes science turns up notions that are stranger than any science fiction. Black holes are an example." Regarding the fantasy of faster-than-light space travel, Hawking contends that "Einstein's general theory of relativity allows the possibility for a way around this difficulty: one might be able to warp spacetime and create a shortcut between the places one wanted to visit." Not much research has been conducted in this area, but the concept, he concludes, "might be within our capabilities in the future."[28]

By contrast, *Star Trek*'s other most popular scientific and technological development, the "transporter," is characterized by Krauss as beyond the pale. The "transporter" was devised by Roddenberry to allow the *Enterprise*'s crew to land on the surface of different planets without having to land the spaceship itself. Mundane budgetary considerations for the weekly television show precluded that. Instead, the crew used what became the show's most famous phrase, "Beam me up," to get the transporter operating. As portrayed in the *Star Trek* television programs and movies, the transporter locks on a target, scans the image to be transported, "dematerializes" it, puts it in a "pattern buffer" for some time, and finally "transmits the 'matter stream' in an 'annular confinement beam' to its destination." "The matter along with the information" is sent out. As Krauss laments,

Building a transporter would require us to heat up matter to a temperature a million times the temperature at the center of the Sun, expend more energy in a single machine than all of humanity presently uses, build telescopes larger than the size of the Earth, improve present computers by a factor of 1000 billion billion, and avoid the laws of quantum mechanics.[29]

According to a 2008 article in *Discovery Channel Magazine*, phenomena such as *Star Trek*'s vanishing spaceships, faster-than-light travel, and dematerialized transport were mere dreams when the original series aired but might yet come about. Others, however, have criticized *Star Trek* for making scientific blunders akin to those found in other science fiction television shows and movies over the years. Hence the literal meaning, I might add, of "science fiction." Still others have noted (as mentioned above) that advances such as the transporter came about because the original series' modest budget precluded providing expensive views of spaceships landing on planets.[30] I always enjoyed the fact that none of the *Star Trek* vehicles had seatbelts, thereby routinely leading to characters falling out of their seats in various action scenes.

Edutopia: George Lucas and Others

Given the critical role of education in various forms in so many visionary schemes, especially those based on scientific and technological advances, it should not be surprising that education at all levels has been embraced by high-tech proponents. Nor should it be shocking that the same faith (blind or not) in computerized and related machinery and gadgetry that pervades, as detailed, so many other sectors pervades this one too. Nor should be a revelation that such faith is hardly new. Nevertheless, there is little memory of the generally unsuccessful "teaching machines" that were widely promoted in the 1960s and 1970s as panaceas for educational ills. True, the world has come a very long way from those days of primitive word processors and the absence of personal computers, but the visionary rhetoric remains intact at present amid the familiar high-tech devices "virtually" embedded in our daily lives and, as detailed above, allegedly transforming our world.[31]

K-12 Edutopia I borrow the term "Edutopia" from the project established by filmmaker George Lucas in 1991. It is not an accident that Lucas is most famous for the *Star Wars* fantasy films, though that fact hardly reduces his educational enterprises to sheer fantasy. Instead, it formally places them in the context of serious-minded visions and visionaries. Formally called the George Lucas Educational Foundation, the project avowedly seeks to address the basic issue of alleged unprecedented change under "Our Vision":

> Kids today—no previous generation has experienced anything like the current pace of transformational societal change. Yet . . . our system of education has been frustratingly slow to adapt . . . . Our vision is of a new world of learning. A place where kids and parents, teachers and administrators, policy makers and the people they serve, all are empowered to change education for the better. A place where schools have access to the same invaluable technology as businesses and universities—where innovation is the rule, not the exception. A place where children become lifelong learners and develop the technical, cultural, and interpersonal skills to succeed in the twenty-first century. A place of inspiration, aspiration, and an urgent belief that improving education improves the world we live in. We call this place Edutopia. And we provide not just the vision for this new world of learning but also the leading-edge interactive tools and resources to help make it a reality.[32]

Through its website Edutopia.org, its *Edutopia* magazine, and its Edutopia videos, the Foundation seeks to provide the "best practices" of educational pioneers and the specific recommendations on how to bring them about elsewhere. "Traditional learning can be extremely isolating," we are told, while "the curriculum is often abstract and not relevant to real life." Meanwhile, many schools are isolated from their surrounding communities. The Foundation thereby emphasizes "project learning, student teams working cooperatively, children connecting with passionate experts, and broader forms of assessment." Cutting-edge digital multimedia and telecommunications are naturally heavily utilized.[33]

Concerning the teaching of science and math, one finds a 2009 article "On Kids Talk Tech" that includes short elaborations on these topics: "visualizing chemistry"; "animating geography"; and "testing [science] for the fun of it." For teaching math, one finds "taxing brain teasers"; "disposable fun"; "counting on lego"; "all the angles"; and a "blast off" computer game. All are touted as parts of an overall explicitly "transformative experience."[34]

The Foundation is not limited to science, mathematics, and technical subjects. It investigates and reports on success stories in all areas of study, including the arts, languages, and social studies. Every September the website and the magazine make predictions for the school year ahead. Recent ones include "Chinese will be the new French"; "Online learning for students and teachers will grow exponentially"; and "Increasing access to digital content will lead to an exponential growth in school-based online communities on the MySpace/YouTube model."[35]

Similar in utopian expectations is the DaVinci Institute, which describes itself as a non-profit "futurist think tank based in the fertile proving grounds of Colorado." The Institute is "a community of revolutionary thinkers and innovators intent on unlocking your future, one idea, one invention, one business at a time. We have seen the future and it is truly a magical place." Their Executive Director and Senior Futurist, Tom Frey, bills himself as "Google's top rated futurist speaker," among other honors recognizing his alleged brilliance. As Colby College's Karen Kusiak characterizes him, he "envisions a Utopian world in which course learning is completed online and the act of learning itself is transformed by participative courseware builders."[36]

According to Frey, fewer than fifty thousand different courses will suffice to cover all conceivable topics. Teaching and learning modules will be designed by "experts" like himself more than by conventional educators who can't think outside the proverbial box. "Classroom-centric" education will decline as education becomes ever more a matter of individuals' convenience of time and place. This educational revolution of sorts should begin very soon.

A third educational project with similarly utopian expectations is T. H. E. Smart Classroom, which provides endless updates on

K-12 hardware and software alike. One has access to "everything it takes to use technology effectively in a school setting." This ranges from interactive projectors to electronic whiteboards to smart phones to 3D glasses to robots. The subtext is clearly that schools without these devices are, in effect, "dumb."[37]

T. H. E. recently put on its website a study commissioned by Cisco Systems and entitled "Technology in Schools: What the Research Says." It offers a mixed record some three decades after computers were first put into school classrooms. "The reality is that advocates have *over-promised* the ability of education to extract a learning return on technology investments in schools." The principal "miscalculation" was not grasping the elementary fact that much more is required beyond "the mere introduction of technology with software and web resources aligned with the curriculum." It requires "the triangulation of content, sound principles of learning, and high-quality teaching," followed by "assessment and accountability." Patience is also an often-overlooked virtue, for false expectations of prompt changes have been pervasive and self-defeating. Still, the research reveals that "technology does provide a small, but significant, increase in learning when implemented with fidelity."[38]

A fourth and final educational project with a utopian thrust is the "virtual school," of which twenty-five states now boast at least one. These schools allow their students to take nearly all of their classes online either at home or in local coffeehouses or in other non-school facilities. They cater to students who are bored in conventional schools or who have disciplinary problems or health issues that make it hard for them to attend regular schools. Most virtual schools have established partnerships with private companies such as K12 Inc. of Virginia. How much students in these settings might lose in terms of social skills usually acquired in traditional schools and classrooms remains to be seen.[39]

Higher Education's Edutopia   If Edutopia and Frey's scenario are primarily designed for K-12 students, teachers, parents, administrators, and community and business leaders, its basic themes are repeated in efforts designed for collegiate education. Curiously, in many contemporary discussions about the future of science and technology in higher education one would never guess that technological determinism and the technological imperative, along with scientific and technological utopianism, are no longer gospel everywhere. Like Noble's and Fleming's scientific and technological elites in space flight, nuclear weapons, artificial intelligence, genetic engineering, and geo-engineering, many educational leaders are locked into old-fashioned bedrock beliefs about science and technology allegedly shaping the modern world, shaping it without question, and shaping it only for the better.

One of my favorite examples is a 1998 speech by James J. Stukel, then president of the multi-campus University of Illinois, entitled "The Future of Land Grant Universities" but relevant to public (and, to a lesser extent, private) universities in general. Stukel was a long-time engineering professor at that institution before moving into administration. He served as president from 1995 to 2005.

In the tradition of Alvin Toffler, Stukel invokes the metaphor of the wave in describing high tech. The wave of the future is the technological imperative taken to an extreme, for one either rides it out and, to this extent, controls one's destiny, or else drowns. There is no middle ground. It is the application of Fuller's *Utopia or Oblivion*. As Stukel puts it, "Our challenge is to act now so that we can control the changes the new technology will [inevitably] make in our institutions instead of allowing them to overwhelm us and cause changes we cannot control"—as if educational leaders actually had much control over the technologically driven changes he otherwise lauds. "To use a nautical analogy," Stukel continues, "I see technology and change as a tidal wave. It is only a very small wave right now"—though the rest of his speech would suggest a much bigger wave even today.[40]

Mainstream higher education, Stukel argues, must master the Internet, under which he includes "telecommunications and computers." If mainstream higher education can do that, a wonderful world awaits us, from the assembly and reconfiguration of "virtual research teams" in endless partnerships with business and industry to the merger of "on-line extension information holdings across the country … into a national website" that will transform cooperative extension and other interactions between higher education and the public. Indeed, according to President Stukel, higher education's research in general will within a decade be conducted almost entirely "in this virtual environment, too. Think of that. When you have a problem, no longer will you phone your local university or your local cooperative extension service." Instead, a five-hundred-dollar desktop computer "will give you access to the most advanced computing and database environment in the world."[41]

Any possible ambivalence about contemporary scientific and technological developments is replaced by a reassurance that higher education will not merely survive but flourish. Any opportunity for providing a more mature middle ground is thereby lost. Instead, one finds here, as elsewhere in education circles, a reassurance reminiscent of the American style of "positive thinking" associated with Norman Vincent Peale above all.

Stukel's vision of high-tech research and cooperative enterprises in higher education complements the more familiar scenarios for televised and computerized distance learning, Web-based online instruction, and full-fledged degrees increasingly being provided by for-profit as well as non-profit institutions. Certainly it makes sense for students who, for whatever reasons, cannot come to a conventional campus to take televised courses at local outreach centers or other nearby facilities. Similarly, wholly online courses, including those taken whenever one wishes, offer opportunities for students with either limited daily learning time or long commuting distances or both. The real issue, of course, is the difference, if any, between distance and in-person instruction, interaction, and learning.

If one is to believe some of the foremost advocates of these high-tech methods, it makes no difference at all. Take, for example, the University of Maine System's George Connick, founding president of the Educational Network of Maine, which was envisioned as the System's electronic campus. Writing in 1994 about the glorious future awaiting Maine's distance learners and their teachers, Connick cited "a major study" in *The American Journal of Distance Education* that revealed "no essential difference in the quality of learning between distance education and more traditional approaches." He added that additional unspecified studies in Maine "have echoed these findings."[42]

Curiously, Connick's enterprise, which focused on interactive television (ITV) spread among over one hundred locations throughout the fairly rural state, was outdated from the outset. When I myself taught a history of technology course through Connick's ITV system, I quickly recognized that the students in my campus classroom had a far better learning environment than those at the "remote" sites. True, the latter students did not have to travel far from either home or work for classes and, if they could not make classes, had easy access to videotapes of each. Whereas, however, they could see me on their television monitors, I never saw them but only heard their voices. And they needed to dial the campus classroom technical assistant when they wished to ask or answer a question or contribute to class discussion, which, not surprisingly, was carried on much more easily with the students in front of me, whom I could see and whose intellectual and facial responses I could immediately take account of as I taught. I tried to provide those outside campus with equal time, but I knew that these students had been shortchanged intellectually whether or not they themselves felt that the savings of time and money were worth it. Others who have also taught ITV courses have repeatedly confirmed similar experiences.

I have subsequently taught in several online and Web-based courses and have similar concerns. If there are no time restrictions as to when students can respond to assignments, to comments on their responses, and to other students' responses to those responses, something is still lost in the transmission—above all, not getting to know any of the students most of the time save in cyberspace.

The denial of these differing educational experiences by Connick and other high-tech educational promoters is frankly disturbing. Significantly, when asked in a 1995 newspaper interview whether he would have wanted "degree by TV" for his own children, Connick revealingly replied that "I would have advised them that the campus experience is wonderful and I would recommend that." He added that "it offers more—especially culturally and socially—than an 'electronic campus' could."[43] Who could disagree?

Equally puzzling is the apparent limited concern with the future of traditional campuses on the part of those with, one presumes, a vested interest in keeping them flourishing, such as President Stukel. Why would most students—and, for that matter, many faculty and their staff—need to be physically present in conventional offices and classrooms if ever more learning, examination, writing, and discussion (as well as research) takes place off campus and online—and with the enthusiastic support of campus leaders? It is one thing for wholly commercial enterprises such as the University of Phoenix to encourage this, but quite another for university presidents and other educational leaders to do so. Is not the logic of Stukel's utopian vision the depopulation of the University of Illinois?

In his 1998 speech Stukel goes on to suggest that, if every American citizen could have the five-hundred-dollar desktop computer and software he describes, "racial, ethnic, and gender conflicts could be at least eased" because everyone would then have direct access to higher education.[44] At one level, this makes good sense. Equality of opportunity is a fundamental American value. But the questionable subtext is the increasingly common mis-equation of sheer access to information with the acquisition of genuine knowledge. For example, in 2010 the chairman of the Federal Communications Commission lamented that the "United States is Falling Behind in Digital Literacy." To him, the solution was painfully obvious: ever greater broadband Internet access. Yet a 2011 news story conceded that "Tests Reveal Most American Students Don't Know Much About US History." Expanded broadband and Internet access was not the panacea here. Far from it![45] Not surprisingly, one of the ways in which so many ordinary Americans and others have become disenchanted with high-tech utopianism is their sense of being overwhelmed with far more information than they can possibly digest, much less apply to their daily lives. The best search engines do not solve this problem.

Interestingly, a recent print advertisement for Thomson Reuters claiming to be "the world's leading source of intelligent information" harks on this point, whereas high-tech promotions generally ignore it. The theme is "Knowledge to Act," but with "The End of Think" being quickly replaced by "The Beginning of Know." "Markets are watching," the advertisement continues. "Your board is waiting. It's no time for 'think.'" The gap between accessing data and making decisions is thereby bridged rather than ignored. That is something that Stukel and thousands of other high-tech promoters might someday appreciate.[46] Moreover, Stukel's proposal, however well intentioned, is reminiscent of those so-called "techno-fixes" that were common in the 1960s and 1970s as government and corporate technocrats struggled to solve the problems of poverty, crime, race riots, and other affronts to affluent America.

A related subtext of Stukel's—and Connick's—visions is that education today is as fundamentally technical a process as it is an intellectual one and that technical experts are therefore at least as important as traditional faculty in curriculum design and implementation. Thus, online peer institutions, led by the University of Phoenix, often offer courses taught by instructors with presumably sufficient technical expertise in the mechanics of online instruction but not necessarily sufficient academic training and, in any case, often with little or no control over course content. Indeed, they might teach courses developed entirely by others, persons the instructors have never communicated with, much less met.[47] Equally significant, course content no longer seems to matter a great deal, so long as the "delivery system" offers the desired "product" as quickly, as efficiently, and as cheaply as consumers want. And the consumer culture that has steadily pervaded higher education now seems to govern almost everything. Traditional faculty are consequently boxed in between high-tech-oriented administrators who generally do no teaching of any kind and students who demand access to instructors and courses at their utter convenience. (True, designing and operating these systems does offer new opportunities for engineers and other technical professions.) As a former colleague with vast experience in high-tech curriculum and instruction has suggested, any administrators who claim that "putting courses on the Web is easy, straightforward, and inexpensive" should themselves "be required to put a course online—over a weekend."[48]

The use of business terms such as "delivery system" and "product" is, of course, no accident, for higher education in America models itself ever more on corporate America. Many might feel akin to the nineteenth-century skilled workers whom the distinguished historian David Montgomery discusses in his *Workers' Control in America* (1979). As Montgomery details, skilled workers in pre-assembly-line, pre-automated industries once controlled the pace of work and in turn the output because they understood more about the machinery than their managers and owners and thus could not easily be replaced. As the radical union organizer whom Montgomery quotes put it so well, "The manager's brains [were] under the workman's cap."[49] Similarly, traditional faculty once controlled curriculum and instruction because they knew more about these than deans, provosts, and presidents and thus commanded considerable respect and deference. But most skilled workers gradually lost control as ever-larger machinery determined the pace and output of work, as "deskilling" steadily reduced the value and application of their expertise, and as manual labor became identified with mindless labor. The analogy to higher education obviously has its limitations, but the growing subservience of traditional intellectual work to high-tech mechanized work is, I believe, a striking comparison. No wonder, then, that "productivity" has become a buzzword for legislators, college and university trustees, and educational administrators almost everywhere.

The aptly named publisher Productivity Press, hitherto oriented toward (purely) commercial enterprises, now markets its books on such topics as *The Visual Factory*, *Implementing a Lean Management System*, and *Performance Measurement for World Class Manufacturing* as tools for the Press to become "the link between the academic world and the manufacturing/corporate areas, providing educators and students with powerful and strategic information." Their book catalog is subtitled *Productivity for the Academic World*.[50]

In the Fall 1999 issue of *Rutgers Magazine*, then Rutgers President Francis Lawrence offered a glimpse of his high-tech vision for Rutgers University. Like former presidents Stukel and Connick, President Lawrence was much taken with the present and prospective technological transformations in higher education. "It seems somehow appropriate that as the world enters a new millennium," Lawrence wrote, "we in higher education find ourselves striding into a new frontier ... Truly, this is a brave new world."[51] On August 25, 2010, Edutopia's website provided readers with ways to "Discover the Brave New World of Online Learning." The apparent absence of irony in these uses of "brave new world" says as much about the resurgence of scientific and technological utopianism in both K-12 and higher education as anything else.

Reengineering the University: The Kellogg Commission's Utopian Aspirations Related to these developments in higher education, but on a much grander scale, was the Kellogg Commission on the Future of State and Land-Grant Universities. The Commission was established in 1996 by one of the United States' leading higher education organizations: the National Association of State Universities and Land-Grant Colleges (NASULGC). NASULGC itself dates back to 1887 (in an earlier embodiment) and is the United States' oldest higher education organization. The Commission's funding came from the highly respected Kellogg Foundation of Battle Creek, Michigan. The Commission was charged by its sponsors with nothing less than trying to "define the direction public universities should go in the future and to recommend an action agenda to speed up the process of change."[52] It became the most significant and most systematic response to date to the changing landscape of higher education, with international implications despite its strictly American locale.

The Commission, composed of the presidents and chancellors of some twenty-five colleges and universities, issued six reports, the final one appearing in 2000. Because NASULGC institutions award roughly a half-million degrees annually (including about thirty-three percent of all United States bachelor's degrees and master's degrees, sixty percent of all doctoral degrees, and seventy percent of all engineering degrees), the Commission's findings and recommendations have had profound effects on American higher education overall and, by extension, higher education abroad. Nothing else since the Commission ended its mission has had a similar impact.[53]

Of particular interest here is the Kellogg Commission's depiction of how contemporary technology is affecting higher education. That old familiar technological determinism pervades the Commission's reports as much as it does contemporary high-tech hype elsewhere. The reports see high-tech advances as transforming the United States and, in due course, the entire world to an unprecedented extent and, no less importantly, at an unprecedented speed.[54] As the Commission sees it, the greatest challenge facing American higher education today is responding to these high-tech advances—or "Taking Charge of Change." That the Commission was, as just noted, simultaneously charged with "speed[ing] up the process of change" is one of several apparent conflicts throughout the Commission's work that was never resolved, perhaps never recognized. This conflict recalls the mixed messages of the Tofflers and other high-tech prophets: change is inevitable and overwhelming, but we alone can nevertheless steer you to safety and progress atop the "third wave" or its equivalent.

Like those high-tech gurus, too, the Commission members are at once dazzled by contemporary scientific and technological developments and fearful that, as in a kind of updated *Frankenstein* tale, those developments will end American higher education as we have known it in the twentieth century—above all the ethos and achievements of the land-grant movement.[55] As the Commission contends,

> The nation's state and land-grant colleges and universities have promised many things to many people and delivered on most of them: world-class research, first-rate service, and access to affordable education for all. They have been a unique source of practical education and lifelong learning, first for farmers and then for just

about everyone else. The value of these institutions is beyond calculation. They have kept the promise.[56]

Revealingly, the title of most of the Commission's reports is "Returning to Our Roots." To do this, however, would undermine the fundamental position of uniqueness, of claiming that today's challenges and crises are truly unprecedented. In effect, the Commission seeks the best of both worlds: avowed connections to the past that do not bind too tightly so that the present and the future can somehow simultaneously reduce the past to simpler, less challenging times. This posture, of course, is routine for avowedly high-tech prophets.

One reason behind this position is surely political: the greater the alleged crisis, the greater the prospects not for just sympathy but for outright financial support from government and, increasingly, the private sector. But there is another, no less genuine reason: ideological. The Kellogg Commission was ultimately convinced that, for all their risks to traditional higher education, high-tech advances are not simply inevitable but generally beneficial, and that they will allow for the re-engineering of land-grant and other public colleges and universities in ways that serve top administrators as well as business/corporate America, local and state if not national governments, K-12 school systems, engineers and other technical professionals, and, not least, self-conscious student consumers.

A persistent theme is the Commission's call for faculty to be reduced from an intellectual elite to the virtual peers of their students. This never extends to the top administrators, who increasingly constitute the actual academic elite. It is no accident that not a single faculty member (or student) served on the Commission. "Faculty, in this conception, change from being the source of all knowledge, 'the sage on the stage,' to mentors helping lead students toward new understanding, 'the guide on the side.'"[57]

Consequently, traditional faculty are boxed-in between high-tech-oriented administrators like Stukel who generally do no teaching of any kind and students who demand access to instructors and courses at their utter convenience. The motto of such institutions might well be that of New York area clothes discounter Sy Syms: "An Educated Consumer is Our Best Customer." What may be a utopia to many administrators and students is a dystopia to most faculty.

The steady loss of faculty autonomy in curriculum development that stems from embracing a student-centered consumer culture is matched by an equally intense desire to please business and industry and to promote that marriage as made in heaven— or a secular utopia. This development recalls Thorstein Veblen's *The Higher Learning in America* (1918), the pioneering and, by now, classic critique "of business control in practically every aspect of the modern university."[58] (Veblen, as noted, was the intellectual mentor of the Technocracy movement.) As in Veblen's day, so here: such pandering to business and industry goes far beyond wishing to cultivate the financial and political support of the private sector amid the declining financial and political assistance offered by most states and national governments in recent decades. We are reminded by the now painfully familiar critique of higher education for selling its soul to high-tech corporate America and elsewhere, as articulated by, among others, historian David Noble.[59]

The Commission compares the crucial importance to the United States' future of the ongoing construction of the high-tech infrastructure to "the construction of our railroads in the 19th century or our national highway system in the 20th century."[60] Dissenters from this faith risk being dismissed as twenty-first-century Luddites.

For, the Commission really envisions not just a wholesale transformation of conventional campuses and extension services, as already outlined, but also a *de facto* social engineering project that would constitute "Returning to Our Roots" on a grand scale. Land-grant and state colleges and universities "must again become the transformational institutions they were intended to be."[61] The project is the application of high-tech advances to: (1) democratize access to higher education; (2) promote the ever-greater "diversity" of students, faculty, and staff; and (3) provide "access to success," or "access to the full promise of American life."[62] The traditional linkage of the land-grant movement with expanding democracy is repeated in the Commission's reports and documents.[63] But the Commission, like its counterparts in other "advanced" countries, overlooks the possible negative consequences for democracy and diversity of the very high-tech advances that lessen the appeal of the traditional classroom and campus experience and so lessen the old-fashioned notions of greater democracy and diversity stemming from the intellectual and social interactions of students, faculty, staff, and community members in "real-time" settings.[64]

It is no accident that "total quality management" (TQM), the epitome of individual empowerment as applied to organizational structures and operations, has by now found a home at American colleges and universities decades after becoming part of offices, factories, and other workplace locales. It is another utopian scheme. "Strategic planning," "active listening," "team development," "conflict resolution," "customer service," and other ingredients of TQM may have already functioned successfully at some levels of college and university administration, but TQM's supreme faith in individuals as "experts on their own work" may prove more difficult to implement.[65]

Thus, the Kellogg Commission faces challenges that go beyond capitulation both to the marketplace in the name of profits and efficiency and to post-modern modes of thought that question the meaning and value of truth and objectivity.[66] High-tech advances, along with the extraordinary sense of individual empowerment that they both encourage and reflect, threaten the Commission's ambitious enterprise and in turn the future of public higher education—and not just in the United States but elsewhere.

The Fate of Books and Newspapers: Utopian and Dystopian Aspirations

Some educators and their business partners at all levels have long dreamed of replacing traditional books, journals, magazines, newspapers, and other printed materials with digitized versions that would save space, save money, and enable students and teachers to access materials electronically. Far from limiting opportunities to those invested in education, the logical extension is the commercial marketplace at large. A number envision the elimination of even libraries and bookstores as outdated and inefficient means of formal and informal education. In recent years the closure of many independent bookstores unable to compete against online booksellers such as Amazon confirms the accuracy of their visions. So, too, does the 2011 bankruptcy and closure of the nearly 400 Borders chain stores. While in the early 1990s there were some six thousand independent bookstores in the United States, by 2010 that number had shrunk to about 2200. Predictions of the downsizing of many newspapers and the disappearance of many others have also proved accurate. If far fewer libraries have closed, it is nevertheless true that ever more students and teachers—particularly at colleges and universities—no longer patronize them as often as in the past, thanks to electronic access. Some predominantly scientific and engineering libraries have sold or discarded many of their technical journals now available in electronic format. This is not as much the case with public libraries, especially those serving poorer communities with fewer patrons who own computers and e-book devices.[67]

Not surprisingly, those who are most passionate about these prospects usually have little or no interest in reading for pleasure. Moreover, the notion of continuing to read conventional printed materials for either business or pleasure is, to them, bizarre. One's reading life should now be conducted through a screen of whatever size—a genuine utopia for all.

Yet something unexpected has happened on the way to the wholesale elimination of books, newspapers, and other printed materials. First came audiobooks, which brought new or renewed attention to thousands of books through enjoyment of them being read by either the authors themselves, professional narrators, or actors.

More recently, books and other printed materials have increasingly been revived in the very electronic form that was predicted to be their downfall. Consider podcasts, for example. In 2004 Ben Hammersley coined the term "podcast"—a mixture of "iPod" and "broadcast." Apple Computer originated the brand of portable media player that first used podcasts, calling it the Apple iPod.

A podcast consists of digital media files that are transferred from the Internet to a computer, iPod, smart phone, or other media player. Podcasts of newspaper, magazine, and journal articles have now become routine.[68]

There is a growing audience of those willing and often eager to listen to podcasts and to read online versions of books, newspapers, magazines, and journals. True, many newspapers and magazines are struggling to find enough revenue to survive in any form, and the availability of free online readership, along with insufficient profits from online advertisements, has proved economically disastrous. But this condition may improve, as with payments for online readers.

As for books, the creation of e-books of all kinds—from bestsellers by leading authors to self-published "indies" to highly specialized academic tracts with insufficiently small readership to justify their conventional printing—has given books a "second wind." E-books are priced far more cheaply than conventional books and can be downloaded quickly at any time, day or night. To date the foremost seller of e-books has been Amazon, which in 2007 introduced the Kindle Reader, a lightweight plastic slab on which one can purchase, at a modest price, hundreds of thousands of e-books. These can then be downloaded quickly and read in various sizes and fonts. There have since been improved versions, including a larger-size Kindle that now allows easier access to selected newspapers that were difficult to read in the earlier Kindle. Meanwhile, rivals to the Kindle have inevitably come about, above all the Apple iPad, released in 2010. This tablet computer offers not only books and periodicals but also games, movies, music, and the Internet. Its origins can be traced back to Apple's first tablet computer, the Newton Message Pad of 1993 (discontinued in 1998), named, of course, after Isaac Newton. Like Apple's extremely popular iPhone and iPod Touch, the iPad uses a multi-touch finger-sensitive touchscreen—a vast improvement over the pressure-triggered stylus used in previous tablet computers.

Studies of human interaction with these devices indicate that touchscreens have become integral components of our daily lives much sooner than other "technological behaviors" because they are "so natural, intimate, and intuitive." Consequently, future devices will focus "on fingertips, with touch at the core" of current and future waves of computer design, now termed "natural user interface." This contrasts with earlier interfaces that concentrated upon a keyboard and mouse and required efforts that were not "engrained human movements" but that instead had to be learned.[69]

In 2010 Amazon announced that sales of its Kindle had by then outpaced its total sales of hardcover books, this after selling hardcover books for fifteen years and the Kindle for only thirty-three months.[70] A French reading device is being tested as a means of helping French newspapers to survive and prosper again. Called Read and Go—the name is in English!—it is similar in size to the larger Kindle but, unlike the Kindle, includes advertisements.[71]

Meanwhile, the popularity of the Kindle has prompted rivals—most notably Barnes and Noble—to offer far more books that can be downloaded onto many iPods and iPhones. That in turn pressured Amazon to open up its e-books to iPods and iPhones. Barnes and Noble then opened its larger list to BlackBerry gadgets. Following these developments, Sony Electronics introduced two new electronic reading devices, the Reader Pocket Edition and Reader Touch Edition, both competitors of the Kindle. They cost less but, unlike the Kindle, must be plugged into a computer to purchase and download their offerings. And so the competition has gone on, with various technical advantages and disadvantages to each utopian scheme. The bottom line in all cases is the wider audience for books and, to varying degrees, journals, magazines, and newspapers. For that matter, the Kindle has won praise, as might the Sony Readers, as a high-tech means of curling up with a book rather than being forced to read it on a conventional computer screen.[72]

At the same time, online booksellers, Amazon again above all, have sold millions of printed books, new and used alike, in the same way as other merchants have sold other products. Amazon's CEO Jeff Bezos has repeatedly stated that he, like many others in bookselling today, sees books as just another product. He is primarily concerned with increasing market share.[73] So popular have online book sales become that Barnes and Noble, America's largest and most powerful bookstore chain, has reported declining sales and in-store traffic—exactly what Barnes and Noble has done to hundreds of small independent bookstores in recent years! The bookstore industry is ever more fearful that chain bookstores might suffer the sad fate of so many record stores when the music business became ever more digital. To stay alive and well, chains are bringing in toys and games to lure customers. Nevertheless, the convenience of being able to shop for books online does not mean the complete fulfillment of the prophecies that hold books and other printed materials in such contempt. Like the early-twentieth-century predictions that movies would wipe out live theater, and the post-World War II predictions that television would eliminate movies and radio, this one about the allegedly dire fate of traditional books is quite likely wrong. As *Newsweek* writer Anna Quindlen has put it about those who dismiss the conventional printed book as a "hopeless dinosaur," "Tech snobbery is every bit as silly as the literary variety. Both ignore the tremendous power of book love."[74]

Beyond the updated Kindle and the other electronic devices that allow newspapers (and other publications) to be read online at one's convenience is the ongoing debate over the viability of newspapers themselves and the disappearance of many newspapers because of declining traditional readership, subscriptions, and advertising. Yet the future of newspapers, like that of books, is far from settled, and apocalyptic predictions of their complete demise are, like those for books, premature. It is now possible for ever more persons to report and analyze news without needing to work for newspapers, ranging from independent small groups to bloggers to individuals who happen upon events and record them on their cell phones' video cameras. No less significantly, it has become increasingly common practice for journalists of whatever kind to offer both unfiltered access to information and unprecedented data, such as unedited interviews formerly condensed for newspapers' limitations. As David Reevely, an editorial writer with the *Ottawa Citizen*, recently put it, "We have to stop thinking of ourselves as newspapers.

We're news organizations, and a printed newspaper is our most important product but not our only one."[75]

For books and newspapers and other publications alike, debate continues as to how much intellectual depth, if any, is lost amid the "distraction" of there being so many outlets in which to focus one's reading time. Some fear that written material—and, for that matter, scientific experiments and inventions—demanding traditional absorption will receive ever less attention and so comprehension and analysis. Others observe that "most of the great scientific and technological innovation over the last millennium has taken place in crowded, distracting urban centers." As Steven Johnson has put it about our being "less focused" than a few decades ago because of the ever-increasing extent to which we read on screens, "Yes, we are reading slightly fewer long-form narratives and arguments than we did 50 years ago," though ever greater use of the Kindle and the iPad may reverse that trend. Moreover, educated people today "are reading more text, writing far more often, than [they] were in the heyday of television." Furthermore, the speed with which we are able to "follow the trail of an idea, or discover new perspectives on a problem, has increased by several orders of magnitude." Consequently, Johnson contends that educated people today are only "marginally less focused, and exponentially more connected. That's a bargain all of us should be happy to make."[76]

Notes

1   According to an article in the Boston Sunday Globe, January 22, 2001, G2, the term "high tech" was coined in 1977 by the founders of the Massachusetts High Technology Council, all of them involved in information technology. See "High Tech Became Future," interview with Howard P. Foley, President of that organization. Although the earliest reference I have found is in David Cushman Coyle, "Decentralize Industry," *Virginia Quarterly Review*, 11 (July 1935), 321–338, he refers there to older forms of technology such as assembly lines and electrical power systems.

2   See, for example, *Newsweek*'s cover story on Apple's latest invention, the iPad, by Daniel Lyons and Nick Summers, "Think Really

Different," 155 (April 5, 2010), 47–51. The issue's cover title was explicit: "What's So Great About the iPad? Everything. How Steve Jobs Will Revolutionize Reading, Watching, Computing, Gaming—and Silicon Valley." Similarly, *Time*'s cover story for 175 (April 12, 2010), 6, 36–43, was "Inside Steve's Pad."

3   On new visions of artificial intelligence, see John Markoff, "The Coming Superbrain: Computers Keep Getting Smarter, While We Just Stay the Same," *Sunday New York Times*, Week in Review, May 24, 2009, 1, 4; and Alex Beam, "Apocalypse Later: Ray Kurzweil Predicts the Not-So-Near Future in 'Post-Biological' Visions of Humanity," *Boston Globe*, June 29, 2010, G23. On nuclear power, see the references in Chapter 6, notes 31–34 and 37–52.

4   See James Fleming, *Fixing the Sky: The Checkered History of Weather and Climate Control* (New York: Columbia University Press, 2010).

5   See David F. Noble, *The Religion of Technology: The Divinity of Man and the Spirit of Invention* (New York: Knopf, 1997), and Noble, *World Without Women: The Christian Clerical Culture of Western Science* (New York: Knopf, 1992).

6   For an early version of these points—one that focuses on the first four visionaries—see Howard P. Segal, *Future Imperfect: The Mixed Blessings of Technology in America* (Amherst, MA: University of Massachusetts Press, 1994), ch. 12. Although, as noted, the Tofflers began writing before contemporary information technology became commonplace, their later works do take those developments into account.

7   See Hugo A. Meier, "Technology and Democracy, 1800–1860," *Mississippi Valley Historical Review* 43 (March 1957): 618–640.

8   Ann Blair, "Information Overload: The Early Years," *Boston Sunday Globe*, Ideas, November 28, 2010, K2.

9   See the ads in *Time*, 174 (July 20, 2009), 4; and *Parade*, August 9, 2009, 21.

10   Alex Beam, "Our Precious Generation," *Boston Globe*, August 23, 2005, C1.

11   See, for example, David M. Potter, *People of Plenty: Economic Abundance and the American Character* (Chicago, IL: University of Chicago Press, 1954) and William Leach, *Land of Desire: Merchants, Power, and the Rise of a New American Culture* (New York: Pantheon, 1993).

12   See, for example, Daniel Akst, *We Have Met the Enemy: Self-Control in an Age of Excess* (New York: Penguin, 2010).

13   See Alex Sherman, *Bloomberg News*, "Facebook Passes Google as Most Visited US Site," *Boston Globe*, January 1, 2011, B6; and Harry

McCracken, "Tech: Social Showdown: Google + Has a Shot at Giving Facebook Serious Competition," *Time*, 178 (July 25, 2011), 58. See also Douglas Edwards, *I'm Feeling Lucky: The Confessions of Google Employee Number 59* (Boston: Houghton Mifflin Harcourt, 2011) and Steve Lohr, "Bits: Rethinking How We Search Online," *New York Times*, August 8, 2011, B6.

14   Deborah Rogers, "I Poke Dead People: The Paradox of Facebook," *Times Higher Education* (London), 1901 (June 18, 2009), 42. See also Ben Mezrich, *The Accidental Billionaires: The Founding of Facebook: A Tale of Sex, Money, Genius, and Betrayal* (New York: Doubleday, 2009); the popular 2010 film based on that book, *The Social Network*, as in Adam Geller and Joseph P. Kahn, "Facebook Film Not Making Friends with Some Harvard Grads," *Boston Globe*, October 2, 2010, A1, A9; David Kirkpatrick, *The Facebook Effect: The Inside Story of the Company that Is Connecting the World* (New York: Simon and Schuster, 2010); Miguel Helft, "Facebook Aims to Expand Its Reach," *Boston Globe*, April 19, 2010, B8; Mark Zuckerberg and Donald E. Graham, "Answering Facebook Privacy Concerns," *Bangor Daily News*, May 25, 2010, A7; Dan Fletcher, "Facebook: Friends Without Borders," *Time*, 175 (May 31, 2010), 32–38; Alex Beam, "Everybody Hates Facebook: For Hundreds of Millions, You Can't Live Without It or Without Complaining About It," *Boston Globe*, August 27, 2010, G39; Kirkpatrick, "It's Time to Clear Up Five Myths About Facebook," *Bangor Daily News*, September 30, 2010, A7; Geller, Associated Press, "Facebook Founder's Story Irretrievably Public," *Bangor Daily News*, October 1, 2010, C9; Kahn, "What Does Friend Mean Now?" *Boston Globe*, May 5, 2011, G16–17; and Alexandra Petri, "Facebook Nation: You Can Never Leave," *Bangor Daily News*, June 15, 2011, A5. See also Timothy Garton Ash, "Look It Up: Wikipedia Is Turning Ten," *Los Angeles Times*, January 14, 2011, http://articles.latimes.com/2011/jan/14/opinion/la-oe-0114-gartonash-wikipedia-20110114; and Noam Cohen, "When Knowledge Isn't Written, Does It Still Count?" Media, *New York Times*, August 8, 2011, B4.

15   See, for instance, Colin Delany, "Can Print Journalism Beat the Tweet?" *Bangor Daily News*, May 23–24, 2009, A11. See also David Talbot, "Can Twitter Make Money?" *Technology Review*, 113 (April 2010), 52–57; Claire Cain Miller, "Advertising Enters Flow On Twitter," *New York Times*, April 13, 2010, B1, B6; and Monica Hesse, *Washington Post*, "Library of Congress' Twitter Archive Spurs Debate," *Bangor Daily News*, May 7, 2010, C10. See also "Texting is not Talking," *Boston Globe*, Editorial, June 16, 2009, A14; and Matt Richtel, "In

Study, Texting Lifts Crash Risk by Wide Margin," *New York Times*, July 28, 2009, A1, A15. See also Verne Kopytoff, "To Match Profit with Popularity, Skype Looks to New Markets," *New York Times*, December 22, 2010, B1, B2.

16 This paragraph and its quotations are adapted from The Center for Land Use Interpretation, "Drop City Site," http://ludb.clui.org/ex/i/CO3134. See also Timothy Miller, "Roots of Communal Revival, 1962–1966," http://www.thefarm.org/lifestyle/root2.html. See John Hendrickson, "They Built this City with Alternative Ideals," *Denver Post*, reprinted in *Boston Globe*, July 18, 2009, G8.

17 See my review in *Technology and Culture*, 28 (July 1987), 697–698 of R. Buckminster Fuller, *Inventions: The Patented Works of Buckminster Fuller* (New York: St. Martin's, 1983) and James Ward, ed., *The Artifacts of Buckminster Fuller: A Comprehensive Collection of His Designs and Drawings*, 4 vols. (New York: Garland, 1985). Both were posthumous publications. The large literature on Buckminster Fuller includes Amy C. Edmondson, *A Fuller Explanation: The Synergetic Geometry of R. Buckminster Fuller* (Boston: Birkhäuser, 1987); Martin Pawley, *Buckminster Fuller* (New York: Taplinger, 1990); Robert R. Potter, *Buckminster Fuller* (Englewood Cliffs: Silver Burdett, 1990); J. Baldwin, *Bucky Works: Buckminster Fuller's Ideas for Today* (New York: John Wiley, 1996); Lloyd Steven Sieden, *Buckminster Fuller's Universe* (Cambridge: Perseus, 2000); Thomas T. K. Zung, ed., *Buckminster Fuller: Anthology for the New Millennium* (New York: St. Martin's, 2001); and Michael John Gorman, *Buckminster Fuller: Designing for Mobility* (New York: Rizzoli, 2005).

18 See Lyman Tower Sargent, *Utopianism: A Very Short Introduction* (New York: Oxford University Press, 2010), 81–85, for a good summary of these recent developments.

19 The foremost history of the kibbutz is Henry Near, *The Kibbutz Movement: A History*, 2 vols. (Oxford: Oxford University Press, 1992; London: Vallentine Mitchell, 1997). The first volume is subtitled *Origins and Growth, 1909–1939*; the second, *Crisis and Achievement, 1939–1995*.

20 Daniel Gavron, *The Kibbutz: Awakening From Utopia* (Lanham: Rowman and Littlefield, 2000), 4. This is a very good introduction to the topic. Further studies of the kibbutzim include Yonina Talmon, *Family and Community in the Kibbutz* (Cambridge: Harvard University Press, 1972); Melford E. Spiro, *Children of the Kibbutz: A Study in Child Training and Personality* (Cambridge: Harvard University Press, 1975); Spiro, *Gender and Culture: Kibbutz Women Revisited* (New York:

Schocken, 1980); Tom Bethell, "Is the Kibbutz Kaput?" *Reason*, 22 (October 1990), 33–37; Alan Cooperman, "A Socialist's Worst Nightmare: Wealth," *U. S. News and World Report*, 122 (March 10, 1997), 41–42; Ilene R. Prusher, "Zionist Dream of Kibbutz Fades in 1990s Lifestyle," *Christian Science Monitor*, December 5, 1997, 6–7; Thanassis Cambanis, "Kibbutz Finds a U. S. Market: Obese Consumers Driving Demand for Israeli Scooters," *Boston Globe*, December 26, 2006, A1; Matthew Kalman, "Capitalism on the Kibbutz: Many Israeli Collectives Shunning System of Financial Equality," *Boston Globe*, February 26, 2007, A1, A8; Sacha Pfeiffer, "Courting Kibbutz, Inc.," *Boston Globe*, June 1, 2007, D1, D6; and Sarah Wildman, "Journeys: Israel: Massage, Not Work, on the Kibbutz," *Sunday New York Times*, Travel, June 29, 2008, A3. My statistics derive from Gavron and from various reports issued by the University of Haifa's Institute for Research on the Kibbutz and the Cooperative Idea—http://research.haifa.ac.il/~kibbutz/main.html.

21 Gavron, *The Kibbutz*, 221.

22 On the many challenges, as of 1996, facing a highly touted "grounded" utopian community that depends on wind bells made at its metal foundry and ceramics factory, see Leo W. Banks, "Cross-Country Journal: In Arizona, Builder Won't Desert Dream," *Boston Globe*, September 9, 1996, A3. Arcosanti, the experimental town discussed in the article, still persists, but so do the basic financial and administrative problems discussed in the article.

23 See Tom Boellstorff, *Coming of Age in Second Life: An Anthropologist Explores the Virtually Human* (Princeton: Princeton University Press, 2008). Boellstorff's multi-year ethnographic study argues both that the "second life" may not be as novel as commonly assumed and, equally important, that all culture may, at heart, be virtual.

24 Hubert L. Dreyfus, *On the Internet*, 2nd edn. Thinking in Action Series (New York and London: Routledge, 2009), 7.

25 John A. Farrell, "The Smithsonian Goes Trekkie," *Boston Globe*, February 29, 1992, 9, 12; Farrell, "Washington's Hottest Summer Ticket—Smithsonian's Tribute to 'Star Trek,'" *Boston Sunday Globe*, June 7, 1992, B7; See James Gorman, "'Star Trek': It's a Wonderful Galaxy," *New York Times*, Arts and Leisure, September 15, 1992, 1, 29; Yvonne Fern, *Gene Roddenberry: The Last Conversation—A Dialogue with the Creator of Star Trek* (Berkeley and Los Angeles: University of California Press, 1994); Eric Schmuckler, "Profits, Reruns, and the End of 'Next Generation,'" *New York Times*, Arts and Leisure, July 24, 1994, 29; Constance Penley, *NASA/TREK: Popular Science and Sex in*

America (New York: Verso, 1997); Frank Ahrens, "Exhibit: A Near Darth Experience," *Washington Post*, October 31, 1997, B1, B5; Julie Cooper, "Las Vegas Beaming Up Trekkies," *San Antonio Express-News*, reprinted in *Bangor Daily News*, Saturday-Sunday, February 7–8, 1998, MW1, MW2; and Stephen Seitz, "'Star Trek' TV Series Lives On Through Conventions Years After its Demise," *New Hampshire Sunday News*, July 29, 2001, A11. Parts of Henry Jenkins, *Textual Poachers: Television Fans and Participatory Culture* (New York: Routledge, 1992) deal with *Star Trek* fans.

26 According to Roddenberry, "we were sending messages and fortunately they all got by the network." This and the quotations are found in several of the works in note 25. See also Joseph P. Kahn, "Boldly Going Where Trekkies Have Gone Before," *Boston Globe*, April 25, 2009, A1, A12; and Steve Daly, "Geeks Rule! We're All Trekkies Now" and Leonard Mlodinow, "Vulcans Never, Ever Smile," *Newsweek* cover stories on "To Boldly Go ... How 'Star Trek' Taught Us to Dream Big," 153 (May 4, 2009), 52–59.

27 See Benjamin Nugent, *American Nerd: The Story of My People* (New York: Scribner, 2008) and Ben Zimmer, "The Word: Birth of the Nerd," Ideas, *Boston Sunday Globe*, August 28, 2011, K1.

28 Stephen Hawking, "Foreword," in Lawrence M. Krauss, *The Physics of Star Trek* (New York: Basic Books, 1995), xii.

29 Krauss, *Physics of Star Trek*, 83.

30 See Gary Sledge, "Going Where No One Has Gone Before," *Discovery Channel Magazine*, 3 (August 2008) and Krauss, *Physics of Star Trek*. Krauss has also written *Beyond Star Trek: Physics From Alien Invaders to the End of Time* (New York: Basic Books, 1997), which examines later science fiction movies for their own scientific accuracy and inaccuracy.

31 See David B. Tyack and Larry Cuban, *Tinkering Toward Utopia: A Century of Public School Reform* (Cambridge: Harvard University Press, 1995); Hank Bromley and David S. Shutkin, "Science and Technology Studies and Education: An Introduction to the Special Issue," *Educational Policy*, 12 (September 1998), 467–483; Cuban, *Oversold and Underused: Computers in the Classroom* (Cambridge: Harvard University Press, 2001); Mark J. Warschauer, *Laptops and Literacy: Learning in the Wireless Classroom* (New York: Teachers College Press, 2006); and Jeffrey R. Young, "When Computers Leave Classrooms, So Does Boredom," *Chronicle of Higher Education*, 55 (July 20, 2009), A1, A13.

32 See the Edutopia website, http://www.edutopia.org.

33 See http://www.edutopia.org.

---

34 See http://www.edutopia.org. The article, by Sara Bernard, also
    appeared in *Edutopia*'s June 2009 issue.
35 See http://www.edutopia.org.
36 See the DaVinci Institute website, http://www.davinciinstitute.com.
    Quotations from the Institute and from Tom Frey are from Karen
    Kusiak, "Students, Laptops, and School Achievement: Identity Con-
    struction in One-to-One Classrooms," unpublished Ed.D. disserta-
    tion, University of Maine, 2011, 46–47.
37 See http://thejournal.com and its regular print publication called
    simply *The Journal*. The motto of both is "Transforming Education
    Through Technology."
38 See Metiri Group, *Technology in Schools: What the Research Says*,
    commissioned by Cisco Systems, 2006, http://www.cisco.com/
    web/strategy/docs/education/TechnologyinSchoolsReport.pdf.
39 See James Vaznis, "Virtual Schools Soon Reality in Massachusetts,"
    Boston Globe, May 5, 2010, A1, A9. See also Julie Rasicot, "Virtual
    Classroom Aims to Offer World-Class Education for Free," *Bangor
    Daily News*, August 8, 2011, A1, D2.
40 James J. Stukel, "The Future of Land Grant Universities," speech of
    February 19, 1998, delivered in Corpus Christi, Texas, 10.
41 Stukel, "The Future," 2, 9, 4, 6.
42 George P. Connick and Jane A. Russo, "Higher Education in the Age of
    Information," *Connection: New England's Journal of Higher Education
    and Economic Development*, 9 (Summer 1994), 18. When Connick
    visited the University of Maine a year or so later to promote his
    vision, I asked him on what basis these studies had reached their
    conclusions. He replied that they did so on only one basis—the course
    grades received by students in conventional classes versus those
    received by students using high-tech methods. When I tried to pin
    him down on how such conclusions could be reached on just one
    basis—as if comparative course grades could ever be relied upon
    exclusively for any definitive judgments even within traditional
    settings—he insisted that the studies were at once completely accu-
    rate and quite sufficient. Not surprisingly, *The American Journal of
    Distance Education* strongly supports the phenomenon it covers.
43 "Trustees to Vote on 'Remote Control' Campus," *Maine Sunday
    Telegram*, January 22, 1995, A1, A10. See an update on what is now
    called "E-Learning" for the University of Maine System in David B.
    Offer, "Expanding Distance Education in Maine," *Bangor Daily News*,
    March 17, 2010, B1, B6; and in an editorial in the *Bangor Daily News*,
    October 18, 2010, A4.

44 Stukel, "The Future," 9.
45 See Julius Genachowski, "U. S. is Falling Behind in Digital Literacy," *Bangor Daily News*, March 18, 2010, A7; and Christine Armario, Associated Press, "Tests Reveal Most American Students Don't Know Much About US History," *Bangor Daily News*, June 15, 2011, A2.
46 The ad appeared in *The Economist*, 391 (June 20, 2009), 5.
47 Gordon Bonin, "Web College Envisioned for Maine: Degrees to be Earned Online," *Bangor Daily News*, November 27–28, 1999, A1. On the value of online learning, see Steve Lohr, "Learning Online May Be Better," *New York Times*, August 24, 2009, B7; Todd Gilman, "Combating Myths About Distance Education," *Chronicle of Higher Education*, February 22, 2010, http://chronicle.com/article/Combating-Myths-About Distance/64299; Iza Wojciechowska, "Continuing Debate Over Online Education," *Inside Higher Ed*, July 16, 2010, http://insidehighered.com/news/2010/07/16/online; and Randall Stross, "Digital Domain: Online Courses, Still Lacking that Digital Domain," *Sunday New York Times*, Business, February 6, 2011, 4. See also Young, "When Computers Leave Classrooms."
48 Paula Evans Petrik, at the time Professor of History at the University of Maine, quoted in Scott Jaschik, "Historians Differ on Impact of Distance Education in Their Discipline," *Chronicle of Higher Education*, 46 (January 21, 2000), A43.
49 Big Bill Haywood, quoted in David Montgomery, *Workers' Control in America: Studies in the History of Work, Technology, and Labor Struggles* (New York: Cambridge University Press, 1979), 9.
50 See *Productivity: Productivity for the Academic World* (Portland: Productivity Press, Summer 1998), 2 and cover. As the accompanying May 28, 1998, "Dear Educator" letter puts it, "Regardless of your academic specialty, the keyword in delivering an education that will serve us in the modern world is change."
51 Francis L. Lawrence, "Connect@Rutgers: Our Link to the World, the Future, and Each Other," *Rutgers Magazine*, 79 (Fall 1999), 22–23. See, by contrast, the understood irony in using the term in discussing Princeton's Center for Information Technology Policy in Christopher Shea, "Brave New World," *Princeton Alumni Weekly*, 111 (November 17, 2010), 32–37.
52 "Announcement of Kellogg Commission: New Commission to Bring Reform to State and Land-Grant Universities Funded by Kellogg Commission," Press Release, January 30, 1996, 1.
53 "Announcement of Kellogg Commission," 3.

54 The fact that no professional historian of technology accepts techno-logical determinism might have given the Commission some pause. But, of course, historians of technology or of anything else were not consulted, even for the periodic references to the history of higher education.

55 The fact that many institutional members of NASULGC and in turn the Commission are not official land-grant schools is not a problem insofar as the issues transcend land-grants themselves yet are rooted in the land-grant ethos.

56 Kellogg Commission, "Taking Charge of Change," brochure, June 1996, cover letter. This is about as much historical context as one finds in any of the Commission reports and other documents, beyond the repeated references to the Morrill Act of 1862. The sole exception is the call for a "Higher Education Millennial Partnership Act" for the twenty-first century that would complement the Morrill Act and other legislation crucial to the evolution and well-being of public higher education. One would never guess from this and related Commission statements that the land-grant movement has been the subject of intense scholarly as well as political discussion since 1862; that the principal motivations for the Morrill Act have themselves been hotly debated by historians and others for decades; and that this retrospective consensus on promises made and kept is thus in some measure an invention.

57 Kellogg Commission, *Renewing the Covenant*, sixth report, March 2000, 7.

58 Laurence R. Veysey, *The Emergence of the American University* (Chicago: University of Chicago Press, 1965), 347. The rest of the paragraph on 347 is a good summary of Veblen's critique.

59 See, for example, David F. Noble, "Selling Academe to the Technology Industry," *Thought and Action: The NEA Higher Education Journal*, 14 (Spring 1998), 29–40. See also David L. Kirp, "The New U," *The Nation*, 270 (April 17, 2000), 25–29, a review of two contrasting books on contemporary higher education, and Arthur Levine, "The Soul of a New University," *New York Times*, Op Ed, March 13, 2000, A25. Ironically, the Commission's January 1996 charge to its members reminded them that Justin Morrill "intended our institutions to provide a practical education, not a classical ideal," and to embrace the "'industrial class'—ordinary laborers, farmhands, workers, and their children" ("Kellogg Presidents' Commission on the 21st Century State and Land-Grant University," Letter to Commission members, January 1996, 1).

60 Kellogg Commission, *Returning to Our Roots: A Learning Society*, September 1999, vii, 31.

61 Kellogg Commission, *Returning to Our Roots: The Student Experience*, April 1997, 1.

62 Kellogg Commission, *Returning to Our Roots: Student Access*, May 1998, 2.

63 See such works as Earle D. Ross, *Democracy's College: The Land-Grant Movement in the Formative Stage* (Ames: Iowa State College Press, 1942); Edward D. Eddy, Jr., *Colleges for Our Land and Time: The Land-Grant Idea in American Education* (New York: Harper, 1957); Allan Nevins, *The State Universities and Democracy* (Urbana: University of Illinois Press, 1962); and Joseph J. B. Edmond, *The Magnificent Charter: The Origin and Role of the Morrill Land-grant Colleges and Universities* (Hicksville, NY: Exposition Press, 1978).

64 On related dilemmas confronting higher education globally, see Ben Wildavsky, *The Great Brain Race: How Global Universities Are Reshaping the World* (Princeton: Princeton University Press, 2010).

65 For elaboration on this paragraph, see Alan I. Marcus and Howard P. Segal, *Technology in America: A Brief History*, 2nd edn. (Fort Worth: Harcourt Brace, 1999), 334–336, 340–342. See also the obituary by John Holusha, of W. Edwards Deming, the foremost advocate of TQM, in *The New York Times*, December 21, 1993, B7.

66 See David D. Cooper, "Academic Professionalism and the Betrayal of the Land-Grant Tradition," *American Behavioral Scientist*, 42 (February 1999), 776–785.

67 See Tracy Jan, "Harvard's Paper Cuts: School Library Works to Maintain Stature in the Shift to Digital," *Boston Globe*, May 24, 2010, A1, A6; and Kristen Wyatt, Associated Press, "As Budgets Shrink, Libraries Fight to Stay Relevant," *Bangor Daily News*, June 24, 2011, A1, A2. See, by contrast, the embrace of electronic devices by the Bangor Public Library, one of the United States' foremost small city libraries in terms of patronage: Katy England, "Electronic Readers and the Changing Face of Books," *The Edge* (Bangor, Maine), September 8, 2010, 14–15. See also the retrospective on the poor timing of Tina Brown's new *Talk* magazine in 1999 by David Carr, "The Media Equation: 10 Years Ago, An Omen No One Saw," *New York Times*, August 2, 2009, B1. A full-page ad in *Time*, 175 (April 19, 2010), 11, by an unspecified proponent of "Magazines: The Power of Print" proclaimed the continuing popularity of magazines: "We surf the Internet. We swim in magazines."

68 See Ben Hammersley, "Audible Revolution," *The Guardian*, February 12, 2004, 27; and James Van Orden, "The History of Podcasting," http://www.how-to-podcast-tutorial.com/history-of-podcasting. htm.

69 See Claire Cain Miller, "To Win Over Today's Users, Gadgets Have to Be Touchable," *New York Times*, September 1, 2010, B1. But see the critique of e-books by Nicholas Carr, "Schools, Beware the E-Book," *Portland Press Herald*, August 15, 2011, A7.

70 See Joseph Galante, *Bloomberg News*, "Amazon Says It Sells More E-Books than Hardcovers," *Boston Globe*, July 20, 2010, B9. See also Julie Bosman, "Pete Hamill, Patriarch of Print, Goes Direct to Digital," *New York Times*, August 12, 2010, C6.

71 See Eric Pfanner, "Reading Device Enlisted to Help French Papers," *New York Times*, July 21, 2008, C8.

72 See Brad Stone, "Amazon Faces a Fight Over Its E-Books," *New York Times*, July 27, 2009, B3; Stone and Motoko Rich, "Sony to Cut E-Book Prices And Offer New Readers," *New York Times*, August 5, 2009, B3; David Pogue, "New Entry in E-Books a Paper Tiger," Personal Tech, *New York Times*, August 6, 2009, B1, B8; Scott Kirsner, "Blog Filter: Catching Up With Kindle Will Be Tough," *Boston Globe*, August 10, 2009, B7; Stone, "Sony Plans to Adopt Common Format for E-Books," *New York Times*, August 13, 2009, B8; Alex Pham and David Sarno, "Electronic Reading Devices are Transforming the Concept of the Book," *Los Angeles Times*, July 18, 2010, A1; and, for comparative analysis, "When Simpler is Better," *Boston Sunday Globe*, Money and Careers, June 20, 2010, G2.

73 See Onnesha Roychoudhuri, "Books After Amazon," *Boston Review*, November/December 2010, http://bostonreview.net/BR35.6/roy-choudhuri.php.

74 Anna Quindlen, "Turning the Page: The Future of Reading is Backlit and Bright," *Newsweek*, 155 (April 5, 2010), 52–53. See also Susan Straight, "Books' Power to Connect Potent as Ever," *Bangor Daily News*, June 24, 2010, A7; and Julie Bosman, "Publishing Gives Hints of Revival, Data Show," *New York Times*, August 9, 2011, C1, C6.

75 David Reevely quoted in Scott Foster, "The Future of Journalism: What's Next for News?" *Carleton University Magazine*, Spring 2010, 23. This is an excellent overview of the topic. See also Josh Quittner, "The Future of Reading," *Fortune*, 161 (March 1, 2010), 63–67, regarding publishing's foolish reliance on simple-minded and ignorant consultants rather than on their foremost reporters to try to grasp the ongoing changes in the industry from the mid-1990s onward.

76 All quotations are from Steven Johnson, "Unboxed: Yes, People Still Read, but Now It's Social," *Sunday New York Times*, Week in Review, June 20, 2010, 3. See also Nicholas Carr, "Is Google Making Us Stupid?" *Atlantic*, 302 (July/August 2008), 56–63. On one couple's differing preference for conventional versus electronic reading materials, see Matt Richtel and Claire Cain Miller, "Of Two Minds About Books: Print or Pixels?" *New York Times*, September 2, 2010, B1, B4. See also Nick Bilton, "Personal Tech: Deciding on a Book, and How to Read It," *New York Times*, August 11, 2011, B10. On one New England prep school's recent experience with eliminating nearly all of its books in favor of a largely digital library, see Sam Allis, "Digital Shift: Going (Almost) Bookless has Made Cushing Academy's Library a Popular Spot," *Boston Globe*, November 6, 2010, G12, G13. By contrast, see Carolyn Y. Johnson, "In Billions of Words, Digital Allies Find Tale," *Boston Globe*, December 17, 2010, A1, A20, regarding "mining the complete text of four percent of the world's books" by Harvard University and Google researchers in order to uncover "surprising insights into language, culture, and history." But see also the somewhat skeptical *Globe* editorial about these revelations, December 21, 2010, A18. See also the 2011 New York federal court decision rejecting Google's plan to create the world's largest digital library and bookstore, in Miguel Helft, "Judge Rejects Google's Deal to Digitize Books," *New York Times*, March 22, 2011, B1.

Chapter 8

The Future of Utopias and Utopianism

The "Scientific and Technological Plateau" and the Redefinition of Progress

The "scientific and technological plateau" noted at several earlier points is a possible successor to scientific and technological utopianism: a redefinition of progress as being as much social and environmental as scientific and technological, with lessened commitment to those sciences and technologies that offer few if any widespread social benefits. Countless examples abound: reduction of nuclear weapons and efforts to minimize their possible use; safer, more fuel efficient cars; elimination of unneeded dams and other structures to restore natural settings; regulation of noise levels of various machines; "limits to growth" campaigns at local, state, and national levels; and "small is beautiful" crusades in both highly industrialized and less industrialized countries.

A historical study, with avowed contemporary implications, of Japan's selective abandonment of one key technology—the gun—without its giving up other, non-military technologies and sciences is Noel Perrin's *Giving Up the Gun: Japan's Reversion to the Sword, 1543–1879* (1980). Prior to 1543, Japan was a warlike country whose fighters relied on swords, spears, and bows and arrows. Things changed completely when two Europeans landed and impressed the warriors with their two guns. Wealthy Japanese noblemen purchased both guns and set about having their

Utopias: A Brief History from Ancient Writings to Virtual Communities,
First Edition. Howard P. Segal.
© 2012 Howard P. Segal. Published 2012 by Blackwell Publishing Ltd.

swordsmiths make many more. By the time of an important battle in 1575, the victorious army had ten thousand gunners! This number dwarfs that for the most powerful European armies of the time.

Such technological success nevertheless had its downside. Non-elite Japanese now had the ability to acquire guns to shoot and kill the elite samurai, for whom fighting was ordinarily highly ritualized and the outcome of which was supposed to reflect superior physical strength and greater moral character. The samurai also disliked the awkwardness of guns versus swords and increasingly resented that they derived from foreigners. In order to preserve their leadership ranks—and themselves—the threatened samurai eventually devised clever means of persuading the non-samurai to give up their guns. Not only did the entire country stop research and development but the samurai also persuaded the non-samurai to have their guns melted down for statues of Buddha, the god of virtually all Japanese.

Guns thereby disappeared from Japan until American explorers "discovered" Japan in the late nineteenth century and ignorantly dismissed the Japanese as primitives partly because they lacked guns. Yet the elimination of guns hardly meant the elimination of all technological advances. Not at all! Water-powered crushing mills, silk production, and gunpowder for blasting loose ore in mining were among those advances after guns were eliminated. In effect, the Samurai had made a "technology assessment" and had proposed and then carried out a "technological plateau."

In addition, as other scholars have detailed, Japan in this same period adopted aspects of not only Western but also Chinese science. Yet Japan also did this selectively and remained a closed society to foreigners. Chinese and Dutch traders, for example, might enter but would have extremely limited contact, if any, with the general population. The Japanese rulers feared Westernization, above all anything akin to Christianity or to republican government.[1]

Perrin may, however, have misrepresented parts of this otherwise compelling story in order to make his basic point. Some scholars of Japan—of which he, a Dartmouth College English Professor, was admittedly not—contend that Japan in fact never gave up the gun entirely. Instead, according to these scholars, the samurai secretly kept many guns in storage for possible future use, but wound up not needing to use them as Japan was sufficiently powerful and united not to fear internal strife or foreign invasion. From 1603 until 1868 Japan was ruled by the Tokugawa shogunate, which came to power in large part because several civil and foreign wars had proved disastrous. Earlier regimes' efforts to expand Japan were no longer popular. While the general Japanese populace was disarmed, until the nineteenth century foreigners largely left Japan alone in favor of discoveries and conquests closer to Europe. The country "turned inward and gave up war, not the gun."[2] Peacekeeping could now be limited to swords and pikes. The number of guns allocated to each lord varied with the lord's power and wealth, but all had at least twenty in their individual armories and the most important had hundreds. As one historian has noted, giving up the manufacturing and improvement of guns reflected no "conscious hostility to firearms per se" and also reflected the fact that "stored guns rot very slowly" and so need not be replaced if not used.[3]

Another historian, William Burns, has observed that, given the long-term peace in Tokugawa Japan, samurai warriors often turned to non-military science and technology to pursue fulfilling careers. This fostered selected scholarship in those areas for the ruling elite: not navigation, for instance, which was no longer important for diminished overseas expeditions, but rather medicine, botany, calendar-making, and mapping.[4]

Curiously, the historian of medieval technology Jean Gimpel has applied the term "technological plateau" to medieval Western Europe after 1375, when, for various reasons, the industrial revolution he details in *The Medieval Machine: The Industrial Revolution of the Middle Ages* (1976) gradually ceased. Whatever else may be said about the medieval period, Gimpel demonstrates that it was definitely not a "dark age" technologically, contrary to the nonsense in Toffler's *Future Shock*. True, as recent scholarship has revealed, Gimpel exaggerated the case for an outright medieval industrial revolution.[5] Yet, where the technological plateau of the late thirteenth and early fourteenth centuries was followed four centuries later by a second industrial revolution in England,

Gimpel fears that the plateau that he discerns in the modern West, including North America, will become a permanent condition. Ironically, the example that Gimpel singles out as symbolic of "the entry of the United States into her aging or declining era"—the refusal of the Congress in 1971 to allocate funds for the supersonic transport (the SST)—has been viewed by others as an immensely hopeful sign. Thirty-some years later, Britain and France, the two nations that were taken in by this "technological imperative," had to bail out entirely, awash in a sea of red ink.[6]

Recall, by contrast, William Morris's celebration of so much of medieval society as he understood it but also romanticized it: not least, its small-scale workshops, with tools in the hands of skilled and dedicated craftsmen and craftswomen. But recall as well Morris's refusal to go back completely to the "good old days" insofar as his *News From Nowhere* envisioned the elimination of the medieval and modern class systems, the creation of genuine democracy, and the development of advanced tools and machines. However backward-looking in several respects, his utopia is in other respects a kind of technological plateau that would infuriate Gimpel.

In their own time, Morris and Henry Adams were lonely voices when they raised questions about scientific and technological change. Now critiques of modern science and technology on comparable grounds are almost routine. David Nye's *America as Second Creation*, for example, calls for new values for our own time. His "recovery narrative" would embrace selective, sustainable scientific and technological development and renew the non-quantitative measures of the "good life" long relegated to the sidelines of serious discussions of "progress." Notwithstanding his abundant faith in science and technology, Fuller understood as early as his young adulthood that the Earth's resources remained finite. To his considerable credit, and long before it became conventional wisdom, he wisely did not equate mankind's growing power over nature with an endless supply of raw materials. In recognizing what was later termed the "limits to growth," Fuller was turning back to the outlook shared by most Americans throughout the eighteenth and early nineteenth centuries, prior to America's own industrial revolution.[7] His inventions accommodated this reality, unlike some of his futurist contemporaries such as Herman Kahn and Julian Simon, who assumed that inventive humans would either discover natural resources in hitherto unexplored places or would readily create adequate substitutes.[8]

True, there was a temporary resurgence of faith in high-tech panaceas during the 1991 Persian Gulf War. Yet that infatuation with seemingly impersonal and sanitized high-tech weapons systems, especially the interestingly named "patriot missiles," proved fleeting, especially once their actual performance was analyzed and found wanting. There appeared to be a growing gap between rhetoric and reality that disillusioned many Americans, among others, about military technology, notwithstanding otherwise seductive commercials in various media fronts trying to lure young men and women into the high-tech armed forces. Moreover, during the war against Iraq beginning in 2003, far fewer Americans were sold on this military version of technological utopia.[9] Meanwhile, the events of September 11, 2001, and their aftermath further demonstrated that "techno-mania" is passé. Notwithstanding the inevitable stress on developing new technological devices for combating terrorism, there was not even a short-lived grassroots love affair with high-tech weapons as in 1991. After September 11 it became increasingly clear that conflicting ideologies, not science and technology—whether box-cutters or airplanes—were the principal culprits.

Some examples of a contemporary plateau are more banal but no less important. For example, in October 2010 Clark University experimented with a "Day of Slowing"—twenty-four hours supposedly without texting or Facebook or iPods or other contemporary electronic devices and activities—only to discover that it was neither popular with most students and other members of the campus community, nor was it acted upon. A minority of students, faculty, and administrators did enjoy the respite, but they were the exceptions.[10]

To take another example, the National Park service now repeatedly urges visitors to its parks *not* to rely on high-tech gadgets as the only means of determining their location, especially not if weather or injuries or other factors lead to their being lost. Those devices at once increasingly lead to carelessness in trip preparations and do not always work in sections of parks. Equally significantly, the very ability to take photos and videos of surroundings and of wildlife has led to ever more injuries and deaths because of inattention to surroundings amid the thrill of capturing nature and its wild creatures. So much for the much-heralded utopian dimensions of those devices in these contexts.[11]

To take a third example, it is increasingly evident that many parents' obsession at home with using domestic electronic gadgets makes their children unhappy at the consequent (relative) lack of attention. True, older children are often equally guilty of ignoring their parents as they use their own gadgets to communicate with friends. In both cases, it sometimes takes an individual or family decision to stay offline during, say, meals or at other family times in order to restore a more traditional conversation. Obviously, the ability to stay in touch with these same devices when family members are apart has its benefits. The point is the ongoing search for balance before an irreversible tipping point is reached.[12]

Harold Loeb's *Life in a Technocracy* (1933) implicitly suggested the prospect of a scientific and technological plateau. His vision was of a world that would go far beyond the Technocracy movement in which he was an important figure before breaking from the narrow-minded leadership of Howard Scott. Loeb understood the value of a society in which there was sufficient affluence for all and in which the time needed for work was sufficiently modest that there would be ample opportunities to engage in various leisure activities. Freed from "that preoccupation with economic security which has always weighted the soul of man except on a few tropical islands," Loeb's utopians would finally be able to devote their principal energies to other, higher pursuits: education, religion, recreation, and, above all, art. Loeb devotes more than half his book to the encouragement of the creative leisure pursuits that Scott and other purely technical types could never imagine, much less allow. Yet no citizen would be compelled to participate in any one or group of these activities.[13]

As Loeb grasped, unlike most other twentieth- and twenty-first-century scientific and technological visionaries, the real challenge is what to do once it is agreed that science and technology, in the words of contemporary philosopher Nicholas Rescher, "cannot deliver on the $64,000 question of human satisfaction . . . because, in the final analysis, they simply do not furnish the stuff of which real happiness is made."[14] Consequently, *Life in a Technocracy* is far more than an intellectual relic in the manner of the vast majority of utopian writings that never reached a large audience. Instead, it is a landmark book that continues to speak to the real present as well as to the imagined future. As the examples cited above suggest, the scientific and technological plateau is becoming the hallmark of mature scientific and technological societies like the United States, albeit in forms never envisioned by Loeb.

A better-known and no less important example of a scientific and technological plateau is a novel by the famous science fiction writer and social critic H. G. Wells: *The Shape of Things to Come* (also, by coincidence, from 1933). In 1936 a popular and much-praised British movie version of the book was made with the title *Things to Come*. Its stars included Raymond Massey, Ralph Richardson, and Cedric Hardwicke. It is the story of Everytown (based on London) from the outbreak of a twenty-five-year-long war in 1936—with remarkable anticipation of the Nazis' highly successful "lightning war" or "blitzkrieg" in Poland three years later that started World War II and of the Nazis' "Blitz" bombing of London and other parts of England. The story continues through various upheavals in the next hundred years until a time of peace and prosperity for all, thanks to the efforts of scientists and engineers. The presumed final stage is what Wells called a "Puritan Tyranny" that values hard work, reliability, productivity, loyalty, and, above all, efficiency.[15]

That calm, however, is shattered by some dissenters who argue that human beings are not meant to venture into outer space. In the final scenes they persuade other citizens to try to prevent the launch of the initial rocket ship, carrying the son and daughter of the society's two foremost leaders around the moon with no guarantee of a safe return. This is a sophisticated and updated Luddite tale: not as mindless destruction of all machinery but instead, in the context of the original Luddites' opposition, as more understandable opposition to that large-scale machinery that threatened their craft labor, *not* to machinery per se. Everytown and all other cities have been completely rebuilt. Society has become highly scientific and technological in the decades since great wars, great famines, great plagues, and oppressive warlords gave way to the progressive, efficiency-minded airmen of "Wings Over the World." Modern cities resembling the 1939–1940 New York World's Fair World of Tomorrow exhibit predominate.

The mob surrounding the launch pad—and actor Massey's foremost opponent, a frightened sculptor named Theotocopulos played by Hardwicke—are demanding only the stoppage of the rocket flight, not the destruction of anything else. Obviously, as with the original Luddites, this is hardly a minor consideration. But there is a profound difference between opposition to science and technology per se versus their alleged excesses and misuse. They seek, then, a scientific and technological plateau and oppose the technological imperative.

Nevertheless, as the out-of-control crowd rushes to destroy the space gun that will propel the rocketship, Massey's character Oswald Cabal—great-grandson of the airmen's founder John Cabal (also played by Massey)—launches the craft ahead of schedule. His speech to his opponent epitomizes the technological imperative and the utopian impulse behind it. "And if," he asks his rival and in turn the whole world, "we're no more than animals, we must snatch each little scrap of happiness, and live, and suffer, and pass, mattering no more than all the other animals do or have done. It is this, or that, all the universe or nothing. Which shall it be ...? Which shall it be?"

Conclusion: Why Utopia Still Matters Today and Tomorrow

During his presidency (1989–1993), George H. W. Bush often mocked the idea of looking ahead as "that vision thing," including such a seemingly vital concept as a "national industrial policy." As someone devoid of ideological purity and persistence of any kind (having repeatedly changed his positions on most major issues in order to advance his political career), Bush's dismissal of "vision" might seem merely self-serving, the crassest kind of practical political bent. But it was sometimes taken up by others who, for whatever reasons, dismissed serious and systematic thinking about the future as a waste of time, an indulgence not fit for respectable leaders daily confronting endless challenges. Fukuyama's provocative *The End of History and the Last Man* (1992) might have been Bush's gospel had he ever read, much less understood, it; but he did neither. Ironically, Bush lost re-election in part because of his inability to present specifics to support the New World Order that he mentioned from time to time in light of the collapse of the Soviet Union. Not having "that vision thing" in the end hurt his presidency and his legacy. (Paradoxically, President Obama has been criticized by some as having too much vision and not enough substance.[16])

Nevertheless, despite the reservations about scientific and technological utopias catalogued in preceding chapters—and perhaps because of them—utopianism in general has blossomed as a field of serious study and scholarship. The Society for Utopian Studies, founded in the United States in 1976, has spawned a journal and complementary organizations in Europe.[17]

Broader public interest in utopianism was legitimized by a major exhibit at the prestigious and avowedly mainstream New York Public Library, in the heart of Manhattan, entitled "Utopia: The Search for the Ideal Society in the Western World." The exhibit ran from October 2000 until January 2001, the last three months of the twentieth century and the first month of the twenty-first century and the start of the Third Millennium. The exhibit drew many visitors and was widely and favorably reviewed. A version of the same exhibit had earlier been at the Bibliothèque Nationale de France in Paris, with similar success.

The subjects of the exhibit ranged from ancient cultures to the Internet. Its roughly 550 objects included often priceless books, manuscripts, documents, drawings, prints, maps, photographs, posters, and album covers. Among these objects were the first editions of More's *Utopia* and of other classic utopian works; Thomas Jefferson's handwritten copy of the Declaration of Independence; "The Green Globe," the first depiction of the Americas as separate continents; The (Christopher) Columbus Letter, the published version of his report from the New World; Shaker drawings; items from the 1939–1940 and 1964–1965 New York World's Fairs; and the original Woodstock poster.

It was unfortunate that non-Western utopias were excluded. As was established earlier, this hardly constitutes evidence that they were few in number, much less non-existent. But the organizers readily defended themselves: no offense was intended, but there was simply no space to be so inclusive. Indeed, the exhibit completely filled the Library's principal display space and had to be continued two floors above.[18] Everything was arranged chronologically and into four major sections: "Sources: Ancient, Biblical, and Medieval Traditions"; "Other Worlds: Utopian Imagination from More to the Enlightenment"; "Utopia in History: From the Revolutionary Age Through the Nineteenth Century"; and "Dreams and Nightmares: Utopias and Dystopias in the Twentieth Century." Within these sections were twenty subsections, ranging from "The Golden Age" and "The Garden of Eden" to "Ideal Cities of the Renaissance" to "The Invention of the New World" to "The Metropolis of the Future." A fifth major section—"Metaworlds: Utopian Visions of the Internet and the Metaphysics of Virtual Life"—remains on the Library's website, as do large portions of the other four sections.

It was reassuring to see utopia taken seriously as an intellectual, social, and cultural tradition, with many tangible expressions ranging from historic manuscripts, books, and maps to contemporary political posters and record album covers. However dismissive many people might be of utopia, these artifacts revealed much about those individuals, communities, and societies that proposed, and sometimes tried to enact, their particular utopia.

Without downplaying utopia's dark manifestations, the exhibit suggested that utopia was not the dead phenomenon it had commonly been assumed to be from World War II until the present. The world had moved beyond utopia's decades-old negative connotation as, at best, the naïve faith of dreamers not grounded in the practical affairs of ordinary, hardworking men and women and, at worst, as the all-too-practical program of dictators willing to murder millions in the pursuit of their version of perfection: for example, Hitler, Stalin, Mao, and Pol Pot. Instead, utopia was evolving into other manifestations—such as virtual communities—primarily based on high tech.

The exhibit's basic arguments were hardly controversial and constituted a useful summary of this book: (1) the quest for an ideal society "has been a staple element in human experience through all of recorded history"; (2) God, gods, and other super-human forces were originally conceived as providing any utopian fulfillment; (3) human beings gradually replaced them; (4) More's *Utopia* (1516) was the first work that moved the prospect of utopia from the hereafter to this world and that did so using ordinary persons rather than saintly souls; (5) the New World, both imag-ined and real, became the focal point of much utopian speculation and enterprise; (6) modern scientific and technological advances eventually allowed for the realization of utopia in the not-too-distant future; but (7) the totalitarian nightmares of Hitler's Germany and Stalin's Soviet Union long associated utopianism with dystopianism (anti-utopianism). Yet the exhibit concluded that (8) utopianism persists in small communities around the world, in fiction and non-fiction writings, and in Internet virtual communities.

True, the inclusion of Nazism and Stalinism might seem bizarre, but utopias reflect their proponents' diverse ideologies. Thus the exhibit illustrated the familiar notions that (1) Europeans' writings of the seventeenth and eighteenth centuries variously depicted Native Americans as either friendly innocents or hostile cannibals, and (2) Europeans' common vision of the New World as an allegedly blank slate varied enormously once the particulars were filled in.

Equally important, however, is determining whether proposed or actual changes will constitute a genuine transformation, as with Nazism or Stalinism, or a modest non-utopian reform, as with, say, American Progressive crusades for the initiative, referendum, and recall. Admittedly, displaying such phenomena as the prospectus for Levittown, Long Island, and items about Jonestown, Guyana, before and after the 1977 mass suicide/murder stretched these conceptual limits. Yet, if the exhibit perhaps inspired visitors to see utopian longings everywhere, encouraging them to contemplate utopianism at all was surely worth it.

As the exhibit acknowledged, utopias are "inseparable from the histories of the people, cultures, and periods that gave birth to them." Greater attention to these backgrounds would have been welcome, however challenging it might have been to include them. Otherwise, one risks marginalizing utopias as the province of only eccentrics, heretics, traitors, and other deviants—the obverse of seeing utopias everywhere. A partial remedy was the accompanying book, *Utopia*, containing twenty-two excellent essays by the editors and other leading scholars along with reproductions of over three hundred of the exhibit's objects.[19]

The fact that 9/11 occurred elsewhere in Manhattan only months after the exhibit closed does not diminish this monumental achievement.

In 2008 and 2009 two major museums, New York's Whitney and Chicago's Museum of Contemporary Art, successively exhibited "Buckminster Fuller: Starting with the Universe." This was the first major retrospective on Fuller since his death in 1983 and, like the New York Public Library exhibit, bespoke a more mature acknowledgment of the continued importance of utopianism, which, in this case, combined utopian writings, structures, and communities.[20]

In 1968 architectural critic Allan Temko published a provocative essay in *Horizon* magazine entitled "Which Guide to the Promised Land? Fuller or Mumford?" Without taking sides, Temko insightfully compared the differing visions of contemporaries Buckminster Fuller (1895–1983) and Lewis Mumford (1895–1990), both then at the height of their power and influence. Despite their vastly differing viewpoints, each had become a hero to younger audiences: Mumford because of his increasingly hostile analyses of modern technological advance gone awry, as in the Vietnam War; Fuller because of his steadily more optimistic views of contemporary technology's potential to transform the world and to create new communities.[21]

The exhibit provided a remarkably rich perspective. Derived largely from the forty-five-ton Fuller Archives at the Stanford University Library, the exhibit covered Fuller's entire life. The exhibit was greatly assisted by his having obsessively saved his correspondence and other paperwork, including notes and sketches, beginning in 1907. Its title came from Fuller's lifelong commitment to solving problems by investigating the basic order of nature and then utilizing the pertinent patterns uncovered there.

The exhibit simultaneously demonstrated how Fuller fulfilled his personal job description of "comprehensive anticipatory design scientist": an interdisciplinary, forward-looking explorer discovering how to benefit the highest number of people while expending the smallest amount of natural resources, akin perhaps to Jeremy Bentham. Here as elsewhere Fuller made up terms that, while sometimes serving to clarify, at other times became irritating jargon. To his great credit, as the exhibit likewise shows, Fuller's emphasis on "spaceship earth"—another of his terms—and on its fragile ecology contributed significantly to the growing post-World War II awareness of a world of integrated parts and people; of complex environmental systems requiring constant care.

Fuller received patents for twenty-eight inventions, a notable achievement in itself. He remains famous for several that were among the exhibit's highlights: the Dymaxion Car (1933), the Dymaxion Bathroom (1936), the Dymaxion Air-Ocean Map (a 1943 projection of the earth consisting of eight triangles and six rectangles), and the Dymaxion House (1945). Fuller envisioned the mass production of all four, but only the car was ever built, and then only three of those. "Dymaxion" combines "dynamic," "maximum," and "ion." After an advertising consultant suggested the term following a 1929 Fuller lecture, Fuller adopted "Dymaxion" as a trademark. He even later named his lifelong archival project, which grew to over two hundred thousand pages, the Dymaxion Chronofile.

Fuller's best-known invention, however, is the geodesic dome. "Geodesic" derives from the Greek words *geo* (earth) and *daiesthai* (to divide). It describes the shortest line between any two points on a surface. Fuller adopted this term as the name for his spherical dome structures that could be erected quickly as extremely strong, lightweight shelters. The exhibit revealed its first practical application as a ninety-three-feet-wide roof for the rotunda of Ford Motor Company's headquarters in Dearborn, Michigan, in 1953. There followed other successful geodesic domes, most famously the United States Pavilion at the Montreal Expo 1967 world's fair.

(Not mentioned is the leakage common to most Fuller domes.) In 1985 three scientists discovered that the structure of the C60 molecule resembles a geodesic dome. They named their discovery *buckminsterfullerene.*

The exhibit omitted the crucial fact that Fuller did not invent the geodesic dome. As revealed years ago, the actual inventor was Dr. Walter Bauersfeld, who designed a structure to cover a planetarium in Jena, Germany, that opened in 1922, three decades before Fuller filed his patent.[22]

Despite his concern that future generations might mismanage "spaceship earth," Fuller was certainly a passionate believer in technology's capacity to transform, if not literally perfect, society. Equally importantly, he was a key figure in the historic Western tradition of utopianism.[23] Fuller was the last popular American utopian who, as indicated, engaged in utopian thinking, speaking, writing, and building for their own sake rather than, as is commonplace today, primarily for commercial reasons. Unlike traditional visionaries, dating back to Thomas More, leading contemporary prophets rarely provide genuine moral critiques of the present or serious efforts to alter society for higher purposes. A notable exception is, as noted, Fuller's fellow Harvard dropout Bill Gates' admirable philanthropy. There is an ethical dimension to Fuller that is rare among technologically oriented visionaries.

Although Fuller never established any actual communities, utopian or otherwise, he invented enough components of potential communities to qualify as a genuine communitarian. As the exhibit illuminates, Fuller proposed land-based cities covered by climate-controlled geodesic domes, tetrahedronal cities floating on the sea, and cloud-structure spheres floating in the air. Many prior communitarians had been far less specific than Fuller in their plans and usually lacked the practical skills to establish successful communities, as with the nineteenth-century Transcendentalists, whose ranks included his great aunt Margaret Fuller. In fact, by designing artifacts that could be both moved and replicated, Fuller readily met a principal challenge facing most earlier (and later) communitarians: how to promote one's vision beyond its base camp, so to speak.[24]

Fuller deserves further recognition as the first major American scientific or technological utopian to argue—as per his bestselling (and already noted) *Utopia or Oblivion: The Prospects for Humanity* (1969)—that the realization of utopia was possible within our own lifetimes rather than, as with all earlier utopians, either possible only at least two generations ahead or virtually impossible. If this ethos has steadily pervaded corporate thinking and advertising, it also suffused such anti-corporate spirits as the hippies at Golden Gate Park, San Francisco, with whom Fuller engaged in 1967, as a delightful forty-four-minute DVD demonstrated at the exhibit. The non-violent, non-ideological, and drug-free guru, with his close-cropped hair and horn-rim glasses, neatly dressed in a conservative suit, impresses the rather differently dressed crowd—just as he did more mainstream audiences who also didn't necessarily understand many of his points.

The exhibit naturally includes an original of the cover the January 10, 1964 issue of *Time*, with Fuller's head caricatured as a geodesic dome. He had certainly "made it" by then. By 1975, however, Mumford could dismiss Fuller as "that interminable tape recorder of 'salvation by technology.'"[25] Hardly modest himself, Mumford was excessively harsh. Yet he reflected the growing disillusionment with technological (and scientific) utopianism and particularly the growing disillusionment with large-scale government projects to cure ills such as poverty and crime, as exemplified by the Reagan Administration of a few years later.

Similarly, Fuller's pioneering environmentalism becomes questionable after viewing his designs for and models of his proposed land-based, sea-based, and air-based cities. Fuller appears more concerned with efficiency than with greening the earth, and we are reminded of Mumford's scathing characterization elsewhere of all three projects as huge tombs akin to Egyptian pyramids.[26] What might be their impact on the environment? Moreover, how much conformity would these huge communities require? And what institutional arrangements would make life interesting once the thrill of being on land or at sea or in the air wore off?

Consequently, Fuller's legacy is by no means assured. Notwithstanding the exhibit's stunning achievement, its uncritical celebration of Fuller, along with its inadequate historical context, will not prevent future, more critical reassessments. Revealingly, however, in the introduction to his *Inventions: The Patented Works of R. Buckminster Fuller* (1983), written shortly before he died, Fuller provided an illuminating end-of-life reflection entitled "Guinea Pig B." Here the normally bombastic, inscrutable, and self-centered utopian is surprisingly restrained, lucid, and modest. He characterizes himself more as God's humble servant than as God's anointed prophet: "I hope this book will prove to be an encouraging example of what the little, average human being can do if you have absolute faith in the eternal cosmic intelligence we call God." Even his familiar utopian rhetoric is tempered by the recognition that the world, alas, is still far from anyone's ideal:

> We have reached a threshold moment where the individual human beings are in what I consider to be a "final examination" as to whether they, individually, as a cosmic invention, are to graduate successfully into their mature cosmic functioning or, failing, are to be classified as "imperfects" and "discontinued items" on this planet or anywhere else in [the] Universe.[27]

Here, then, might be an appropriate starting point for reconsidering the place of Buckminster Fuller and other twentieth- and twenty-first-century utopians.

In the first decades of the twenty-first century, utopian communities continue to be established and maintained, utopian writings continue to be published, world's fairs continue to be held, and, as noted at the outset, a popular Boston-area beer manufacturer offers New Englanders a highly potent "Utopias" beer. The search for utopia thus continues. True, no single model fits contemporary utopian endeavors any more than it fitted their predecessors; their contents remain as varied as ever. Yet it is increasingly clear that the ongoing computerization and digitalization of the world and the extraordinary growth of instantaneous communications and of unprecedented access to information have generated a renewed stage of utopian expectations despite, as already detailed, a legitimate and mature skepticism about especially scientific and technological "advances."

I myself advocate utopianism. For, in its most substantial forms, utopianism remains a provocative means of offering constructive criticism of existing society in order to improve it, not to abandon it. But, to be effective as social criticism, a utopian vision should be concrete enough to be applicable to the real world but also detached enough to be truly critical. I repeat: far from being escapist, utopianism in this sense is intended to be played back upon the real world in order to try to change it. Utopianism provides a vision of how the real world could be made more nearly perfect.

As James Dator, the head of the highly respected Hawai'i Research Center for Futures Studies at the University of Hawai'i, put it in a speech on May 9, 1997,

> I can assure you, there is no single, correct, view of the future, but many different views, depending on where you stand—your culture, your language, your age, your gender, your education, your unique personal experiences.... Nothing in society beyond the most trivial can be precisely predicted.... On the other hand, it is not the case that it is hopeless to try to anticipate things to come, or that anyone's guess is as good as anyone else's.... There are theories and methods which futurists have developed, tested, and applied in recent years which have proven useful, and exciting.

And, if "the future" cannot be predicted, then "alternative futures" should still be sought out, along with "preferred futures." Dator is not shy about suggesting that several tidal waves or "tsunamis of change" are probable, such as the relegation of Western civilization to a lesser place in shaping the twenty-first-century world behind "Confucian cultures," Islam, and Indian Hindu cultures; the replacement of territory-based nation-state governments with global "virtual governments"; and the phasing out of conventional schools and workplaces everywhere by online versions. But, unlike Toffler and educator Stukel, for example, Dator offers possibilities, not certainties. He manifests humility, not arrogance.[28]

Moreover, to be useful, utopianism need not consist of detailed blueprints. Building on Marx and Engels' critique of excessively detailed "utopian" blueprints, the philosopher Ernst Bloch (1885–1977) emphasized "traces" of existing society as being more important. Bloch stressed the potentials in the past and the present, "the memories," to link them to the "not yet," as he called the future and the multiple possibilities contained therein. Bloch likened utopias to daydreams, waking fantasies of objects, relationships, and conditions we presently lack and may either have once had or may never have had. True, few such daydreams constitute anything resembling full-fledged utopian visions. But daydreams can be positive steps in that direction. In fact, unlike most prior advocates of particular utopian visions, Bloch relished a plurality of utopian visions to reflect the desired plurality of everyday experience in both the real and the ideal worlds. He was advocating a choice of visions to ensure that utopianism served most fully its role as critic.[29]

Like Marx and Engels, and like Wells in, say, *Men Like Gods* (1923), Bloch appreciated the need for any actual utopias to allow for change once established. Too many utopias fail to do so and, even on paper—much less in practice in the case of communities—fall victim to self-defeating rigidity, monotony, and possible decay. Wise pioneering utopian writers such as More and Bacon also appreciated this, and More's Utopians, for example, welcome Christianity, while Bacon's New Atlantis sends out explorers to see whether the outside world has anything of use for them.

Historian Jay Winter has recently offered a different cast in support of several twentieth-century European utopias, which he labels "moments" or "minor utopias." Like Bloch, he advocates a diversity of utopian expressions. These moments constituted serious and, in some cases, nearly forgotten projects for partial transformation of the world rather than for its wholesale revolution or destruction. Yet they were legitimate utopian undertakings, often with greater long-time influence than better-known utopian enterprises. Rarely if ever examined from the angle of utopianism, these projects are the Paris World's Fair of 1900 and, in the same year, the photographs commissioned by French banker Albert Kahn and the Socialist Second International led by Frenchman Jean Jaurès; the Paris Peace Conference of 1919 and the League of Nations; the Paris exhibit of 1937 celebrating science, technology (especially electric lights), and art; French lawyer René Cassin's Universal Declaration of Human Rights of 1948; the French student revolt and the "Prague Spring" of 1968, plus, in the same era, Latin American liberation theology and communities; and the 1992 emergence of visions of global citizenship following the emergence of a powerful European Union through the Maastricht Treaty.

In each case, Winter reveals arguments and artifacts that demonstrate the appropriateness of the utopian label, yet without romanticizing the projects. For example, President Woodrow Wilson's 1919 vision of self-determination for all peoples as the royal road to peace was conspicuously at odds with his contempt for non-whites and non-Europeans. At the peace conference Wilson arrogantly refused to meet with W. E. B. Du Bois and Chinese Ambassador to the United States Wellington Koo to discuss Pan-African and Asian concerns. For the morally superior Wilson, racial hierarchy trumped universal rights. So much for the universality of his utopia.

Equally importantly, Winter strikingly connects these utopian enterprises with their decidedly non-utopian contexts. As noted in Chapter 2, the Spanish Civil War coincided with the 1937 Paris exposition's celebration of technology and science, which was at variance with the mass bombing of the city of Guernica weeks earlier. Recall that this deliberate attack on civilians inspired Pablo Picasso's famous painting, first shown in the Spanish pavilion. Meanwhile the Tower of Peace dwarfed the highly nationalistic German, Italian, Soviet, and Japanese pavilions, along with the Palestinian one boasting growing Jewish settlement. Similarly, the 1948 Declaration of Human Rights was shadowed by the recent liberation of the Nazi death camps. (These contradictions do not dismay but rather intrigue Winter.)

Not surprisingly, science and technology are the subtexts of Winter's minor utopias. His starting point is Kahn's project to photograph the entire world, to preserve it in Paris as the Archive of the Planet, and, by demonstrating more kinship than differences between nations and cultures, somehow to avoid further war. This might be considered a precursor of some contemporary projects to use the world's most powerful computers to try to determine once and for all what makes people tick and likewise to reduce conflicts (and, in some cases, to attempt to increase profits in stocks and other commercial ventures).[30] Similarly, the 1900 Paris fair, among the grandest of all, promoted capitalism, imperialism, and consumption as other means toward permanent world peace. By contrast, Jaurès opposed that very world order and instead sought peace by appealing to workers' presumed commitment worldwide to an equal distribution of products and to control over industrialization.

In these early utopian moments, Winter observes a genuine sense of globalization overlooked by those who associate it with only the past two decades. But he updates global citizenship to include "trans-national rights," women's rights, and environmental rights, such as the lawsuits against Union Carbide following the disastrous chemical spill in Bhopal, India, in 1984. Winter notes that recent minor utopians "have focused less on nation and social class and more on civil society and human rights." (Curiously, Winter does not follow countless others in deeming the Internet, the Web, and other "high-tech" advances utopian.)[31] Unlike those popular high-tech prophets, Winter wisely does not indulge in shallow speculation about the future. Winter's reconstruction of these past and present visionary projects offers "a margin of hope" (as Irving Howe entitled his autobiography) for recognizing their positive legacies for today.

Utopian visions of globalization, however, are as diverse as prior utopias. As Sargent observes, advocates of free markets and free trade offer a utopian scenario increasingly condemned as dystopian by opponents who seek to preserve distinctive local, regional, and national cultures from being trampled by multi-national corporations and by homogenized markets, manufactures, media, and so forth. These opponents frequently cite "civil society and human rights" as their fundamental utopian structure.[32]

Meanwhile, one of the most avowedly practical of American federal government agencies, the Department of Homeland Security, has enlisted futurists to assist with developing possible inventions and programs. There is now a Homeland Security Science and Technology Stakeholders annual conference, many of whose members are outright contractors seeking government contracts. Its members, however, generally provide their basic information for free as a civic patriotic duty. Some are professional scientists and engineers. They are not traditional utopians with full-fledged blueprints. Hence their kinship with Bloch's "traces."[33]

From a wholly different angle, literary scholar Kenneth Roemer has tested the responses of 733 contemporary readers from twenty years in four countries (Austria, Canada, Japan, and the United States) to *Looking Backward* as a means of trying to determine how significant utopian writings might affect those who absorb them. Roemer also examined eighty-three initial reviews of the book and found that many of those early reviewers themselves designated what they deemed appropriate audiences for that seminal book by, of course, a fairly obscure writer and journalist at the time of its 1888 publication. And some reviewers, for example William Morris, were definitely hostile. Roemer incorporated several literary methods, most notably reader response and book culture, in analyzing the results of modern readers' responses to his questionnaires.

In his provocative afterword, Roemer imagines a gathering to preview those exhibits on utopianism at the Bibliothèque Nationale de France and the New York Public Library. The viewers arrive by conventional and unconventional means alike: automobiles and rocketships, sailing ships and time machines, dreams and deep freezes. Their numbers include actual authors; living descendants of those authors; such professional readers as reviewers, illustrators, critics, and scholars; activists seeking to effect utopian visions; those 733 respondents; and the imagined readers inscribed in utopian texts by authors and scholars. Their discussions reveal, first, that the common assumption of most ordinary readers' estrangement from utopian writings can be reduced by the incorporation of conventional narratives and appealing characters; second, that a variety of utopian writings, both fiction and non-fiction, will enlarge the reading audience with its varied tastes; and third, and finally, that serious utopian writings of all kinds can still move readers in any number of ways.

Sterling Delano's *Brook Farm: The Dark Side of Utopia* (2004) details the basic facts of daily life of that famous utopian community's residents and also their reading habits. Most interestingly, they did not appear to have read many (if any) utopian works once they had chosen to try to establish an actual community. Instead, they read primarily non-utopian works. "Living the dream," so to speak, presumably sufficed and, despite Bellamy's preference for writings over communities later in the nineteenth century, was certainly a passionate commitment to utopianism. In a sense, moreover, the Brook Farm residents had acted upon their earlier readings of Fourier and other visionaries. This places them within the realm that Roemer explores as one-time readers obviously moved to action and attempted fulfillment.

These approaches could surely be broadened to include both responses to online utopian writings and other high-tech communications such as e-mail and text messages—again, full-fledged blueprints are not necessary.[34] Going further: if, thanks to high-tech advances, "virtual reality" has become widely used in other realms, it could surely be utilized here to test and develop alternative futures. Those wishing to experience alternatives can do so "safely," before committing themselves to actual decisions and actions. What could be a more appropriate application of this scientific and technological advance? And what better way than this of experiencing alternatives before deciding about whether to try to change existing societies? Consequently, utopianism may thus have a bright future after all.

Notes

1   See the excellent summary of Japan's ambivalence toward Chinese and Western science in William E. Burns, *Knowledge and Power: Science in World History* (Upper Saddle River: Pearson, 2011), 14–15, 94–95, 107–120.
2   Alex Roland, review of Kenneth Chase, *Firearms: A Global History to 1700*, in *The Journal of Interdisciplinary History*, 35 (Spring 2005), 618.
3   Conrad Totman, review of Noel Perrin, Giving Up the Gun: Japan's Reversion to the Sword, 1543–1879, in *The Journal of Asian Studies*, 39 (May 1980), 601.
4   See Burns, *Knowledge and* Power, 108.

5   See Adam Robert Lucas, "Industrial Milling in the Ancient and Medieval Worlds: A Survey of the Evidence for an Industrial Revolution in Medieval Europe," *Technology and Culture*, 46 (January 2005), 1–30.

6   Jean Gimpel, *The Medieval Machine: The Industrial Revolution of the Middle Ages* (New York: Holt, Rinehart and Winston, 1976), 249.

7   See Howard P. Segal, "Eighteenth-Century American Utopianism: From the Potential to the Probable," *Utopian Studies*, 11 (2000), 5–13.

8   See, for example, Herman Kahn, *The Coming Boom: Economic, Political, and Social* (New York: Simon and Schuster, 1982); Kahn et al., *The Next 200 Years: A Scenario for America and the World* (New York: Morrow, 1976); and Julian L. Simon, *The Ultimate Resource* (Princeton: Princeton University Press, 1981).

9   On the questionable performance of high-tech weapons systems during the 1991 Persian Gulf War, see Howard P. Segal, *Future Imperfect: The Mixed Blessings of Technology in America* (Amherst, MA: University of Massachusetts Press, 1994), ch. 12, n. 1. On the initial situation during the 2003 Iraq War, see Anne Bernard, "Gritty Ground Footage Topping Smart Bombs," *Boston Globe*, March 25, 2003, A19. See also George N. Lewis and Theodore A. Postol, "Truth or Consequences for Missile Defense," *Boston Globe*, May 28, 2010, A13; and letter from Patrick J. O'Reilly criticizing that Op Ed column in *Boston Globe*, June 16, 2010, A12.

10 See David Abel, "School's Call to Unplug Welcomed by Some, Unanswered by Others," *Boston Globe*, October 7, 2010, B1, B15.

11 See Leslie Kaufman, *New York Times*, "Parkgoers Find Trouble with Gadgets: Devices Factor in More Incidents, US Rangers Say," *Boston Sunday Globe*, August 22, 2010, A3.

12 See Julie Scelfo, "The Brain on Computers: R U Here, Mom?" *New York Times*, June 10, 2010, D1, D7. See also Susan Maushart, *The Winter Of Our Disconnect: How Three Totally Wired Teenagers (and a Mother Who Slept with Her iPhone) Pulled the Plug on Their Technology and Lived to Tell the Tale* (New York: Tarcher/Penguin, 2011); and interview by Bella English with William Powers, "Plugged In," *Boston Globe*, July 17, 2010, G: Living, 3.

13 Harold Loeb, *Life in a Technocracy: What It Might Be Like* (Syracuse, NY: Syracuse University Press, 1996 [1933]), 45. For an extended discussion of Loeb's entire life, his other writings, the evolution of his thought, and the fate of technocracy over time, see the new introduction to *Life in a Technocracy* by Howard P. Segal.

14   Nicholas Rescher, "Technological Progress and Human Happiness," in *Unpopular Essays on Technological Progress* (Pittsburgh: University of Pittsburgh Press, 1980), 19.

15   The term is mentioned by David C. Smith in his *H. G. Wells: Desperately Mortal: A Biography* (New Haven: Yale University Press, 1986), 324. Smith's definitive biography summarizes both the book and the film on 324–325.

16   See Charles Krauthammer, "Obama's Economic Vision," *Bangor Daily News*, June 18, 2010, A13.

17   The following is taken from the website of *Utopian Studies*' new publisher, Penn State University Press. For more information on the journal see http://muse.jhu.edu/content/alerts/journals/utopian_studies.

    Utopian Studies is a peer-reviewed publication of the Society for Utopian Studies, publishing scholarly articles on a wide range of subjects related to utopias, utopianism, utopian literature, utopian theory, and intentional communities. Contributing authors come from a diverse range of fields, including American studies, architecture, the arts, classics, cultural studies, economics, engineering, environmental studies, gender studies, history, languages and literatures, philosophy, political science, psychology, sociology, and urban planning. Each issue also includes dozens of reviews of recent books.

18   Despite this overflow of intellectual riches, the exhibit was extremely well organized and very accessible to the proverbial general public. Most of these treasures were placed in forty-four new steel, glass, and stone exhibition cases, with special lighting that, for preservation purposes, was kept low.

19   "Utopia: The Search for the Ideal Society in the Western World." The New York Public Library, Humanities and Social Sciences Library, http://www.nypl.org/utopia. Temporary exhibit, October 14, 2000 to January 27, 2001. Curator: Roland Schaer; research curator: Holland Goss; advisory team: Gregory Claeys, Paul LeClerc, and Lyman Tower Sargent. Catalog: Schaer, Claeys, and Sargent, eds. *Utopia: The Search for the Ideal Society in the Western World* (New York: New York Public Library and Oxford University Press, 2000). See also Howard P. Segal, "Exhibition Review: 'Utopia: The Search for the Ideal Society in the Western World,' New York Public Library," *Journal of American History*, 88 (June 2001), 152–155.

20   "Buckminster Fuller: Starting with the Universe." The Whitney Museum, New York, http://www.whitney.org/www/buckminster_ fuller. Temporary exhibit, June 26 to September 21, 2008. Also The Museum of Contemporary Art, Chicago, http://www.mcachicago.

org/exhibitions. Temporary exhibit, Summer 2009. Catalog edited by K. Michael Hays and Dana Miller (New York: Whitney Museum; and New Haven: Yale University Press, 2008). The exhibit included approximately 220 models, videos, photographs, and works on paper.

21 See Allan Temko, "Which Guide to the Promised Land? Fuller or Mumford?" *Horizon*, 10 (Summer 1968), 25–30. Mumford's life and work have received serious posthumous treatment—see, for example, Donald Miller, *Lewis Mumford: A Life* (New York: Weidenfeld and Nicholson, 1989) and Agatha and Thomas Hughes, eds., *Lewis Mumford: Public Intellectual* (New York: Oxford University Press, 1990), but Fuller's have not. Partial reconsideration have now been remedied by Hsiao-Yun Chu and Roberto G. Trujillo, eds., *New Views on R. Buckminster Fuller* (Stanford: Stanford University Press, 2009).

22 One of the catalog's essays—by K. Michael Hays—includes a photo of that dome's construction but doesn't elaborate.

23 The exhibit's press kit states that "Fuller has often been called a utopian thinker, yet it is important to note that he was not overly optimistic about the future." His concern that future generations might mismanage "spaceship earth" was understandable, but the exhibit failed to put Fuller into sufficient historical context. Hays' essay does discuss Fuller's utopian bent.

24 On Margaret Fuller, see the helpful summary by Jenny Rankin, "A Writer, Thinker, and Trailblazer," *Boston Globe*, May 24, 2010, A11. Fuller's readiness to work for Stalinist Russia in 1932 and for the Ford Motor Company in 1953 does not reflect any growing political conservatism on his part but rather the tough reality of the necessity of seeking sources for funding and for bringing his designs to fruition. The exhibit might have noted this. Similarly, one cannot associate Fuller with any fascist tendencies akin to the uniformed right-wing Technocrats of the 1930s in this label about his 1933 Dymaxion Car: "Several of the car's mechanics can be seen wearing jumpsuits emblazoned with a winged fish that Fuller used for his company's logo." Furthermore, when Fuller was criticized by some during the Vietnam War for allowing the American military to consider using geodesic domes, he defended himself by noting that they would be employed elsewhere in the world, and for non-military purposes, and that he hadn't taken a position on the war.

25 Lewis Mumford, *Findings and Keepings: Analects for an Autobiography* (New York: Harcourt Brace Jovanovich, 1975), 373.

26 See Howard P. Segal, *Future Imperfect: The Mixed Blessings of Technology in America* (Amherst, MA: University of Massachusetts Press, 1994), 152.

27 Richard Buckminster Fuller, *Inventions: The Patented Works of R. Buckminster Fuller* (New York: St. Martin's, 1983), xxxii, xx.

28 James Dator, "Will You Surf the Tsunamis of Change?" Lecture before the Pacific Islands Club, Hawai'i, May 9, 1997. My colleague in the University of Maine's Department of Public Administration, Kenneth Nichols, provided me with a copy of this lecture as part of the readings for the annual fall Pop Tech online course we co-teach, along with several others at the University of Maine.

29 On Ernst Bloch, see, for example, his *A Philosophy of the Future*, tr. John Cumming (New York: Herder and Herder, 1970), esp. 84–144. His most important work is the three-volume *The Principle of Hope*, tr. Neville Plaice, Stephen Plaice, and Paul Knight (Cambridge: MIT Press, 1986). Jacoby offers an appreciation of this aspect of Bloch's work. See also Yves Charles Zarka, "The Meaning of Utopia," *New York Times*, Opinion Pages, August 28, 2011, http://opinionator. blogs.nytimes.com.

30 See, for example, "Google: Books by the Numbers," *Boston Globe*, Editorial, December 21, 2010, A18; Graham Bowley, "Computers that Trade on the News," *New York Times*, December 23, 2010, B1, B4; Gareth Morgan, "Earth Project Aims to 'Stimulate Everything," *BBC News Technology*, December 27, 2010, http://www.bbc.co.uk/news/ technology-12012082; and Scott Kirsner, "Innovation Economy," *Boston Sunday Globe*, January 2, 2011, G3.

31 Jay Winter, *Dreams of Peace and Freedom: Utopian Moments in the Twentieth Century* (New Haven: Yale University Press, 2006), 190, 6.

32 See Lyman Tower Sargent, *Utopianism: A Very Short Introduction* (New York: Oxford University Press, 2010), 115–117, for some specific writers and writings.

33 David Montgomery, "Sci-fi Writers on Mission to Imagine Unimaginable," *Washington Post*, reprinted in *Boston Globe*, May 23, 2009, A4. This is a different David Montgomery from the labor historian mentioned earlier.

34 See Kenneth M. Roemer, *Utopian Audiences: How Readers Locate Nowhere* (Amherst: University of Massachusetts Press, 2003).

Further Reading

General Histories of Utopian Writings, Communities, and Movements

Claeys, Gregory, Paul LeClerc, and Lyman Tower Sargent, eds., *Utopia: The Search for the Ideal Society in the Western World* (New York: New York Public Library and Oxford University Press, 2000).

Claeys, Gregory, and Lyman Tower Sargent, eds., *The Utopia Reader* (New York: New York University Press, 1999).

Clarke, I. F., *The Pattern of Expectation, 1644–2001* (New York: Basic Books, 1979).

Manuel, Frank, and Fritzie P. Manuel, *Utopian Thought in the Western World* (Cambridge, MA: Harvard University Press, 1979).

Sargent, Lyman Tower, *Utopianism: A Very Short Introduction* (New York: Oxford University Press, 2010).

Studies of Utopian Writings and Movements

Bauer, Wolfgang, *China and the Search for Happiness: Recurring Themes in Four Thousand Years of Chinese Cultural History*, tr. Michael Shaw (New York: Seabury, 1976).

Ferguson, John, *Utopias of the Classical World* (Ithaca, NY: Cornell University Press, 1975).

Jacoby, Russell, *Picture Imperfect: Utopian Thought in an Anti-Utopian Age* (New York: Columbia University Press, 2005).

Kateb, George, *Utopia and Its Enemies* (New York: Free Press, 1963).

Utopias: A Brief History from Ancient Writings to Virtual Communities,
First Edition. Howard P. Segal.

Kumar, Krishan, *Utopia and Anti-Utopia in Modern Times* (Oxford: Blackwell, 1987).

Kumar, Krishan, *Utopianism* (Minneapolis, MN: University of Minnesota Press, 1991).

Levitas, Ruth, *The Concept of Utopia* (Syracuse: Syracuse University Press, 1991).

Manuel, Frank E., ed., *Utopias and Utopian Thought: A Timely Appraisal* (Boston, MA: Houghton Mifflin, 1966).

Sargent, Lyman Tower, "The Three Faces of Utopianism Revisited," *Utopian Studies*, 5 (1994), 1–37.

Surveys of Utopian Literature

Davis, J. C., *Utopia and the Ideal Society: A Study of English Utopian Writing, 1516–1700* (New York: Cambridge University Press, 1981).

Gregory Claeys, ed., *The Cambridge Companion to Utopian Literature* (Cambridge: Cambridge University Press, 2010).

Kilgore, De Witt Douglas, *Astrofuturism: Science, Race, and Visions of Utopia in Space* (Philadelphia, PA: University of Pennsylvania Press, 2003).

Longxi, Zhang, "The Utopian Vision, East and West," *Utopian Studies, 13* (2002), 1–20.

Patai, Daphne, ed., *Looking Backward, 1988–1888* (Amherst, MA: University of Massachusetts Press, 1988).

Plath, David W., ed., *Aware of Utopia* (Urbana, IL: University of Illinois Press, 1971).

Roemer, Kenneth M., *America as Utopia* (New York: Burt Franklin, 1981).

Roemer, Kenneth M., *The Obsolete Necessity: America in Utopian Writings, 1888–1900* (Kent, OH: Kent State University Press, 1976).

Roemer, Kenneth M., *Utopian Audiences: How Readers Locate Nowhere* (Amherst, MA: University of Massachusetts Press, 2003).

Utopian Communities

Bestor, Arthur E., Jr., *Backwoods Utopias: The Sectarian Origins and the Owenite Phase of Communitarian Socialism in America, 1663–1829*, 2nd edn. (Philadelphia, PA: University of Pennsylvania Press, 1970).

Delano, Sterling F., *Brook Farm: The Dark Side of Utopia* (Cambridge, MA: Harvard University Press, 2004).

Foster, Lawrence, *Women, Family, and Utopia: Communal Experiments of the Shakers, the Oneida Community, and the Mormons* (Syracuse, NY: Syracuse University Press, 1991).

Francis, Richard, *Fruitlands: The Alcott Family and Their Search for Utopia* (New Haven, CT: Yale University Press, 2010).

Garrett, Clarke, *Origins of the Shakers: From the Old World to the New World* (Baltimore, MD: Johns Hopkins University Press, 1998).

Gavron, Daniel, *The Kibbutz: Awakening From Utopia* (Lanham, MD: Rowman and Littlefield, 2000).

Guarneri, Carl J., *The Utopian Alternative: Fourierism in Nineteenth-Century America* (Ithaca, NY: Cornell University Press, 1991).

Kern, Louis J., *An Ordered Love: Sex Roles and Sexuality in Victorian Utopias: The Shakers, the Mormons, and the Oneida Community* (Chapel Hill, NC: University of North Carolina Press, 1981).

Lejeune, Jean-Francois, ed., *Cruelty and Utopia: Cities and Landscapes of Latin America* (New York: Princeton Architectural Press, 2005).

Near, Henry, *The Kibbutz Movement: A History*, 2 vols. (Oxford: Oxford University Press, 1992; London: Vallentine Mitchell, 1997).

Stein, Stephen J., *The Shaker Experience in America* (New Haven, CT: Yale University Press, 1992).

World's Fairs

Findling, John E., ed., *Historical Dictionary of World's Fairs and Expositions, 1851–1988* (Westport, CT: Greenwood, 1990).

Meikle, Jeffrey L., *Twentieth-Century Limited: Industrial Design in America, 1925–1939*, 2nd edn. (Philadelphia, PA: Temple University Press, 2001 [1979]).

Rydell, Robert, John Findling, and Kimberly Pelle, eds., *Fair America: World's Fairs in the United States* (Washington: Smithsonian Institution Press, 2000).

Winter, Jay, *Dreams of Peace and Freedom: Utopian Moments in the Twentieth Century* (New Haven, CT: Yale University Press, 2006).

The Idea/Concept of Progress

Adas, Michael, *Machines as the Measure of Men: Science, Technology, and Ideologies of Western Dominance* (Ithaca, NY: Cornell University Press, 1989).

Burns, William E. *Knowledge and Power: Science in World History* (Upper Saddle River, NJ: Pearson, 2011).

Bury, J. B., *The Idea of Progress: An Inquiry Into Its Origin and Growth* (New York: Macmillan, 1932 [1920]).

Duffy, Enda, *The Speed Handbook: Velocity, Pleasure, Modernism* (Durham, NC: Duke University Press, 2009).

Nisbet, Robert, *History of the Idea of Progress* (New York: Basic Books, 1980).

Olson, Theodore, *Millennialism, Utopianism, and Progress* (Toronto, ON: University of Toronto Press, 1982).

Rescher, Nicholas, *Unpopular Essays on Technological Progress* (Pittsburgh, PA: University of Pittsburgh Press, 1980).

Smith, David C., *H. G. Wells: Desperately Mortal: A Biography* (New Haven, CT: Yale University Press, 1986).

Wagar, W. Warren, *Good Tidings: The Belief in Progress from Darwin to Marcuse* (Bloomington, IN: Indiana University Press, 1972).

Visions of America

Corn, Joseph J., ed., *Imagining Tomorrow: History, Technology, and the American Future* (Cambridge, MA: MIT Press, 1986).

Honour, Hugh, *The New Golden Age: European Images of America from the Discoveries to the Present Time* (New York: Pantheon, 1975).

Jennings, Francis, *The Invasion of America: Indians, Colonialism, and the Cant of Conquest* (New York: Norton, 1976).

Nye, David E., *America as Second Creation: Technology and Narratives of New Beginnings* (Cambridge, MA: MIT Press, 2003).

Science, Technology, and Public and Foreign Policy

Balogh, Brian, *Chain Reaction: Expert Debate and Public Participation in American Commercial Nuclear Power, 1945–1975* (New York: Cambridge University Press, 1991).

Bedford, Henry F., *Seabrook Station: Citizen Politics and Nuclear Power* (Amherst, MA: University of Massachusetts Press, 1990).

Bess, Michale, *The Light-Green Society: Ecology and Technological Modernity in France, 1960–2000* (Chicago, IL: University of Chicago Press, 2003).

Bix, Amy Sue, *Inventing Ourselves Out of Jobs? America's Debate Over Technological Unemployment, 1929–1981* (Baltimore, MD: Johns Hopkins University Press, 2000).

Brown, Valerie A., John A. Harris, and Jacqueline Y. Russell, eds., *Tackling Wicked Problems: Through the Transdisciplinary Imagination* (Washington and London: Earthscan/James and James, 2010).

Bueno de Mesquita, Bruce, *The Predictioneer's Game: Using the Logic of Brazen Self-Interest to See and Shape the Future* (New York: Random House, 2009).

Haney, David Paul, *The Americanization of Social Science: Intellectuals and Public Responsibility in the Postwar United States* (Philadelphia, PA: Temple University Press, 2008).

Hart, David M., *Forged Consensus: Science, Technology, and Economic Policy in the United States, 1921–1953* (Princeton, NJ: Princeton University Press, 1998).

Hecht, Gabrielle, *The Radiance of France: Nuclear Power and National Identity After World War II* (Cambridge, MA: MIT Press, 1998).

Kevles, Daniel J., *The Physicists: The History of a Scientific Community in Modern America* (Cambridge, MA: Harvard University Press, 1995 [1977]).

Kleinman, Daniel Lee, *Politics On the Endless Frontier: Postwar Research Policy in the United States* (Durham, NC: Duke University Press, 1995).

Marcus, Alan I and Amy Sue Bix, *The Future Is Now: Science and Technology Policy in America Since 1950* (Amherst, MA: Humanity Books, 2007).

Matarese, Susan M., *American Foreign Policy and the Utopian Imagination* (Amherst, MA: University of Massachusetts Press, 2001).

Nelson, Richard, *The Moon and the Ghetto: An Essay on Public Policy Analysis* (New York: Norton, 1977).

Prakesh, Gyan, *Another Reason: Science and the Imagination of Modern India* (Princeton, NJ: Princeton University Press, 1999).

Stokes, Donald E., *Pasteur's Quadrant: Basic Science and Technological Innovation* (Washington, DC: Brookings Institution Press, 1997).

Critiques and Defences of Science and Technology

Brende, Eric, *Better Off: Flipping the Switch on Technology* (New York: HarperCollins, 2004).

Chu, Hsiao-Yun and Roberto G. Trujillo, eds., *New Views on R. Buckminster Fuller* (Stanford, CA: Stanford University Press, 2009).

Cornish, Edward, *Futuring: The Exploration of the Future* (Bethesda, MD: World Future Society, 2004).

Ezrahi, Yaron, Everett Mendelsohn, and Howard P. Segal, eds., *Technology, Pessimism, and Postmodernism* (Amherst, MA: University of Massachusetts Press, 1995 [1994]).

Gross, Paul R. and Norman Levitt, *Higher Superstition: The Academic Left and Its Quarrels with Science* (Baltimore, MD: Johns Hopkins University Press, 1994).

Holton, Gerald, *Science and Anti-Science* (Cambridge, MA: Harvard University Press, 1993).

Hoos, Ida R., *Systems Analysis in Public Policy: A Critique*, 2nd edn. (Berkeley and Los Angeles, CA: University of California Press, 1983).

Horgan, John, *The End of Science: Facing the Limits of Knowledge in the Twilight of the Scientific Age* (Reading: Addison-Wesley, 1996).

Ross, Andrew, *Strange Weather: Culture, Science, and Technology in the Age of Limits* (New York: Verso, 1991).

Ross, Andrew, ed., *Science Wars* (Durham, NC: Duke University Press, 1996).

Turner, Fred, *From Counterculture to Cyberculture: Stewart Brand, the Whole Earth Network, and the Rise of Digital Utopianism* (Chicago, IL: University of Chicago Press, 2006).

Three Twentieth-Century Leading Visionaries

Chu, Hsiao-Yun and Roberto G. Trujillo, eds., *New Views on R. Buckminster Fuller* (Stanford, CA: Stanford University Press, 2009).

Hughes, Agatha and Thomas, eds. *Lewis Mumford: Public Intellectual* (New York: Oxford University Press, 1990).

Smith, David C., *H. G. Wells: Desperately Mortal: A Biography* (New Haven, CT: Yale University Press, 1986).

Educational Utopias

Cuban, Larry, *Oversold and Underused: Computers in the Classroom* (Cambridge, MA: Harvard University Press, 2001).

Johnson, Marilyn, *This Book Is Overdue: How Librarians and Cybrarians Can Save Us All* (New York: Harper, 2010).

Tyack, David B. and Larry Cuban, *Tinkering Toward Utopia: A Century of Public School Reform* (Cambridge, MA: Harvard University Press, 1995).

Warschauer, Mark J., *Laptops and Literacy: Learning in the Wireless Classroom* (New York: Teachers College Press, 2006).

The Social Media

Boellstorff, Tom, *Coming of Age in* Second Life*: An Anthropologist Explores the Virtually Human* (Princeton, NJ: Princeton University Press, 2008).

Dreyfus, Hubert L., *On the Internet*, 2nd edn. (New York and London: Routledge, 2009).

Edwards, Douglas, *I'm Feeling Lucky: The Confessions of Google Employee Number 59* (Boston, MA: Houghton Mifflin Harcourt, 2011).

Kirkpatrick, David, *The Facebook Effect: The Inside Story of the Company that Is Connecting the World* (New York: Simon and Schuster, 2010).

Mezrich, Ben, *The Accidental Billionaires: The Founding of Facebook: A Tale of Sex, Money, Genius, and Betrayal* (New York: Doubleday, 2009).

Turkle, Sherry, *Alone Together: Why We Expect More from Technology and Less from Each Other* (New York: Basic Books, 2011).

Contemporary Utopian Megaprojects

Fleming, James, *Fixing the Sky: The Checkered History of Weather and Climate Control* (New York: Columbia University Press, 2010).

Franklin, H. Bruce, *War Stars: The Superweapon and the American Imagination*, 2nd edn. (Amherst, MA: University of Massachusetts Press, 2008 [1988]).

Noble, David F., *The Religion of Technology: The Divinity of Man and the Spirit of Invention* (New York: Knopf, 1997).

Popular Culture and Utopias/Dystopias

Fisch, Audrey A., *Frankenstein: Icon of Modern Culture* (Hastings: Helm Information, 2009).

Kirby, David A., *Lab Coats in Hollywood: Science, Scientists, and Cinema* (Cambridge, MA: MIT Press, 2011).

Index

1959: The Year that Changed Everything (Kaplan) 191
1984 (Orwell) 14, 124, 166

Absent-Minded Professor, The 202
Aburdene, Patricia 161, 162, 168, 186
Ackerman, Forrest J. 8
Adams, Brooks 98
Adams, Henry 82–83, 98, 168, 237
Adas, Michael 169, 170
Affluent Society, The (Galbraith) 101
Africa 102, 170
  and Western technology 170–171
Afrocentrism 171
ahistorical/anti-historical trend 191
AIDS 171
All Things New: American Communes and Utopian Movements, 1860–1914 (Pogarty) 25

Alone Together: Why We Expect More from Technology and Less from Each Other (Turkle) 194
alternative futures, necessity to consider 250
Amazon (website) 218, 219, 220
  see also Kindle
Amazons (mythological) 92
ambivalence toward the modern 191
America as Second Creation (Nye) 81, 168, 237
American Association for the Advancement of Science 116
American Interplanetary Society 9
American Progressive campaigns 244
American Revolution 56, 74
American Technocracy Crusade 90, 109, 110, 123, 216, 239
  history of 96–99
  in UK 98
  see also Thorstein Veblen

Andreae, Johann Valentin   52, 53,
   54, 164
"Anglophone world"   98
*Another Reason: Science and the
   Imagination of Modern India*
   (Prakesh)   171
anti-corporatism   114–115
anti-utopians   7, 147, 161
Apocalyptic Presentiments   191,
   211
Apollo Program   7, 139–140, 141
   spin-offs from   7, 140
Appalachia, United States   101
Apple Computer   158, 187, 202,
   218
Archive of the Planet   252–253
area studies   102
Argentina   22
Arnold, Matthew   98
artificial intelligence   187
Asia   19, 102, 172, 196, 252
"Atom, Electricity, and You!, The"
   143–144
Atomic Energy Act, US   143
Atomic Energy Commission,
   United States   143
Atoms for Peace program   143
Atwood, Margaret   9
audiobooks   218

Bacon, Francis   52, 53, 54, 55,
   164, 251
Baigan, Ishida   19
Balogh, Brian   155, 156
Barnwell, South Carolina   148
Barnes and Noble   220, 221
Bauersfeld, Dr. Walter   247
Beard, Charles   51
Beijing Olympics   188
Being Digital (Negroponte)   163
Bell, Alexander Graham   157
Bell, Daniel   115, 109, 114, 122

Bellamy, Edward   10, 24, 29–32,
   59, 90, 255
   Bellamy-led Nationalist move-
      ment   10, 24, 27, 32
   and technology   31–32
   see also Looking Backward
Bello, Andrés   22
Bentham, Jeremy   62, 246
Berry, Brian   30
Best and the Brightest, The   99ff,
   111, 160
*Best Game Ever, The: Giants vs. Colts,
   1958, and the Birth of the
   Modern NFL* (Bowden)   191
Bezos, Jeff   220
Bhopal, India   253
Bible   47
Bibliothèque Nationale de France,
   Paris   254
Big Brother   166
Bigelow, Jacob   52
Bikle, George   20, 21
Billington, David   52, 121
Bimber, Bruce   118
biomass, energy from   157
biotechnology   186
BlackBerry gadgets   220
Blair, Ann   190
Blake, William   83
Blithedale Romance (Hawthorne)
   25
Bloch, Ernst   251, 254
Bohr, Niels   120
Bolívar, Simon   22
Bonald, Vicomte de   60
Bono (pop star)   163
Book of Revelation and utopianism
   25
books, attitudes toward   190
   persistence of print   217–222
bookstores, US, closure of   218
Boorstin, Daniel   101, 102

Borders chain stores, closure
    of   218
Boston Beer Company   3
Bova, Ben   9
Bowden, Mark   191
Bradley, Mary E.   92
Brand, Stewart   154
Brave New World (A. Huxley)   123,
    166
Brazil   23
*Bright-sided: How the Relentless
    Promotion of Positive Thinking
    has Undermined America*
    (Ehrenreich)   168
Brin, Sergey   158
British Empire   114
Brook Farm   24, 25–26, 27
Brook Farm: The Dark Side of Utopia
    (Delano)   254–255
Brooklyn Bridge   139
Brooks, David   124
Bryan, William Jennings   29
Bryant, Howard   191
Buckminster Fuller: Starting with
    the Universe (exhibition)
    245
buckminsterfullerene   247
Buddhist eschatological
    traditions   21
Bundy, McGeorge   104, 106
Bunji, Suzuki   20
Burma (Myanmar)   19
Burns, William   236
Bury, J. B.   51
Bush, President George H. W.
    115, 241, 242
Bush, President George W.   11,
    140, 142, 151
Bush, Vannevar   103, 122
  on science policy   99–101,
    119–120, 121
  and Stokes   120, 121–122

  *see also Science – The Endless
    Frontier*

California-Pacific Exposition, San
    Diego   34
Campanella, Tommaso   52, 53,
    164
*Camperdown; or, News from Our
    Neighbourhood* (Griffith)
    91
campuses, real and virtual
    207–210
"Can Technology Replace Social
    Engineering"
    (Weinberg)   107
Canada   10, 28, 254
cancer, detection and treatment
    126, 146
Cape Wind, United States   150
capitalist viewpoint   104
"capture" of improvement   6
Carlyle, Thomas   58, 59
Carnegie, Dale   168
Carter, President Jimmy   111–112
Cassin, Rene   252
Castro, Fidel   22
"cataclysmic thought"   98
cell phones   193, 194
Century of Progress International
    Exposition, Chicago   34
Chabon, Michael   202
*Chain Reaction: Expert Debate and
    Public Participation in
    American Commercial Nuclear
    Power, 1945–1975*
    (Balogh)   155
Chavez, Hugo, President of
    Venezuela   23
Chen Shuai   38
Chernobyl, Ukraine   147, 153,
    155
Chester, John   145

Chiapas Indians, Mexico   23
Chicago fair 1893   37
Chicken Soup for the Soul   168
China   2, 188
 Chinese science   170
 and Internet   189
 utopianism in   17–19, 196
Christianity   48
 and Pansophia   53
Christian messianic utopian
  movements   20–21
Christianopolis (Andrea)   53
Churchman, C. West   112
Cisco Systems   206
City of the Sun, The (Campanella)
  53
civil society   253
Clark University   238
Clarke, Arthur C.   9
Clinton, President Bill   115, 119
cloning   125
Cold War   9, 36, 102, 143
 end of   1, 156
 India and   172
 and Space Program   139–140
 and utopias   2
Coleridge, Samuel Taylor   112–113
Colored People's Day   37
Columbus, Christopher   242
communist viewpoint   104
 collapse of communism   156
computers, development
  of   160–161, 186
Comte, Auguste   52, 56, 57–58
Condorcet, Marquis de   52, 56, 61
Confucius   18
Congress, US   111, 115, 117, 118
 and Superconducting Super
  Collider   122, 237
 and the White House   99
Connick, George   208–210, 213
cooperation as a movement   31

Corruption of Improvement, The
  159
corruption   23, 31
Council of Economic Advisors, US
  101
counterculture   25, 84–85
Cours de philosophie positive (Comte)
  58
Covey, Stephen   168
Cruelty and Utopia: Cities and
  Landscapes of Latin America
  (exhibition and text)   22
Crystal Palace Exhibition, London,
  1851   34, 36
Cuba   22
*Culture of Improvement: Technology
  and the Western Millennium,
  A* (Friedel)   6, 158–159
*Cure for Chaos: Fresh Solutions to
  Social Problems Through the
  Systems Approach* (Ramo)
  110
cyberspace communities   12, 24,
  194, 198–199, and "real
  world"   198
cyberspace   1, 2, 24, 199
 cyberspace relationships   192
 and universities   209

Dahl, Robert   106, 108, 109, 114,
  119, 122
Dator, James   250
DaVinci Institute   205
"Day of Slowing"   238
daydreams and utopias   251
Declaration of Independence,
  US   93
"Decline of Politics and Ideology in
  a Knowledgeable Society,
  The" (Lane)   106
Del Sesto, Stephen   146
Delano, Sterling   254–255

democracy and technology
189–190
Denmark 151
Department of Homeland Security,
United States 253–254
Dertouzos, Michael 161, 164, 186
Descartes, Rene 55
deskilling 212
development studies 102
digital utopianism 154
digitization and the market
217–218
Dikotter, Frank 19
Diothas, The; Or, A Far Look Ahead
(Macnie) 82, 89
"Discover the Brave New World of
Online Learning" 213
Disneyland 36
Dispossessed, The (LeGuin) 92
diversity, concept of 190
Dolly the sheep 125
Donnelly, Ignatius 98
dot-com revolution 190, 201
Doublespeak 166
Douglass, Frederick 36–37
Dreyfus, Hubert 199
Dreyfuss, Henry 34
Drop City 195
Du Bois, W. E. B. 252
Duffy, Enda 164, 165
Dulles, John Foster 143
Dymaxion Chronofile 246
Dymaxion products 195–196,
246
"Dymaxion" as a trademark 246
dystopia 19, 83, 147, 151, 171
dystopian aspects of Internet
194, 199
science fictional 166
and utopia 5, 123, 186, 216,
243, 244, 253
see also utopia

Eastman, George 157
e-books 219
Echeverría, Esteban 22
Edison, Thomas 120, 142, 157
education and technology 203ff
and Internet 207–208,
209–210, 211
higher education and technology 207–208, 214
Education of Henry Adams, The
(H. Adams) 82–83
Educational Network of
Maine 208
Edutopia 203–213
higher education and Edutopia
206–213
Edwards, Robert 127
Ehrenreich, Barbara 168
Einstein's general theory of
relativity 202
Eisenhower, President Dwight D
108–109, 115, 143
el dorado, Latin America 21
Electricité de France 152
"electronic battlefield" 105, 112
"electronic campus" 208, 210
Elements of Technology (Bigelow)
52
Elizabeth II, Queen, on economic
crisis 166–167
Ellicott, Thomas 77
Embree, Ainslie 171
Emerson, Ralph Waldo 84
empowerment of the
individual 122–123
End of History and the Last Man, The
(Fukuyama) 188, 242
End of Ideology, The (Bell) 101
end of science 116
Endangered Species Act, United
States 111
Energy Policy Act, US 153, 157

Engels, Friedrich   32, 53, 60, 66–67, 250, 251
engineers and scientists compared   52
engineering as a culture   121
Engineers and the Price System, The (Veblen)   97, 106
"Enlightenment Project"   104, 116
Enlightenment   50, 55–56, 104, philosophies of   160
environmental disasters   115
environmental rights   253
Epode   47
Equality movement Washington state   25
equality   56
equality of genders   26, 92–93, 196
equality of opportunity   31, 54, 210
Erasmus   190
Espy, James   188
ethnopsychiatry   170
Etzler, John Adolphus   78, 79–80, 81
eugenics   159, 188
Evans, Oliver   77
Ewbank, Thomas   78, 80
experts   109, 112
  and activism   107
  attitudes toward   114, 115, 155–156, 157–160, 192
  and changing of society   97
  and education   205, 211
  experts and scientists   100, 119, 121
  need for   57
  and nuclear power   155–156
  as social engineers   108
  systems experts   160
  and Systems Analysis   110
  and TQM   217

Expo 2010 Shanghai, China   38

Fabianism   20
Facebook   193, 194, 238
Fair America: World's Fairs in the United States (Rydell, Findling, Pelle)   36
fascism   98, 104
Federal Communications Commission   210
Female Man, The (Russ)   92
Findling, John   36
Flanagan, Judy   145
Fleming, James   187–188, 207
Flubber   202
Fogarty, Robert   25
Ford Motor Company   139, 246
Ford, Henry   104, 157, 165
Ford, President Gerald   108
Fourier, Charles   25, 53, 60, 64–66, 67, 255
  utopian views   64–65
Fourierists   29
Fourth Eclogue   47
Fragments (Pindar)   47, 237
France:
  and energy   157
  French Revolution   57, 60, 64
  French student revolt 1968   252
  nuclear industry in   152
  utopian housing projects in   2
  utopianism in   24
Frankenstein (M. Shelley)   90–91, 128–131, 188, 192
  misreading of   129–130
Frankenfood"   130
"Frankenstudents"   130
Franklin, Benjamin   168
Franklin, H. Bruce   141
free markets, free trade and utopianism   253
Frey, Tom   205, 206

Friedel, Robert 6, 158
Friends of the Coast-Opposing
    Nuclear Pollution
    147–148
From the Earth to the Moon
    (Verne) 8
From the Legend of Biel (Staton) 92
Fukushima Daiichi plant, Japan
    152, 242
Fukuyama, Francis 188
Fuller, Margaret 247
Fuller, R. Buckminster 14,
    245–249
  influence 195–196, 207
  and "limits of growth"
    237–238
  sense of social responsibility
    163
  as visionary 162
  Fuller Archives 245–246
  see also Utopia or Oblivion
Fulton, Robert 142
Funding for science and
    technology 121–122
Future and its Enemies, The
    (Postrel) 164
"Future of Land Grant Universities,
    The" 207
future of print 217–222
  online readerships 219
Future Shock (Toffler) 118,
    163–164, 236

Galbraith, John Kenneth 12, 101,
    109, 122, 161
Gandhi, Mohandas
    (Mahatma) 173
Garden City movement 196
Garden of Eden 47, 243
Gates, Bill 157–158, 161, 163,
    186, 201
  philanthropy 247
Gates, Melinda 163

Geddes, Norman Bel 34, 35
geeks, image of 201
General Electric 167
genetic engineering 121, 124,
    159, 187
genetic modification of
    animals 125–126
genetic testing 126
Genius of American Politics, The
    (Boorstin) 101
geodesic dome 195–196,
    246–247
George Lucas Educational
    Foundation 204–205
George, Henry 82
German Ideology The (Marx/
    Engels) 66–67
Germany 38, 79
  Nazi Germany 104, 244
  and nuclear power 152
Gernsback, Hugo 9
Ghost Busters 202
Gilbert, Daniel 124–125
Gillette, King Camp 90
Gilman, Charlotte Perkins 92
Gimpel, Jean 236–237
Gingrich, Newt 118, 189
*Giving Up the Gun: Japan's Reversion
    to the Sword, 1543–1879*
    (Perrin) 234–235
global citizenship, visions of 252,
    253
God is Back (Micklethwait and
    Wooldridge) 11
Golden Gate International Exposi-
    tion, San Francisco 34
Google 158, 193, 205
Gore, Vice-President Al 119, 189
Great Delusion, The (Stoll) 79
Great Depression, 1930s 9, 83,
    96, 102, 109
Great Famine, China 19
Great Society 159

Greater East Asian Japanese
    colonialist movement   21
"Green Globe, The"   242
Griffith, Mary   78, 81, 90, 91
Guernica   35, 252
Gulliver's Travels (Swift)   200
Gutenberg, Johann   190

Hammersley, Ben   218
Hardwicke, Cedric   240, 241
Hare Krishnas (International
    Society for Krishna
    Consciousness)   196
Harrington, Michael   101
Hawai'i Research Center for
    Futures Studies   250
Hawking, Professor Stephen   202
Hawthorne, Nathaniel   25, 130
*Heaven: Our Enduring Fascination
    with the Afterlife* (Miller)   12
Heinlein, Robert   9
Hemingway, Ernest   90
Henry VIII, King   48
Herf, Jeffrey   104
Herland (Gilman)   92
Hesiod   47
Hewlett, William   158
Hewlett-Packard   158, 192
higher education–military research
    nexus   115
Higher Learning in America, The
    (Veblen)   216
high-tech:
  advances   2
  and cyberspace   192, 253, 255
  and education   203, 209,
      211–213, 214
  India   172
  industry   110, 121, 158, 163, 198
  Kellogg Commission and
      211–213, 214, 215, 216–217
  and military   238
  negative aspects   121, 217, 243

research   115, 121
  and techno-fixes   211
  and techno-mania   187
  utopias and utopianism   1, 16,
      159, 162, 163, 164,
      165–168, 186, 207–208
  zealots and   188–189
  see also cyberspace
Hilton, James   13
Hinduism   171
hippies at Golden Gate Park   248
history: nature of   19, 51
  distortion of   84
  persistence of   163–164
  prophets' ignoring of   163, 166,
      188–193
Hitler, Adolf   243, 244
Ho Chi Minh trail   105
Ho, Koon-ki   17
Homeland Security Science and
    Technology Stakeholders
    253–254
Honey, I Blew Up the Kid   202
Honey, I Shrunk the Kids   202
Hoover, President Herbert   88,
    102, 110
Horace   47–48
Howe, Irving   253
Hubble space telescope   121
human behavior   123, 125
Human Genome Project   124
human rights   23, 39
  suppression of   168
  utopias and   253
human satisfaction   240
Huxley, Aldous   123, 164, 166
Huxley, T. H.   98

*Idea of Progress, The: An Inquiry into
    its Growth and Origin*
    (Bury)   51
Immelt, Jeffrey   153, 154
immigration as an issue   31

Implementing a Lean Management System, The   212
in vitro fertilization (IVF)   127
India:
  Indocentrism   171–172
  utopian visions in   171–173, 196
  and Western technology   171
Industrial Revolution: English
      50, 57, 60, 61–62, 65, 163,
      164, 169
  US   83–84
"industrialization"   31
  critics of   60
inequality, racial   159
"information overload"   190
interactive television (ITV)   209
international studies   102
Internet   2, 186, 187, 199, 243,
      253
intractable social problems,
      problems termed "wicked"
      112–113
intraorganizational individualism
      122
*Inventions: The Patented Works of R.
    Buckminster Fuller* (Fuller)
      249
iPads   187, 193, 219, 222
iPhones   187, 219
iPods   2, 163, 187, 193, 219, 220,
      238
Iran   189
Iraq War of   2003 11, 140
Iso, Abe   20
Israel   8, 24
  kibbutzim in   24, 196–198
Italy   98

Jaher, Frederick Cople   98
Japan   115, 196
  and Chinese science   235
  "discovery" by American
      explorers   235
  and guns   234–236
  interwar politics   20–21, 170
  Japanese rulers' fear of
      Westernization   235
  Meiji period   20
  nuclear industry in   152
  socialist movement   20
  and space   141
  Taisho period   20
  and technological development
      234–236
  Tokugawa period   19, 236
  utopianism in   19–20
Jasons (secret group)   105
Jaures, Jean   251, 253
Jefferson, Thomas   242
Jobs, Steve   158, 187, 201
Johnson, President Andrew
      94
Johnson, President Lyndon   101,
      104, 111, 159
Johnson, Steven   222
Jonestown, Guyana   244
Journey to the Center of the Earth
      (Verne)   8
Judaism   10
J-wear   141

K-12 school system   215
  Edutopia   204
  K-12 hardware and software
      205–206
  K-12 participants   206
Kaczynski, Theodore   84
Kahn, Albert   251, 252–253
Kahn, Herman   238
Kaplan, Fred   191
Karloff, Boris   128
Kateb, George   6–7
Kellogg Commission on the Future
      of State and Land-Grant
      Universities   213–215,
      216–17

Kellogg Commission (*Continued*)
political and ideological compo-
nents of report   215
Kellogg Foundation   213
Kelmscott Press   59
Keniston, Kenneth   116
Kennedy President John F   101,
104, 105–106, 111, 192
Kennedy, Senator Ted   104
Khang Yu-Wei   18–19
Kibbutzim, Israel   24, 196–198
Kilby, Jack   158
Kilgore, Senator Harley   100–101,
113, 115–116, 120
Kindle Reader   219, 220, 222
Kondratiev, Nikolai   30
Kondratiev theory   30–31
Koo, Wellington   252
Krauss, Lawrence   202–203
Kumar, Krishan   9–10, 92
Kusiak, Karen   205

labor unrest as a problem   31
Labour Party, UK   114
Lane, Mary E. Bradley   92
Lane, Robert   106–107, 108, 109,
114, 117–118, 119, 122
Laos   104
Lartigue, Jacques-Henri   165
Las Vegas   36
Lasser, David   9
Last Hero, The: A Life of Henry Aaron
(Bryant)   191
Latin America   102
and European ideas   21–22
indigenous cultures and move-
ments   21, 23
liberation theology and
communities   52
Spanish conquest   21
utopias in   21–23
Lawrence, Francis   212
Lea, Homer   98

League of Nations   251
Lease, Mary   98
Lee, Ann   26
Lefkowitz, Mary   171
Left Hand of Darkness, The (LeGuin)
92
legitimation crisis in US science and
technology   122
LeGuin, Ursula   92
LeMay, General Curtis   105
Lemontey, Pierre Edouard   60
Lenin, Vladimir   104
Lessing, Doris   9
Levitas, Ruth   7
Levittown, Long Island   244
Ley, Willy   9
library usage   218
*Life in a Technocracy: What It Might
Be Like in 1933* (Loeb)   89,
106, 239, 240
limits to growth   234, 237
Literary Digest   97
"literary intellectuals"   114
"living the dream"   254
Loeb, Harold Albert   89, 90, 95,
96, 239
and politics   109
Loewy, Raymond   34
London, Jack   98
Longxi, Zhang   18
Looking Backward: 2000–1887
(Bellamy)   10, 13, 24, 27,
31–32, 34, 90, 194
attitudes toward   59–60, 254
Lost Horizon   13
Lucas, George   204
Luddites   240, 241

Maastricht Treaty   252
*Machine in the Garden: Technology
and the Pastoral Ideal in
America, The* (Leo Marx)
84

Machines as the Measure of Men: Science, Technology, and Ideologies of Western Dominance (Adas)   169
Macnie, John   82, 87
Maine and nuclear power   142–157
Maine Yankee Atomic Power Company   142–143, 145, 146–148, 149, 151
  as "cargo cult"   147
  closure of   148
  opposition to   156–157
  referenda on   147, 155
  utopian and dystopian aspects   156
  views of   156–157
Malthus, Thomas   63
Mandela, Nelson   171
Manhattan Project   156
"Manifest Destiny," American   11
Manuel, Frank and Fritzie   16
Manuel, Frank   6
Mao Tse-Tung   18, 243
  utopian vision   19
Mao's Great Famine (Dikotter)   19
Maraniss, David   191
marginalizing utopias   29, 245
Marx, Karl   32, 53, 60, 66–67, 105, 250–251
  Marxism   22
Marx, Leo   84, 85
Massachusetts Institute of Technology   52
Massey, Ranymond   240, 241
Mauchly, John   160
Mayer, Anna-K.   98, 114
Mbeki, Thabo, President of South Africa   171
McDonald, Michael J.   111
McIntyre, Vonda N.   9
McKinley, President William   94

McNamara, Robert   104–105, 106, 112, 113, 166
"McNamara Line"   105
Medieval Machine, The: The Industrial Revolution of the Middle Ages (Gimpel)   236
"megachurches"   11
megaprojects:
  and climate change   187–188
  retreat from   139ff, 157
  skepticism toward   141–142
  taxpayer support for   122, 150
Megatrends and *Megatrends 2000* (Naisbitt and Aburdene)   168
Men Like Gods (Wells)   251
mercantilism   77
Metamorphosis (Ovid)   47
Mexico   23
mice, as subjects of research   125
Micklethwait, John   11
Microsoft   158, 192
"middle landscape"   85
military technology   238
millenarian movements   8
  God and millenarianism   8, 10
  Christians and millenarianism   8, 10
  Judaism and millenarianism   8, 10
  Mormonism   10
  and Pansophism   54–55
  and utopia   55
Miller, Lisa   12
Mitchell, General Billy   142
Mizora: A Prophecy (Lane)   92
Model T car   165
Modern Times in Maine and America, 1890–1930   191
  over-reliance on technology   105
"Modernization" theory   102ff, 114

Mojave Desert, California   151
monkeys, genetically modified
     125
Montgomery, David   212
Montreal Expo   1967 246
*Moon and the Ghetto: An Essay on
     Public Policy Analysis, The*
     (Nelson)   117
Moon landing   139, 140, 141,
     190, 200
moon landing fraud claims   141
More, Thomas   23, 42, 58, 247
   coining of term utopia   5
   and history   164
   and utopias   251
   utopia described   48–50
   see also Utopia
Morison, George Shattuck   89–90
Mormonism   10
Morozov, Evgeny   189
Morris, William   17, 32, 58–59,
     60, 237, 254
   see also News from Nowhere
Mosquito Coast, The   202
Mumford, Lewis   1, 106, 245, 246
music, digitization of   221
Mussolini, Benito   98
MySpace   205

Naisbitt, John   161, 162, 168, 186
Nantucket Sound   150
NASA   7, 140
National Association of State Uni-
     versities and Land-Grant
     Colleges (NASULGC)
     213–214
National Park Service   238–239
National Science Foundation (NSF)
     99, 100, 115
Native Americans   81
natural user interface   220
Nazi Germany   104, 244
   Nazism and utopia   188

Negroponte, Nicholas   161–162,
     163, 186
Nehru, Jawaharlal   172
Nelson, Richard   117
Neo-Confucian thought   19–20
*Net Delusion, The: The Dark Side of
     Internet Freedom* (Morozov)
     189
Neumann, Franz   109
Neumann, John Von   160
New Atlantis, The (Bacon)   53, 251
   Condorcet on   56
*New Christianity, The (Le Nouveau
     Christianisme)* (Saint-
     Simon)   57
New Deal   106, 159
New England   3, 24, 27, 147, 150,
     156, 249
New Harmony, Indiana. settlement
     at   60
New Lanark Mills, Scotland   60,
     62, 64
New View of Society A (Owen)   62
New World and Old World com-
     pared   24, 244
New World Order   242
*New World, The; Or, Mechanical
     System to Perform the Labours
     of Man and Beast by Inanimate
     Powers, that Cost Nothing*
     (Etzler)   78
New York City's New School for
     Social Research   97
New York Public Library   242,
     245, 254
New York World's Fair World of
     Tomorrow   1939–1940
     164, 240
News from Nowhere (Morris)   17,
     32, 59–60, 237
newspapers and digital media
     218, 221–222
Newton Message Pad   219

Newton, Isaac   55, 219
Nexi the robot   126
Nixon, President Richard   108,
      155
Noble, David F   187, 190, 207, 216
non-utopian reform   244
North Americans, early European
      perceptions of   244
North Vietnam   105–106
*Not Out of Africa: How Afrocentrism
      Became an Excuse to Teach
      Myth as History* (Lefkowitz)
      171
Noyce, Robert   158
Noyes, John Humphrey   10, 27,
      28
nuclear industry:
   France   152
   Germany   152
   Japan   152
   US   142–156
nuclear power   142–157
   being "too cheap to meter"   156
   changing attitudes
         toward   146–147
   experts and   155–156
   leakage of tritium   153
   and power station decommis-
         sioning   148, 149–150
   possibility of disaster   154–155
nuclear weaponry   187
Nuclear Regulatory Commission
      (NRC)   148, 149, 153, 154
Nutty Professor, The   201
Nye, David   81, 168, 169, 190, 237
Nyhan, David   148–149

O'Neil, Gerard   9
Obama, President Barack   140,
      151
Office of Science and Technology
      Policy   108

Office of Technology Assessment
      (OTA)   117–119, 121
One Laptop per Child   161
Oneida community   10, 24, 27–28
   daughter communities   28
   open marriage in   27, 199
Oneida Limited   28
"Oneida Perfectionists"   28
ordinary readers and utopian
      writings   11, 139, 254
Organization Man, The (Whyte)
      114–115
original sin   8
Orwell, George   14, 124, 166
Other America, The (Harrington)
      101
Ovid   47
Owen, Robert   53, 60–64, 66, 67
   and drawbacks of
         industrialization   62
   influence on Japan   196
   utopian plans   62–63
   see also New Harmony, Indiana,
         New Lanark Mills
ozone layer, monitoring of   121

pacifism   26
Packard, David   158
Page, Larry   158
Palestine   25, 35
Pansophists   48, 52, 53–55
*Paradise Within the Reach of All Men,
      Without Labor, By Powers of
      Nature and Machinery, The*
      (Etzler)   79
parents, children, and technology
      239
Paris exposition 1937   35,
      251–252
Paris Peace Conference 1919   251
Paris World's Fair 1900   251, 253
Pasteur, Louis   120–121

Pasteur's Quadrant: Basic Science and Technological Innovation (Stokes)   120
patriot missiles   238
Peale, Norman Vincent   168, 208
Pelle, Kimberly   36
Pentagon   109
People of Plenty: Economic Abundance and the American Character (Potter)   101
Performance Measurement for World Class Manufacturing   212
Perrin, Noel   234, 235
Perry, Commodore Matthew   20
Persian Gulf War 1991   238
Pew Forum on Religion and Public Life   11–12
Pew Research Center for the People   116
phalansteries   29, 64–65
Physics of Star Trek, The (Krauss)   202
Picasso, Pablo   35, 252
Piercy, Marge   92
Pilgrims, US   24
Pindar   47
Plato   13, 47, 48, 50, 123
podcast   218–219
Point East Maritime Village, Wiscasset   150
Pol Pot   243
"Politics of Consensus in an Age of Affluence, The"   106
politics, affluence, and knowledge   106–107
    significance of political power   109
Positivism   58
Post Shredded Wheat   191
post-9/11 period   142
"post-colonial" critique of Western imperialism   169–173
post-Millennialists   8, 27

post-modern skepticism and relativism   160
Postrel, Virginia   161, 164, 186
post-World War II period, beliefs, and projects   160
Potter, David   101, 102
poverty and progress   82
Prague Spring   1968 268
Prakash, Gyan   171, 172
Preface to Democratic Theory, A (Dahl)   106
pre-Millennialists   8
Press and the American Association   116
primitivism   92
Productivity for the Academic World   212
Productivity Press   212
professional forecasting   160–169
    failures of   160–161
Progress and Poverty (George)   82
proletariat   66
public faith in government and scientific-technological advance   113
Puffer, Erma   145
Puritans, US   24

"Quick Technological Fixes"   107–108, 117
Quindlen, Anna   221

racism   9, 169, 172
radiation, issues with   144–145, 155
Ramo, Simon   110–111, 112, 113, 122, 160
    utopian vision of   110, 166
rationalism   55
Reactionary Modernism (Herf)   104
Read and Go   220
Reader Pocket Edition and Reader Touch Edition   220

Reagan, President Ronald   8, 108, 115, 140, 142, 248
real world and the internet   194–195
Recent Social Trends in the United States (Hoover)   102
recovery narrative   81, 237
Reevely, David   221–222
Religion of Technology, The: The Divinity of Man and the Spirit of Invention (Noble)   187
religion   169
    attitudes toward belief   56
    declining beliefs   11–12
    freedom of religion   168
    religious beliefs and utopianism   9–12, 24, 29–30, 31, 90, 96, 239
    in US   25, 26, 103
    Western   172
Report to the County of Lanark (Owen)   62, 63
Republic (Plato)   13, 47, 48, 50, 123
Rescher, Nicholas   239–240
Research Applied to National Needs"   115
"Returning to Our Roots"   215, 216
Revenge of the Nerds   201
revolution of rising expectations   50
Ricardson, Ralph   240
Rittel, Horst   112
Road Ahead, The (Gates)   163
Robinson, Kim Stanley   9
robotics, development of   126–127
Roddenberry, Gene   200, 201, 202
Rodriquez, Simon   22
Roebling, John   79
Roemer, Kenneth   254
Rogers, Deborah   193

Rome 1960: The Olympics that Changed the World (Maraniss)   191
Roosevelt, President Franklin   94, 102, 159
Rosas, Juan Manuel de   22
Rostow, Walt   104, 105
Roszak, Theodore   111, 112
Rural Electrification Administration   94
Ruskin, John   58, 59, 60
Russ, Joanna   92
Rydell, Robert   36, 37

Saddam Hussein   11
Saint-Simon, Henri de   22, 52, 56–58, 65, 66
Sale, Kirkpatrick   117
"salvation by technology"   248
Samurai "technology assessment"   235
Sargent, Lyman Tower   16, 253
Satellite (machine developed by Etzler)   79–80, 81
Saunders, Doug   105
Schindler, Solomon   10
Schuller, Robert   168
Science Advisory Committee   106
science and technology   57
science fiction   8–9, 199–203, and utopias   201
Science in the National Interest   119–122
Science Wars"   159
"science-driven globalization"   8
Science – The Endless Frontier (V. Bush)   99, 119
scientific and technological elites   98, 188, 207
scientific and technological plateau   53, 59, 81, 234–241
    in Europe   236
    in Japan   234–236

scientific (*Continued*)
  modern 237, 238
  and utopianism 67
Scientific Management 104, 164
Scientific Revolution 160
"Scientific" Socialism (Marx and Engels) 66–67
scientist, coining of word 51
Scott, Howard 96, 97–98, 106, 109, 239
Scottish Parliament and Robert Owen 64
Seabrook Station, New Hampshire 149
second life 198
"Selling the World of Tomorrow" 37
September 11, 2001 238, 245
Serenbe, near Atlanta 2
Shadis, Raymond 147, 148
Shakers 24, 26–27, 194, 196, 242, celibacy 26, 28, 199
Shalam, New Mexico 25
Shape of Things to Come, The (Wells) 240
Shelley, Mary 90–91, 128, 129–130
Shelley, Percy Bysshe 128
Sierra Club 169
Silicon Valley 192
Simon, Julian 238
Sketch of a Historical Picture of the Progress of the Human Mind (Condorcet) 56
Skype 187, 194
small is beautiful 234
Snow, C. P. 113–114, 121, 122
social engineering 107–108, 109–110
social forecasters and utopianism 12–13
social media 193–194

social sciences 101, 102–104, 107, 121, and social engineering 110, societal benefits of science and technology 119
socialism 2, 10, 24, 26, 31
  Morris and 59
  Marx and Engels and 66–67
  see also Fabianism
Socialist League 59
Socialist Second International 251
Society for Utopian Studies, The 242
Sokal, Alan 160
solar power 150, 157
Sontoku, Ninomiya 20
Sony Electronics 220
Sorai, Ogyū 20
South Africa 171
Soviet Union 104, 108, 113, 244
  collapse of 1, 156, 242
space flight 187
  space shuttle disasters 140
"spaceship earth" 245–246, 247
Spanish Civil War 35, 252
Speed Handbook, The: Velocity, Pleasure, Modernism (Duffy) 164
speed, significance of 164–165
Spent Fuel Storage Installation, Bailey Point Peninsula, Wiscasset, US 149
Spinoff (NASA journal) 140
Spirit Fruit in Ohio and Illinois 25
Sputnik I 108, 113
Stages of Economic Growth, The (Rostow) 105
Stalin, Joseph 243, 244
Stalinism and utopia 244
Star Trek (series) 200
Star Trek Empire 199–203

Star Wars films   202, 204
"Star Wars" missile defense sys-
     tem   115, 141, 187–188
Staton, Mary   92
Steele, Allen   9
Stokes, Donald   120–121 120
Stoll, Steven   79
Story of Utopias, The   1
Strategic Defense Initiative   142
Strauss, Lewis   143
Stukel, James J.   206, 207–208,
     210, 211, 213, 215, 250
Sun Yat-Sen   18
Superconducting Super Collider,
     Texas   122, 141
supersonic transport (SST)   237
Swift, Jonathan   200
Sy Syms (company)   216
"System"   78
Systeme de politique positive (Comte)
     58
Systems Engineering   110–111
critiques of   112
  failure of   112
systems experts   160

T. H. E. Smart Classroom   205–206
ta thung and *thai phing*   18
Ta Thung Shu (Book of the Great
     Togetherness)   18
Takemura, Eiji   19–20
"Taking Charge of Change"   214
Taoist concepts   19
Taylor, Elizabeth   195
Taylor, Frederick   104, 164
teaching machines   203
Teague, Walter Dorwin   34
technocracy   24, 96
  false prophets of technocracy
     106
  science fiction and technocracy
     9
  social impact of technocracy   96

technocracy and progress   106
techno-fixes   159, 187–188, 211
technological advances   78, 113,
     235, 255
  high-tech attitudes toward
     203
  Industrial Revolution   50, 163
  reservations and skepticism
     about   58, 167, 245
  Technocrats and   96
  US attitudes   78, 82, 84, 116
  utopianism and   19, 32, 35, 53,
     54, 56, 58, 60, 63, 127–131,
     244
technological behaviors   219–220
technological determinism   82,
     102, technological impera-
     tive   82, 237
technological inadequacy   165
technological
     unemployment   83–84
technology and utopianism   2, 51,
     67, 89–96, 239
  assembly line model of
     technology   119
  development of term   51–52
  perceptions of technology   192
"Technology in Schools: What the
     Research Says"   206
techno-mania   187, 190
Tellico Dam   111–112
Temko, Allan   245
Tenner, Edward   167
Tennessee Valley Authority (TVA)
     94–95, 111–112
text messaging   193
Thomson Reuters   211
Thoreau, Henry David   79
*Thoughts on Matter and Force: Or,
     Marvels that Encompass Us*
     (Ewbank)   80
Three Hundred Years Hence
     (Griffiths)   91, 92

Three Mile Island, Harrisburg,
    Pennsylvania   147, 152,
    155
Thurston, Robert Henry   90
tidal power   157
Time Warner Cable   192–193
Toffler, Alvin and Heidi   118, 161,
    162, 167–168, 186
    Alvin   163, 207, 236, 250
Tokyo   20
*Too Much to Know: Managing Schol-
    arly Information Before the
    Modern Age* (Blair)   190
"total quality management"
    (TQM)   217
touchscreens   219–220
Tower of Peace   252
traces of existing societies and
    utopias   251, 254
Transcendentalism   25–26, 247
"trans-national rights"   253
Truman, President Harry S.   108
TRW (company)   110
"tsunamis of change"   250
Turkle, Sherry   194
Turner, Frederick Jackson   37
Turner, J. M. W.   165
*TVA and the Tellico Dam, 1936–1979:
    A Bureaucratic Crisis in Post-
    Industrial America* (Wheeler,
    McDonald)   111
*Twenty Thousand Leagues Under the
    Sea* (Verne)   8
Twitter   193
Two Cultures, The (Snow)   113–
    114, and engineering   121

Unabomber   84
"underdeveloped" or "Third
    World"   102, 105, 172
Union Carbide   253
United Kingdom   151
    Fabianism in   20

relationship with the United
    States   114
    utopianism in   24
    and wind power   151
United Nations International Year
    of Cooperatives   64
United Society of Believers in
    Christ's Second Appearing
    see Shakers
United States   187
    "aging or declining era"   237
    America as "Second Creation"
        81–85
    America as utopia   10, 24–25,
        74–78, 188–189
American "exceptionalism"   89
    attitudes toward inventors,
        engineers and scientists
        157–160
    attitude toward rulers   159
    attitudes toward technological
        progress   78, 82, 84, 116
    citizens' demand for separation
        from external world   122
    Civil War   76, 77
    concept of System   78
    exportation of science and tech-
        nology   102–103, 109–110
    fairs   36, 37
    gap between science and public
        beliefs   116–117
    immigration   77–78
    imperialism   9
    influence of European
        utopianism   76
    moral superiority   11
    nature of Americaness   78–79
    and nuclear plants   142–156
    "nuclear renaissance"   154
    and Old World   74
    "positive thinking"   168
    potentiality of utopia in
        75–76

reconceptualization of America 78

religious beliefs 11–12

science and technology 108–109

sense of identity 77

technology and opportunism 75, 77

2011 earthquake 153

United States and digital literacy 210

United States Constitution 74, 93

utopianism and contemporary disorder 93

utopianism 5, 24–32, 24

views of industrialization and technology 83, 84

see also technological utopia

Universal Declaration of Human Rights 1948 252

universal rights 252

Universal Studios 36

universities 130, 204, 207, 213, 214

Kellogg Commission 215, 216

and "power of knowledge" 104

and TQM 217

see also electronic campus

University of California 112

Berkeley, protests at 111

University of Illinois 207, 210

University of Maine System 208

University of Phoenix 210, 210, 211

urban crises 115

"urbanization" 31

utilitarianism 62

utopias:

defined 1, 5–7

alternative energy 150–151

American 24–32, 89–96

artifacts and utopia 196, 243, 252

attitudes toward utopia 124, 192, 242–244

background to 50ff

in China and Japan 17–21

contemporary utopias 194–199

creation of 13

critics of utopia 48ff, 74ff, 123–131

critiques 169–173, 243

and cyberspace 198–199

declining faith in 158

digital utopianism 154

and dystopias 5, 216, 244

educational 205, 206–213

and electrification 94

expectations of achievability 50–51, 248–249

failures of 186

as fantasies 251

feasibility of establishment 13–14

forecasters' claims 160–169

future of utopias 255, 234ff

genres of utopianism 24ff

and globalization 253–254

high-tech 1, 2, 16, 118, 162, 163, 172, 186, 210, 214–215, 253, 255

negative components 165–166, 167–168

inherent impracticality of 123

intent of utopias 7, 205

internal criticism 28

Kellogg Commission's utopianism 213–217

Latin American utopias 21–23

literary accounts 1–2, 47–50, 54–55

location of 13

utopias (*Continued*)
  and megaprojects 139–142
  and millenarian movements
    8–9
  minor utopias 251, 252–253
  and modernization 105–106
  and "near future" 164, 186
  necessity for ability to
    change 5, 251
  non-utopianism 7, 147, 252
  non-Western utopian-
    ism 16–23, 196, 243
  nuclear power 146, 153–154,
    156
  ongoing significance of utopia
    241–255
  origin of term 5, 48
  overdetailed descriptions
    250–251
  print and utopianism 217–222
  and real world 1, 5–6, 7, 12–13,
    244–245
  reflecting societies 1, 31
  and religion 9–12, 56
  and science fiction 8–9,
    199–201
  and scientific and technological
    plateau 67, 234–241
  significance of utopianism
    241–255
  significance of utopian writers
    95–96
  skepticism toward 2
  and social media 193–194
  spiritual qualities and formal
    religion 9–12
  spread of utopias 16–17
  technological utopias 3, 32, 34,
    53ff, 99, 102, 107, 109, 202,
    247, 253
  potential failure of 187
  tradition of 188–189
  timescale of utopias 13–11

  true and false utopias 5–6, 7,
    106
  utopia and history 244–245
  utopian communities' political
    viewpoint 25
  utopian writings 47, 254
  utopianism and availability of
    choice 123
  utopias and role of women 25,
    63, 90–92, 173
  utopias, millenarianism and sci-
    ence fiction 8–9
  and virtual reality 255
  Western utopias 16, 242, 250,
    252
  see also particular authors, Best
    and Brightest, Edutopia,
    Pansophists, Shakers, Tech-
    nocracy, World's fairs
utopian communities 194–198,
    247
  and France 2
  negative aspects 254–255
  quasi-utopian societies 201
  religion-based 2, 10
  utopian settlements, US 98
Utopian Socialist Society,
    Venezuela 79
Utopia (New York Library exhibi-
    tion catalog) 245
Utopia (Thomas More) 5, 13, 23,
    47, 48, 123, 242, 244
*Utopia or Oblivion: The Prospects for
    Humanity* (Fuller) 14, 164,
    207, 248
Utopia Road, Southern
    California 2
Utopia, Texas, United States 2
Utopia: The Search for the Ideal
    Society in the Western
    World (exhibition, New
    York Public Library)
    242–245

utopianism (movement)   5,
        100–101, 245, 247, 250, 254
Utopianism: A Very Short Introduction
        (Sargent)   16
utopians   98, 161, 186–192
Utopias (beer)   3, 249
*Utopias in Conflict: Religion and
        Nationalism in Modern India*
        (Embree)   171

Veblen, Thorstein   97, 106, 216
Venezuela   23, 189
Venter, Craig   127
Vergil   47
Vermont Yankee Nuclear
        Plant   145, 148, 154
Verne, Jules   7, 8
Vernon, Vermont, United
        States   145, 147–148
Vietnam War   104–105, 111, 112,
        115, 158, 159, 160, 245
Vincenti, Walter   52, 121
virtual governments   250
virtual reality   255
"virtual school"   206
"vision thing" (H. W. Bush)
        241–242
Visual Factory, The   212
von Braun, Wernher   9

Wallingford, Connecticut   28
"War on Poverty"   101
*War Stars: The Superweapon and
        the American Imagination*
        (Franklin)   141–142
water power   150
Watergate scandal   158, 159
Watt, James   8
We (Zamyatin)   123, 166
Webber, Melvin   112
Weinberg, Alvin   106, 107–108,
        109, 110, 114, 122
Wells, H. G.   9, 35, 240, 251

Wen Jiabao, Prime Minister   38
Western ethnocentrism and
        industrialisation   169–170
Westinghouse, George   157
What Will Be (Dertouzos)   164
Wheeler, William Bruce   111
Whewell, Rev. William   51, 52
"Which Guide to the Promised
        Land? Fuller or Mumford?"
        (Temko)   245
"white man's burden"   170
Whitney, Eli   157
*Who Governs? Democracy and Power
        in an American City* (Dahl)
        106
Whole Earth Catalog, The (Brand)
        153–154
*Why Things Bite Back: Technology and
        the Revenge of Unintended
        Consequences* (Tenner)   167
Whyte, Jr., William H.   114–115,
        122
Wikipedia   193, 194
Williams, Rosalind   8
Wilson, President Woodrow   252
wind power   150–152, 154, 157,
        utopian aspects   150
Winfrey, Oprah   168
Winter, Jay   251–253
Wiscasset, Maine, US   143, 145,
        146–147
Woman on the Edge of Time (Piercy)
        92
women   114–115
    and education   22
    equality   26, 92–93
    and *Frankenstein*   130–131
    marginalizing of   67, 170, 188
    and utopianism   25, 63, 90–92,
        173
    women's rights   18, 253
Women's Commonwealth,
        Texas   25

wood, energy from   157
Woodstock   242
Wooldridge, Adrian   11
workers:
  exploitation of   81
  and industrial revolution   75,
    83, 212
  and speed   165
  and utopia   61, 62
Workers' Control in America
    (Montgomery)   212
"Works and Days" (Hesiod)   47
World a Workshop, The: Or the
    Physical Relationship of Man
    to the Earth (Ewbank)   80
World Future Society   166
World of Tomorrow exhibit, 1939–
    1940 New York World's
    Fair   14, 34–35, 37, 164
World War I   170
World War II   21, 35, 240
World Wide Web   186
World's Columbian Exposition,
    Chicago   36–37

World's Fairs   33–39
  decline of   38
  and impact of communications
    35–36
  impact   37
  listed   34, 36, 37–38, 39
  New York   242
  perceptions of   33
  as temporary utopias   34
Wozniak, Stephen   158, 202

Young Mill-Wright and Miller's
    Guide, The (Evans and
    Ellicott)   77
Young West (Schindler)   10
YouTube   193, 205
Yuaikai (Friendly Society), Japan
    20

Zamyatin, Eugene   123, 166
zealots, high-tech   188, 189
Zimbabwe   170
Zionists   8
Zuckerberg, Mark   193